The Quest for the Rose

The Quest for the Rose

Roger Phillips & Martyn Rix

Historical research by Nicky Foy, Alison Rix
Design & layout by Jill Bryan, Gillian Stokoe &
Anne Thatcher

BBC BOOKS

Acknowledgements

We would like to thank everybody that helped with this book, especially: David Austin, Peter Beales, David and Norma Beattie, Margrit Blackburn, Fred Boutine, Judith Bronkhurst, Tessa Clark, Yvonne Cocking, J N Coldstream, Margaret Collinson, Aline Converset, Harvey Davidson, Dale Ditmanson, Beverly Dobson, Margaret Drower, Pamela Egremont, Brent Elliott, Irving Finkel, Gianfranco Fineschi, George Fuller, Iris Furlong, Bill Grant, Peter Harkness, Chris Hill, Marie-Claire Howe, Muriel and Bill Humenick, Rosalind Janssen, Kirk Johnson, John Killen, Kleine Lettunich, Greg Lowery, Barbara Levy, Sam McGredy, Clair Martin, Ian Martin, John Mattock, John Moffett, Ralph Moore, Lyvia Morgan, Jacques Mouchotte, Sarah O'Brien-Twohig, Charles d'Orban, Charles Quest-Ritson, Catherine Raczynska, Richard Rix, Ted Rix, Philip Robinson, Kim Rupert, Gillian Snowden, Marten Stol, Graham Stuart Thomas, Sharon Van Enoo, John Walden, Miriam Wilkins, Scott L Wing, Jack Wolfe, Ed Wilkinson, Keith Zary.

We would like to thank the following museums and gardens for all the help that we have received: The David Austin Garden, Shropshire; The Auckland Botanic Garden, New Zealand; The Bagatelle Gardens, Paris; Peter Beales Roses, Norfolk; The staff of the British Museum; Cants of Colchester; The Botanic Garden, Christchurch, New Zealand; Courtauld Institute of Art, London; The Denver Museum of Natural History, Colorado; Dickson Nurseries, Co. Down; Eccleston Square Garden, London; Florissant National Monument, Colorado; The Garden of the Rose, St Albans; La Roseraie de l'Haÿ-Les-Roses near Paris; Harkness Roses, Hertfordshire; Huntington Botanical Gardens, San Marino, California; The Institute of Archaeology, London; The Institute of Classical Studies, London; Jackson & Perkins, Oregon; The Royal Botanic Gardens, Kew; The staff of the Lindley Library, London; The staff of the London Library; The Château de Malmaison; Mattock Roses, Oxford; Meilland Richardier, France; The National Trust Mottisfont, Hampshire; The staff of the Petrie Museum, University College, London; Rose Acres, California; Queen Mary's Rose Garden, Regent's Park, London; The Savill Gardens, Windsor; The School of Oriental and African Studies, London; Sequoia Nursery, California; The Smithsonian Museum, Washington; The Sydney Botanical Garden; Vintage Gardens Nursery, Califonia.

PICTURE CREDITS

Accademia Italiana page 21 and back cover; **Archaeological Museum, Heraklion, Crete** page 13; **Bridgeman Art Library** pages 19 (Galleri degli Uffizi, Florence), 20 (Private Collection), 26 (Bibliothek National, Vienna), 28 (St Martin, Colmar) and 29 (Victoria and Albert Museum); **Flinders Petrie Museum, London** page 10; **Lauros-Giraudon** page 32; **Réunion des Musées Nationaux, Paris** page 37; **Royal Horticultural Society, London** pages 38, 46, 52, 55, 56, 77 and 116. We would also like to thank the following for allowing us to use their photographs: **David Austin** Happy Child page 240, St Swithuns page 243, Mrs Doreen Pike page 245, **Harvey Davidson** pages 248 (Smooth Perfume) and 249 (Smooth Prince); **Kim Rupert** pages 194 (Careless Love) 197 (Café) and 197 (Brownie). All the remaining photographs Roger Phillips and Martyn Rix.

This book is published to accompany the television series entitled The Quest for the Rose which was first broadcast in 1993
Published by BBC Books,
a division of BBC Enterprises Limited, Woodlands, 80 Wood Lane
London W12 0TT

First Published 1993
© Roger Phillips and Martyn Rix 1993
ISBN 0 563 36442 4
Set in Monophoto Garamond by Selwood Systems,
Midsomer Norton
Printed and bound in Great Britain by Butler & Tanner Ltd,
Frome and London
Colour separation by Dot Gradations Ltd, Berkhamsted
Jacket printed by Laurence Allen Ltd, Weston-super-Mare

Contents

Introduction

I have been growing roses for many years now in the garden at Eccleston Square in London where I live, and I have often discussed their qualities, history, growth and background with Martyn Rix, my friend and co-author. Five years ago we published our first book on roses but I felt that I still knew so little about them. Yes, I knew their individual names and if they were Hybrid Teas or Bourbons or whatever. But exactly what a Bourbon Rose is and how it differs from a Hybrid Perpetual was a complete mystery. Who developed them? Why? When? What about the China and Tea Roses which do so well in a London garden? How did they get to the West? Do their wild parents still exist in the mountains of China? These were some of the questions Martyn Rix and I set out to answer in our quest for the rose.

The ancient history proved fascinating because the origins of many of the oldest rose groups like Damask and Alba are still largely a mystery. Seeing and touching actual remnants of 2000-year-old roses excavated by Flinders Petrie in the tombs of ancient Egypt was an extraordinary experience that I had never dreamed of when we started on our quest; and 35-million-year-old rose fossils in Florissant, Colorado were another unexpected discovery.

Writing and photographing for this book, and filming for the television series, has been very exciting. We found a great many wild Chinese roses during our trip through the Himalayan foothills of Yunnan and Sichuan, as well as many strange garden varieties that the visiting botanists of 100 years ago had taken little interest in. Every village seemed to have its own garden rose, many of which are unknown in the West.

California was another revelation. First, we went hunting through the cemeteries of the gold-mining country and discovered that the pioneers obviously loved their roses; the graveyards are full of exciting Tea Roses that have survived in the region's hot, dry conditions while dying out elsewhere. We also found gardening in Los Angeles very different to gardening in Britain. It seemed that all the rose gardeners we met were really rose collectors – their gardens were packed to the gills exclusively with roses: Sharon Van Enoo, for instance, has well over 300 different varieties in a tiny back garden in Torrance, Los Angeles. One of her passions is for the English Roses of David Austin so it made me feel ashamed that I only had twelve of them when she had about fifty! There are thriving Old Rose groups all over America.

New Zealand and Australia are at least on a par with the USA in their passion for roses, especially Old Roses. Many that have died out in the countries in which they were bred have been refound in old gardens there.

Il Roseto di Cavriglia near Florence, Italy. Professor Fineschi's collection of roses is one of the world's greatest.

How the book is laid out

Chapters One, Two and Three deal with the history of roses, tracing their development up to and including the advent of Josephine Bonaparte. These chapters are written as an ongoing story and are illustrated with appropriate paintings or archaeological pictures, together with photographs of roses belonging to the ancient rose groups. Chapter Four is a diary of our trip to China, illustrated with the roses that we found there.

From Chapter Five onwards the roses are in their groups or sections. We start with Wild Roses, then move on to the Old Rose chapter which is subdivided by section from Mosses to early Hybrid Teas, arranged chronologically by the date of their introduction. Most of the subsequent chapters are self-explanatory. Modern Roses contains the Hybrid Teas and Floribundas. We have used the original terminology rather than modern terms like 'clustered-flowered' or 'large-flowered' roses – I think changing names that have been used for a hundred years or so is totally confusing for beginners and experts alike. Within the chapters the roses have usually been arranged by colour: white, pink, red, orange, yellow.

The formal rose gardens at Bagatelle, on the edge of the Bois de Boulogne in Paris.

Dotted throughout the text, positioned with the roses that they developed, are pocket biographies of many important rose growers, to give readers more background information about the development of the rose.

The photographs

What you see is what you get. In other words we do not go around picking one flower from one bush and then wiring it on to another, and so on, to get a bunch of perfect flowers. That we leave to the rose cataloguers. In reality, roses flower over a period of time and a plant will therefore bear buds, half-open flowers, open flowers and dead flowers at the same time. What we hope is that if you buy a rose you find in this book and grow it successfully you will not be disappointed; with any luck it will turn out just like our shot.

The captions

We have given consistent information under each rose. The first name given is that which is generally accepted as correct; other names are either incorrect, or commonly found alternatives. We do not describe the colour – that we leave to the photographs. The breeder and the rose parentage are given if known. When a rose suffers badly from disease this is mentioned; if it is especially healthy this is mentioned (a list of healthy roses is on page 250). Information about flowering is also included: whether roses are spring flowering (once in spring), summer flowering (once in summer) or repeat or flower continuously. Heights are on the basis of average conditions. Scent is normally given. If not mentioned, it means it is very slight, or absent.

BONICA and SEXY REXY vie for attention in the garden of Dr Ernest Scholtz on the outskirts of Los Angeles, California.

ROSA NUTKANA, NOOTKA ROSE A shrub with stout stems, straight prickles and flowers 4–6 cm ($1\frac{1}{2}$-$2\frac{1}{4}$ in) across. Native of California and Colorado, northwards to Alaska, growing in damp places, often in redwood forest. Once flowering, between early and midsummer. Height to 100–200 cm ($3\frac{1}{2}$-7 ft). Slight scent.

ROSA GALLICA, *ROSA RUBRA*, RED ROSE A low, suckering shrub with red to deep pink flowers. A native of France (and possibly Belgium) east to Turkey, Iraq and the Caucasus, growing in stony open places and on sunny banks. Once flowering in late spring. Height to 80 cm ($2\frac{1}{2}$ ft). Good scent.

CHAPTER ONE

The Rose in Ancient History

This chapter starts with archaeology then moves on to mythology followed by ancient history. It finishes at the end of the Middle Ages. The ancient rose groups illustrated are Damasks, Albas and the early Gallicas.

When Did the First Rose Exist?

There is little doubt that roses grew on Earth at least 35 million years ago. Evidence of their existence comes from rose fossils that have been found in rocks from the Oligocene epoch in North America, Europe and Asia. The fact that there are far fewer fossils of roses than of other plants such as *Gingko* and *Pinus* has aroused the curiosity of palaeontologists, particularly as roses now grow in almost all regions in the northern temperate zone.

A very credible explanation for this paucity of rose fossils has been put forward by an American palaeontologist, Charles Resser. His theory is that if prehistorical roses can be assumed to have flourished in a dry climate similar to that in which modern roses grow the likelihood of them fossilizing over millions of years is slim. Fossilization frequently takes place in muddy or swampy areas where rapid burial that prevents decay setting in can occur. Therefore, if prehistorical roses grew in drier places than plants that require more than average moisture, the chance of fossilization taking place is greatly reduced. This might explain why there are so few rose fossils world-wide.

Resser's explanation for the rose fossils that have been found is as follows. When an enormous amount of dust, volcanic ash or mud (created by a mixture of dust and rain) descends on an area, suddenly trapping plants and animal life and preserving them from rapid decay, fossilization that is not found elsewhere may occur. These unexpected conditions prevailed at two of the major palaeo-botanical sites where rose fossils have been found in North America: at Florissant, a small village in South Park Colorado, 2500 m (8193 ft) above sea-level, 35 miles west of Colorado Springs; and at Bridge Creek and Crooked River, 850 m (2800 ft) above sea-level, in central Oregon.

The rose fossil specimens collected at these two sites have been named as: *Rosa hillae, Rosa wilmattae, Rosa scudderi* and *Rosa ruskiniana*. Perhaps these four species are really only a single species. The living roses they most resemble today are *Rosa nutkana* or *Rosa palustris*.

The Rose in Pre-classical Times

Myth, legend, literature and art have all perpetuated the idea that the rose itself and, more importantly, the rose as a symbolic image extend far back into the mists of time. What actual evidence is there that this is so?

Archaeology is the key. Excavations at ancient cities, towns, settlements and burial sites throughout the world have given us insights – sometimes very clear, sometimes less so – into past cultures. Unravelling the past by analysing their artefacts can often be a fascinating but tantalizing business, particularly as archaeological techniques have become increasingly precise and comprehensive over the last hundred years. Whereas excavators originally searched primarily for large scale, striking or valuable artefacts, it is now recognized that seemingly insignificant objects like baskets or containers can reveal a great deal about day-to-day life in a previous civilization.

This is where roses come in. Archaeologists working on early excavations in Greece, Italy or western Asia may have unwittingly disregarded dried plant matter in tombs or houses when they were searching for, and finding, larger objects. Much valuable information and evidence must therefore have been lost over the centuries. Nevertheless, archaeological digs on very ancient sites have provided the rose historian with some tantalizing, if inconclusive, evidence to suggest that roses were used in pre-classical cultures for the same or similar purposes as in Greek and Roman times: medicinal, cosmetic, religious and artistic.

The Olive Oil Tablets of Pylos

The excavations in the palace of Nestor at Pylos on the south-western tip of the Peloponnese provided just the kind of hard evidence for the existence and use of roses in ancient times that historians were itching for.

A fossilized rose-leaf dating from around 35 million years ago. The rose is thought to be close to the *Rosa nutkana* that grows in the area now.

FINDING THE WILD GALLICA We found this rose in the Alpes-Maritimes after much searching. Before we left London on the French leg of our quest we visited the Royal Horticultural Society's Lindley Library in London and noted the localities given for *Rosa gallica* in Burnat's *Flora des Alpes-Maritimes* (1876). One of the villages mentioned was Sigale, so when we reached Grasse, where we were very saddened to find that the production of rose oil was no longer important, we pushed on to this tiny village high in the foothills of the Alps.

The drive took us through spectacular gorges and wooded hills. Although we found Dog Roses, Sweet Briars and lots of wild Scotch Roses there was no sign of Gallica, until we were within a mile of Sigale, when suddenly its bright red flowers were scattered all over low bushes by the roadside – exactly as described by Burnat a hundred years earlier. Nearby we found a few other plants, all growing in loose, stony soil below limestone cliffs, ideal for a plant that spreads so freely by underground suckers.

Gigantic Redwood stumps dot the landscape. Most of them were exposed about 100 years ago when farmers used to sell bits taken from them to fossil-hunters.

Florissant was a lake 35 million years ago. Gradually deposits of mud settled at the bottom of the lake forming the paper shales in which fossils are found today.

ROSA × *RICHARDII*, *ROSA SANCTA*, HOLY ROSE, ST JOHN'S ROSE An ancient garden rose, brought from Ethiopia to Europe in 1895. (Possibly *Rosa gallica* × *Rosa phoenicea* or *abyssinica* which makes it a primitive Damask.) A bushy shrub with flowers 5–7.5 cm (2–3 in) across. Summer flowering. Height to 120 cm (4 ft). Good scent. Thought to have formed the chaplets found by Flinders Petrie.

DAMASK ROSES are mysterious in origin. They are thought to have arisen in antiquity from crosses between Gallicas and *Rosa phoenicea*, a native of the Middle East. They resemble Gallicas, but are taller and lankier, with large thorns and leaves with greyish-green, hairy undersides. The flowers are usually pink or white, without the purple of the Gallicas, and are often in sprays. The hips are long and thin. Very fragrant, they are still used in the production of attar of roses.

SIR WILLIAM FLINDERS PETRIE (1853–1942) His meticulous attention to the detritus of past civilizations led him to discover the oldest rose remnants ever seen. The men who went before him used high explosives to excavate; those who came after used paint brushes.

After years of discussion, planning and exploratory digging, full-scale excavations by the joint Hellenic-American Expedition started in 1952, almost eighty years after Heinrich Schliemann (1822–90) had first recognized the probable significance of the site. In the various rooms of the palace, which was destroyed by fire around the end of the thirteenth century BC, a number of stone tablets were found on which a variety of information was recorded in Linear B script. Many that were excavated in 1955 give detailed information about quantities and transactions connected with oil – obviously an important industry. They have subsequently been named the Olive Oil Tablets of Pylos and have been studied in great detail by the Linear B specialist Emmett L. Bennett Jr (1918–).

Bennett's analysis of the ideograms on the tablets has led him to the conclusion that while the principal commodity listed and described is oil, probably olive oil, various recurrent marks or ligatures represent different qualities and kinds of oil, particularly those used for anointment or perfume. Of the scented ones there seem to have been three kinds: rose scented, sage scented and Cyperus scented. He also believes that his interpretation of the ideogram for rose-scented oil is written in the same way as in Homer's *Iliad* which refers to Hector being embalmed with rose oil (page 16).

The Rose Found in an Egyptian Tomb

In 1908 the French horticulturist and rose specialist Pierre-Charles-Marie Cochet (1853–1912) known as Cochet-Cochet, wrote to Georges Schweinfurth (1836–1925), a German botanist who specialized in identifying plant remains from ancient sites.

> Dear Sir,
> Although the French language is said to be very rich, I must admit that I cannot find the words to express, deeply enough, all my gratitude for the parcel you sent me, of such great interest!!! Thank you, a thousand times, Sir, for these remains of Roses which arrived in perfect condition.
> I have received from the four corners of the world samples of roses, plants and earth; but I have never experienced such emotion as that on opening your small parcel!!!

Schweinfurth was amused by his correspondent's 'Latin enthusiasm' but he himself had been equally excited some twenty years earlier when he first set eyes on its cause. In 1888 he had visited Sir William Flinders Petrie (1853–1942), an English archaeologist excavating a previously untouched cemetery at Hawara, in the Fayum Province of Lower Egypt, and Petrie had shown him a large box full of wreaths of roses and other flowers that had been found in the tombs. Percy E. Newberry (1869–1949), who was working on the dig with Petrie, wrote the following account of the finding of the wreaths:

> Although these remains [the wreaths etc.] were found merely covered with dust and sand, they have been preserved with scarcely any change, and therefore permit the closest examination and comparison with their existing representatives. Many of the most delicate flowers, indeed, have been preserved without sustaining the slightest damage. The roses, for instance, had evidently been picked in an unopened condition, so as to prevent the petals from falling. In drying in the coffin, the petals had shrivelled and shrunk up into a ball, and when moistened in warm water and opened, the androecium appears before the eye in a wonderful state of preservation. Not a stamen, not an anther is wanting – one might almost say that not a pollen grain is missing.

The wreaths date back to *c.* AD 170 and are the earliest known record of extant roses. Like Schweinfurth and Cochet-Cochet, the Belgian, François

A box of rose remnants from the wreaths found during Petrie's excavations of the tombs at Hawara in Egypt. They are thought to date from AD *c*.170. We photographed the specimens with fresh *Rosa* × *richardii* (formerly known as *Rosa sancta*), which is what the remnants are thought to be. Seen in the Herbarium at Kew Gardens, London.

ROSA × DAMASCENA VERSICOLOR,
YORK AND LANCASTER A Damask with
greyish-green leaves, white, pink or striped
flowers and long sepals. Known since
1550. Summer flowering. Height to
200 cm (7 ft). Very good scent.

TRIGINTIPETALA, KAZANLIK, ROSE À
PARFUM DE GRASSE A Damask. An old
variety, long grown for producing attar of
roses. Summer flowering. Height to
200 cm (7 ft). Very good scent.

VAN HUYSUM A Damask. Jan van
Huysum was a famous Dutch flower
painter. Summer flowering. Height to
150 cm (5 ft). Good scent.

Crépin (1830–1903), the most famous rhodologist of his day, was 'highly excited' when he learnt about Petrie's discovery. After studying specimens of the wreaths which were sent to him from Kew Gardens, London (where several are still held in the Herbarium), he identified the roses as The Holy Rose or *Rosa sancta*, now known as *Rosa richardii*.

Sir William Flinders Petrie (1853–1942)

Petrie was a great Victorian eccentric whose reputation was made in the heyday of British Egyptology. His discoveries and methods influenced generations of archaeologists, some of whom are now household names. Howard Carter first went out to Egypt on a dig with Petrie in 1891, at the age of seventeen, and learnt much from him about archaeological method. Ironically, it is Carter who is remembered today because of his discovery of Tutankhamun's tomb. Petrie, whose famous finds such as the encaustic portrait paintings from the tombs at Hawara were exhibited at the Egyptian Hall in Piccadilly in London, drawing large crowds a century ago, is today largely unknown by the general public.

Petrie is renowned among archaeologists for his interest in the detritus of Egyptian life that he found in the tombs and burial mounds he excavated. Although every excavator is excited by the prospect of a spectacular discovery, Petrie recognized that much could also be learned about the past from unspectacular finds. While many archaeologists and tomb robbers, both before and contemporaneous with him, had discarded anything not obviously valuable, he collected numerous everyday artefacts that they had ignored: pottery, basketwork, textiles, plant remains. It was this last group that has proved so interesting to archaeo-botanists and rosarians.

Roses on Ancient Coins

In the eighteenth century there were claims that some very ancient coins dating back to 3000 BC and bearing 'some impression of a full blown rose' had been found in the graves of an Aryan people called the Tschudes. However, this has never been verified by any hard evidence and nobody knows where the coins are now – if they ever existed! The oldest coins with roses imprinted on them date back to *c.*500 BC and come from Rhodes.

Archaeologists believe that the island was named after the nymph Rhode of Greek mythology, whose symbol was the rose and who was loved by the sun god Helios. Rhodes was the centre of the cult of Helios which lasted from 400–80 BC and his head can be seen on one side of the coins that have been found in excavations there. A rose is represented on the other side.

The First Rose Painting

In 1900 the British archaeologist Sir Arthur Evans (1851–1941) began to excavate the palace of Minos and the surrounding town, at Knossos in northern Crete. It had been built between *c.*1900 and 1700 BC and was destroyed, possibly as a result of a volcanic explosion which took place on the island of Santorini, in *c.*1450 BC. Sir Arthur discovered that many walls of the palace and surrounding houses were decorated with beautiful frescos, some of which exist today. One that he excavated, in a house off the Royal Road leading to the palace, known as 'The House of Frescos', is called the 'Fresco with Blue Bird' and it caused enormous excitement among rosarians at the turn of the century because it depicts a number of monkeys, birds and plants including, undoubtedly, a rose. Sir Arthur described the fresco as follows:

'To the left, for the first time in Ancient Art, appears a wild rose bush, partly against a deep red and partly against a white background, and other coiling sprays of the same plant hang down from a rockwork arch above. The flowers are of a golden rose colour with orange centres dotted with deep red. The artist has given the flowers six petals instead of five, and has reduced the leaves to groups of three like those of the strawberry.'

As Sir Arthur said, this was the oldest painting of a rose ever discovered but, as with almost all archaeological discoveries, controversy abounds. C.C. Hurst (1870–1947), a botanist, had worked with him in England on identifying the rose and thought it bore 'a striking resemblance to the Holy Rose of Abyssinia, Egypt and Asia Minor.' That is, *Rosa sancta* (now known as *Rosa × richardii*). However, Hurst's widow Rona reopened the discussion after she visited Crete in 1964. An archaeologist as well as a botanist, she was able to provide archaeological information that supported a view somewhat at odds with the one generally held as a result of Sir Arthur's original description and her husband's subsequent identification. The problem is that the 'Fresco with

LEDA, PAINTED DAMASK A Damask. Known since 1827. Summer flowering; produces a few late flowers. Height to 100 cm ($3\frac{1}{2}$ ft). Good scent.

CELSIANA Leaves are greyish-green. Known at least since 1732. Summer flowering. Height to 150 cm (5 ft). Very good scent.

PALMYRE A Damask Perpetual. Raised by Vibert in France, 1817. Repeat flowering. Height to 120 cm (4 ft). Very good scent.

THE 'FRESCO WITH BLUE BIRD' (*c.* 1900–1700 BC) Most of the roses have been repainted, but the very faint specimen to the bottom left is an original rose. As far as one can see it seems to have five petals like a wild rose.

LA VILLE DE BRUXELLES A Damask with very long leaflets. Growth is loose and floppy if unsupported. Raised by Vibert in France, launched 1849. Repeat flowers a little. Height to 160 cm (5½ ft). Good scent.

AUTUMN DAMASK, QUATRE SAISONS, *ROSA × DAMASCENA* BIFERA The original Autumn Damask. A very ancient rose, possibly known to the Greeks in the 5th century BC, and probably the twice-flowering rose of Paestum described by Virgil. (Probably *Rosa gallica × Rosa moschata*.) Repeat flowering. Height to 130 cm (4½ ft). Very good scent.

AUTUMN DAMASK roses are a small but ancient group, and are thought to have arisen from a cross between *Rosa gallica* and the autumn-flowering musk rose, *Rosa moschata*. The original, twice-flowering Damask, Quatre Saisons, is said to have been known on the island of Samos since the late 10th century BC when it was used in the Greek cult of Aphrodite, and to be the rose of Paestum mentioned by Virgil in the *Georgics* (37–30 BC) and by the Romans in the worship of Venus. The flowers are pink and very well scented. The plant is rather tall and thorny, with grey-green leaves that reach right up to the flower. This character is seen in later Autumn Damasks such as Rose de Rescht, and in their descendants, the Portlands and Hybrid Perpetuals.

Blue Bird' was restored by E. Gillieron Fils under Sir Arthur's aegis and there are a number of roses on the fresco: some with six petals which have a yellowish tinge, as Rona Hurst agrees, and one, much fainter, pink rose which appears to have only five petals with strong veining on them. This feature is a distinctive characteristic of Gallica Roses, according to Rona Hurst. However, the most recent study of these frescos by the late Mark Cameron (to be published in his forthcoming book *Minoan Frescos*, edited by Lyvia Morgan) says that the six-petalled flowers occur 'with and without brown-veined leaves'. He calls them the wild dog rose, *Rosa canina*.

So the commonly held view seems to be that the fresco contains the earliest known painting of a rose but there is disagreement as to whether it is *Rosa sancta*, *Rosa gallica* or *Rosa canina*. In reality, it is the in-filling painting between the surviving fragments of the ancient fresco to 'clarify' the situation which casts doubt everywhere.

The Rose on Cuneiform Tablets

Many thousands of cuneiform tablets have been retrieved from archaeological sites in ancient Mesopotamia (the area principally covered by modern-day Iraq). Such tablets can reveal an enormous amount of information about the successive dynasties that ruled that part of the world and the lives of the people who lived under them. Many of the tablets record administrative information such as lists of stores and commodities; others preserve letters, omens, sign lists, vocabularies and even literature. A passage from the *Epic of Gilgamesh* and what Assyriologists call 'plant lists' and 'medical texts' are particularly important to the rose historian. The most comprehensive version of the *Epic*, which is on twelve separate tablets, and the majority of the plant lists and medical texts, were found at Nineveh. Others were unearthed at Assur, Babylon, Uruk, Nippur and Borsippa and one or two came from the enormous number of tablets found by Sir Leonard Woolley (1880–1960) in the course of his excavations at Ur and many other sites.

The Royal Library at Nineveh

Nineveh, near Mosul in northern Iraq, was an important and prosperous city as far back as 2000 BC. Assurbanipal, the last great king of the Assyrians who reigned from 668–627 BC, greatly expanded it when he came to power. At the north-west end of the Acropolis he constructed a palace to house the great library he assembled. He ordered his scribes to collect and copy on to tablets ancient texts from all over Babylonia to create the most comprehensive collection of written information in existence. Nineveh was conquered by the Medes in 612 BC and the library and tablets were buried in rubble when the palace was destroyed.

In the 1850s Sir Austen Henry Layard (1817–94) excavated the city and unearthed Assurbanipal's library in the large Kuyundjik mound. (Artefacts found there are usually referred to as the 'K' collection.) Some tablets were damaged by fire, and all had been broken as the walls of the rooms in which they were housed had caved in. Nevertheless there, in one collection, was a superb intellectual treasure trove. A vast amount of information about the cultural history of ancient Mesopotamia has been reconstructed from the tablets in the 'K' Collection, and there is a great deal more to be learnt when a systematic study of the library's contents and the provenance of the tablets is completed.

The 'plant lists' and the tablets called 'medical texts' have revealed much about the kinds of plants grown, and how they were used in pharmacology, in ancient Mesopotamia. Some of them have been easy to identify but the majority have proved more difficult to link to known flora, and this has resulted in many conflicting theories and counter-theories. One scholar, Reginald Campbell Thompson (1876–1941), a cuneiform expert who specialized in translating and interpreting the medical and plant texts, was convinced that the word *kasu* meant rose. It occurs 181 times on the 600 tablets known as the Assyrian Medical Texts and is the third most commonly mentioned plant after *burasu* (identified as *Pinus*) and *kukru* (now known to be *Abies*). Others have argued that *kasu* be identified with mustard, beetroot and liquorice. However, recent work by a Dutch Assyriologist, Marten Stol, has concluded that *kasu* is probably the word for *Dodder*. This is a species of *Cuscuta*, a parasitic plant that was used to flavour beer, and perhaps explains why it was mentioned so often: the Babylonians were more than fond of brewing. Although it is disappointing not to have overwhelming proof that roses were used medicinally in numerous ways, as Thompson had claimed, the word *amurdinnu*, which crops up in some of the medical texts and which even Thompson somewhat reluctantly agreed may have referred to a 'bramble' or 'wild rose', is now considered to mean wild rose by most contemporary Assyriologists.

The latest justification for this identification comes from a Russian scholar, Igor M. Diakonoff, who cites its use in the *Epic of Gilgamesh*. There *amurdinnu* appears to be a thorny flower with a strong smell (which a bramble does not have, as Diakonoff points out, while a rose does). The etymological connection between *amurdinnu* (M often became w in later Babylonian times) and the Arabic *ward* (rose) has been increasingly commented on by linguists. Some commentators claim that *amurdinnu* could just as easily apply to a bramble. However, as a bramble (*Rubus*) has a delicious edible fruit one would expect to find this mentioned on the tablets in conjunction with *amurdinnu*, but it never is. The task of deciphering and interpreting the cuneiform tablets will continue for centuries and hard evidence is needed before any theory can be conclusively proved.

CLAY TABLET K2252 FROM THE ASKENAZI LIBRARY AT NINEVEH The tablet tells the story of the *Gilgamesh Epic*. The word thought to represent rose appears five lines down from the top left.

IMPORTANT ROSE BREEDERS I

Alexandre Hardy was for many years chief horticulturist at the Luxembourg Gardens in Paris, and an amateur rose breeder. Between 1829 and 1847 he raised many thousands of seedlings and introduced many new roses, of which around ten are still grown. The perfect white Damask, Félicité Hardy, named after his wife, is his most famous, but there were also several Teas including the unusual Bon Silène (page 106).

ROSA × ALBA SEMI-PLENA An Alba. A large, tall shrub with arching stems. This is probably one of the oldest cultivars of roses, perhaps even Roman in origin. Thought to be a hybrid between a Damask and a Dog Rose. Graham Thomas records that it appeared as a sport on Alba Maxima in 1959. Height to 180 cm (6 ft). Very good scent.

ALBA ROSES are one of the four very ancient groups of garden roses, probably grown by the Romans and earlier. The original Alba, Semi-plena, is thought to be a hybrid between a Damask and a Dog Rose. Several of the latter have greyish leaves and white or pale pink flowers, both typical characters of the Alba. The shrubs are strong growing, with arching shoots, well set with flowers. All are once flowering, with good scent.

FÉLICITÉ HARDY, MME HARDY (WAS THE ORIGINAL NAME) A Damask. The rather leafy sepals and green eye are characteristic. Raised by Hardy in France, launched 1832. A Damask-Portland or possibly a Damask-Alba hybrid. Summer flowering. Height to 200 cm (7 ft). Very good scent.

THE WHITE ROSE OF YORK, *ROSA × ALBA* MAXIMA, THE JACOBITE ROSE, GREAT DOUBLE WHITE. A very ancient Alba rose, probably a sport from Alba Semi-plena, with very strong-growing foliage. Summer flowering. Has been known to sport a single white. Very resistant to disease. Height to 240 cm (8 ft). Well scented.

BLANCHE DE BELGIQUE, BLANCHE SUPERBE An Alba. The tight central rosette is characteristic of this variety. Raised by Vibert in France, launched 1817. Summer flowering. Height to 150 cm (5 ft). Good scent.

LA VIRGINALE An Alba. More double than Semi-Plena, less double than Maxima. Raised by Moreau-Robert in France, launched 1840. Summer flowering. To 180 cm (6 ft). Good scent.

Geographically and climatically, roses have been flourishing in the area known previously as Mesopotamia for many millennia. It seems likely that they existed and were used there in ancient times, especially since we have learnt from other archaeological excavations that they were known and used in the first millennium BC both in the Peloponnese and in China.

The Rose and the Greeks

We know from archaeological discoveries that the rose was well known to the Greeks: the mention of rose-scented oil on the Olive Oil Tablets of Pylos (page 9), and the painting of a rose on the 'Fresco with Blue Bird' at Knossos (page 13) are two concrete examples. But it is from numerous Greek writings that we realize its importance in many aspects of Greek life: botanical, medicinal, cosmetic and, above all, symbolic.

The earliest reference to the use of rose oil for medicinal and funeral purposes comes in Book XXIII of the *Iliad*, Homer's epic poem describing the siege of Troy. Although it was not written down until the eighth century BC, the events it records, passed down through oral tradition, are believed to date back to the eleventh century BC. The *Iliad* tells how the body of Hector, killed by Achilles to avenge Patroclus' death, was anointed with rose oil and then embalmed by the goddess Aphrodite.

Aphrodite herself by day and by night, she washed the skin with rose oil ...
Iliad Book XXIII (translated by W. H.D. Rouse)

At that time rose oil was made not by distillation (which came later) but by steeping petals in olive, sesame or almond oil. As huge quantities are required to scent oil this way it seems highly probable that the Greeks must have cultivated roses specifically for the purpose. Much has been written about which particular species they would have grown. Because later writers like Theophrastus (*c.* 372–*c.* 287 BC) and Pliny the Elder (AD 23–79) mentioned the hundred-petalled rose it has sometimes been suggested that *Rosa centifolia* was cultivated by the Greeks. In fact *Rosa centifolia* is, relatively speaking, a modern rose, developed in Holland in the sixteenth century.

The Greek rose was probably either a very fully petalled form of *Rosa gallica* or *Rosa damascena* or possibly a double form of *Rosa alba*. This seems to be supported by the Greek historian Herodotus (*c.* 480–425 BC) who wrote of the sixty-blossomed rose grown by King Midas of Phrygia when he was exiled to Macedonia in the sixth century BC. The exact location in Macedonia of Midas' garden is uncertain (although A.D. Godley, one of Herodotus' translators, says it was in the fertile valley of Aegae or Edessa (modern-day Vodena) in Macedonia). However, we can be certain from Herodotus' account that the roses growing there were more strongly perfumed than any other rose he had ever smelt:

The garden of Midas son of Gorgias, wherein roses grow of themselves, each bearing sixty blossoms and of surpassing fragrance ...'

At about the same time that Theophrastus, the philosopher, scientist and first major botanical writer, was describing roses in considerable detail, explaining methods of propagation and their blossoming periods in Egypt, another Greek philosopher, Epicurus (*c.* 341–270 BC), had his own private rose garden in Athens. Presumably the never-ending stream of fresh roses it supplied enabled him to achieve the high degree of pleasure that his philosophy advocated as being the natural and highest good of mankind.

Unfortunately, Greek cities and towns were generally too compact for any except the wealthiest to have rose gardens like Epicurus. Those who did have gardens at the backs of their houses grew roses for their perfume which they believed kept illness at bay, as well as for ornament and for use in wreaths. Theophrastus records that in some gardens, known as 'Gardens of Adonis', exceptionally pretty roses were cultivated in silver pots. Later writers, such as Dioscorides (first century AD) in *Materia Medica*, describe numerous cosmetic and medicinal uses for roses which had, presumably, been handed down over the centuries.

Greek Poetry and Mythology

It is in Greek poetry and legend that the symbolic nature of the rose is first explored. In the seventh century BC Sappho, the Greek poetess from the island of Lesbos, wrote, 'The rose each ravished sense beguiles' and called the rose the 'Queen of Flowers' – images that were to be used repeatedly over the centuries. In the fifth century BC Anacreon composed an ode dedicated to praising every aspect of the rose's beauty: its perfume, its power to heal, the esteem in which it was held among the gods.

> The rose the poet's song perfumes,
> And in each muse's bosom blooms,
> How sweet to seize the blushing Prey,
> And snatch it from the Thorn away!
> …
> Before the Rose pale sickness flies;
> The Rose can ev'n the dead rejoice:
> 'Gainst Time itself it keeps the field,
> To Time its odours scorn to yield.
> *Ode 51*, Anacreon (translated by
> Addison, 1735)

The wearing of rose wreaths had symbolic connotations. Solon (640–560 BC), a Greek lawyer, tells us that girls who had lost their virginity were not allowed to wear rose wreaths; these were presumably reserved only for virgins, symbols of their innocence and purity. At about the same time Stesichorus (602–555 BC), a Greek poet who lived in Himera, a town in northern Sicily colonized by the Greeks, associated the rose with drinking and feasting. In his heroic ballads he wrote of the rose wreaths revellers wore at banquets. Eros, son of Aphrodite and god of love and sexual desire, is frequently depicted wearing a wreath of roses, as is Dionysus, the god of wine. This association between roses and revelry was to reach its peak in Roman times.

Greek myths accentuate the symbolic nature of the rose. The most famous is probably that surrounding Aphrodite (Venus), goddess of love. According to Anacreon, she sprang forth into life from the sea's foam (as celebrated in the fifteenth century in Botticelli's *Birth of Venus*) and where the foam fell to the ground white roses grew. This and later myths about Aphrodite capture the dual nature of love that she symbolizes: purity and innocence represented by white roses; desire and sexual gratification by red ones. In one story she runs to help her lightly wounded lover, Adonis, and catches her flesh on the thorns of a white rose bush. Her blood falling on the bush turns the roses red. White roses become red, symbolizing the way innocence and purity change to fecundity and motherhood when blood is shed through menstruation and parturition. Another myth, about the creation of rose bushes, concerns Rhodanthe, the queen of Corinth, whose name means rose bloom. Her beauty was such that she had three suitors who pestered her until she took refuge in the temple of Artemis, virgin goddess of the hunt. However, visitors to the temple were so struck by her looks that they began to worship her instead of Artemis, whose temple it was. Apollo (Artemis' twin brother) was so furious at their treatment of his sister that he turned Rhodanthe into a rose bush and her suitors into a fly, a worm and a butterfly.

ROSA ALBA (A SINGLE SPORT) An Alba. This appeared on a plant of *Rosa alba* in 1992. We are uncertain whether it is a sport or an Alba-like stock. Summer flowering. Height to 150 cm (5 ft). Photographed at Symnel Cottage, Kent. Growing roses from seed may throw up plants that have reverted to some earlier form, the wild species from which the rose has been bred. Could this be a lost parent of the Alba Roses?

SMALL MAIDEN'S BLUSH An Alba. Slightly smaller than 'Great' but similar. Known since 1797. Summer flowering. To 120 cm (4 ft). Very good scent.

FÉLICITÉ PARMENTIER An Alba. Small and shrubby for this section. Known since 1834. Summer flowering. Height to 120 cm (4 ft). Very good scent.

MME PLANTIER Probably a hybrid
Alba × Noisette, though often classed as
an Alba. Raised by Plantier in France,
launched 1835. Summer flowering, over
a long period. Height to 240 cm (8 ft),
more if supported. Well scented.

Sharon Van Enoo can trace the history
of the Mme Plantier in her garden at
Torrance, near Los Angeles back to its
arrival in America: Thomas Bullock
(1816–85) was born in Staffordshire and
converted to Mormonism while a young
man. Because of his conversion he lost
his job, and so migrated to Nauvoo,
Illinois where he became personal
secretary to Joseph Smith. After Joseph
Smith was murdered, Thomas became
secretary to Brigham Young, and joined
the trek to Utah.

In 1858 he went back to England on a
Church mission and to visit his family.
On his return he wrote to his cousin in
Staffordshire asking for plants, seeds and
cuttings to grow in Utah, and among the
plants that arrived were cuttings of Mme
Plantier. Thomas' daughter Pamela was
born in 1842, and married James Mason,
who had a nursery of sorts in Morgan,
Utah. By the early 1880s Mason had two
wives and in 1884 moved with his family
to establish a new settlement in Idaho.

When Utah decided to become a state
the Mormon Church declared polygamy
illegal, and men had to make the choice
of which wife to keep. Like many men
of his day (or any other) James Mason
chose the younger of his two wives,
leaving Pamela alone in the backwoods
of Egin Bench, Idaho with her children
and her roses. (*Egin* is the Indian word
for 'cold and windy' and is located on the
north fork of the Snake River.) However,
it was from Merna Davenport de Spain,
the daughter of Genie the second wife of
James Mason, that Sharon received her
cutting of Mme Plantier.

Roses in Roman Myths

As in Greek mythology, the rose plays a recurring and symbolic role in Roman
legends. Although the names are different there is a basic similarity in many
of the stories. The rose as a symbol for youth, beauty, desire, fecundity and
a kind of panacea or substitute for death crops up over and over again. The
Roman story of Roselia draws several parallels with that of Rhodanthe.
Roselia's life, from birth, had been dedicated to Diana, virgin goddess of the
hunt and moon, so when the goddess discovered her acolyte had married
Cymedor she killed her with an arrow. However, when she saw the despair
she had inflicted on Roselia's distraught husband, she was filled with remorse
and changed the lifeless corpse into a beautiful rose bush.

Another myth parallels that of Aphrodite rescuing Adonis and symbolizes
the connection between blood, sexual fulfilment and red roses. Venus loved
Adonis but was also pursued by Mars, the god of war, who would have killed
Adonis had not Venus warned her lover of the danger he faced. In her haste
to save him, she slipped in a rose bed and scratched her legs. Red rose bushes
grew from the blood that flowed from her wounds on to the ground. Similarly,
a story about Bacchus, the god of wine, relates how a pretty girl he was trying
to seduce became entangled in a thorn bush. The god was so grateful to the
plant for helping him achieve his desire that he rewarded it by covering its
branches with red roses. The Greek connection between wine, love and roses
lives on in the Roman story in which Cupid, the god of love, accidentally
knocked a bowl of wine standing on Bacchus' table on to the ground. A rose
bush sprang from the pool of wine.

Several myths involve Flora, the goddess of spring and flowers. In one, she
asks all the gods to help her change a most beloved, dead nymph into a
wonderful flower. Apollo gave the corpse the breath of life; Bacchus washed
her in nectar; Vertumnus gave her a beautiful perfume; Pomona gave her
fruit; and Flora gave her a crown of petals. Thus was the rose, the Queen of
Flowers, created. Another tells how Eros shot Flora with one of his arrows
and she, overcome with love, was unable to pronounce his name in full but
just murmured 'rose'. From that time Eros and roses have, together, symbolized
love, desire and beauty.

Roses in Everyday Roman Life

The Romans admired, and were enormously influenced by, what we would
call the Greek 'life style': their philosophy, culture and education; the way
they lived their everyday lives. Consequently the Greeks' love, and use, of
roses percolated into the Roman life style, presumably from the time of the
Greek colonization of southern Italy and Sicily in the eighth century BC. But
what was a love for the Greeks was a passion for the Romans; admiration
turned into obsession. Everything the Greeks had done with roses the Romans
did ten times over. They wore rose wreaths, grew roses in their gardens,
incorporated roses (or bits of them) into a thousand dishes and used roses in
a huge variety of cosmetics, unguent oils and remedies. They lay on rose
pillows, painted roses in frescos, wrote of roses in myths, perfumed water
with roses, buried their dead with roses, deified roses and even, occasionally,
suffocated their guests with roses.

These excesses did not pass without critical comment. Cato (234–149 BC),
a Roman senator and statesman who denounced the moral decay that he
claimed existed in Rome, believed that this decline was symbolized by awarding
rose wreaths for every minor military victory instead of only as a mark of
honour for a major success. Two and a half centuries later Tacitus (AD 56–
117), the Roman historian, was still incensed because the military honour
conferred on a man awarded a rose wreath had been diluted. When the

Emperor Vitellius (AD 15–72) visited the corpse-strewn battlefield of Bedriacum (now Calvatone near Cremona) in northern Italy, laurels and roses were scattered in his path implying that the honour of the victory was his. In fact, he had not participated in the fighting. Roses, the symbol of courage and bravery, were being degraded.

Cicero (106–43 BC) criticized the governor of Sicily for his excessively lavish life style, paid for by heavily taxing the ordinary people. He particularly condemned his habit of wearing a rose wreath on his head and easing the discomfort of travel by placing a soft, petal-filled cushion under his bottom. The governor kept the smells and diseases of the plebeians at bay by holding a bag of scented petals under his nose!

However, the extraordinary extravagance with which roses were used came to the fore early in the first millennium AD. Nero (AD 37–68), a notoriously cruel and hedonistic emperor, started the fashion for raining rose petals on guests at feasts. On one occasion, it is said, he spent four million sesterces (about £200 000) on roses to decorate the banqueting hall. On another, an entire beach at Baiae, near Naples, was strewn with roses at a cost of about two million sesterces.

Two centuries later the Emperor Heliogabalus (AD 204–224) wanted to commemorate the start of his reign – at the age of fourteen – with a memorable feast. He certainly fulfilled his ambition. Locking all his guests in the banqueting room to ensure their attention to the spectacle he had devised, he showered them three times with roses. The quantities of petals he used were so overpowering that a number of people were suffocated. If given the chance to say so, those who died at Heliogabalus' feast would probably have preferred to have nothing further to do with roses. However, it is unlikely that their wishes would have been granted, for the Romans used them in abundance at funerals. The rose was a symbol of life because of its beauty, a symbol of death because of the inevitable withering of its blooms and a symbol of eternal life because of its association with the gods.

The rose's association with wine and revelry had originated during the height of the Roman Empire. Rose chaplets were worn at feasts to cool the brow and counteract the smell of stale wine. Roses sculpted or painted on a ceiling symbolized secrecy and ensured that whatever was said in the room,

CHLORIS, ROSÉE DU MATIN An Alba with dark green leaves. Known since 1848. Summer flowering. Height to 150 cm (5 ft). Good scent.

POMPOM BLANC PARFAIT An Alba. Known since 1876. Summer flowering but long lasting. Height to 120 cm (4 ft). Good scent.

THE BIRTH OF VENUS (APHRODITE) BY SANDRO BOTTICELLI (1440–1510) Aphrodite is shown rising from the sea with the white roses that are associated with her purity falling from her like foam from the waves.

GREAT MAIDEN'S BLUSH, CUISSE DE NYMPHE, INCARNATA, LA SÉDUISANTE, ROSIER BLANC ROYALE An Alba. Known since before the 15th century. Summer flowering. Height to 180 cm (6 ft). Very good scent.

CELESTIAL, CELESTE A semi-double Alba that flowers beautifully in summer. Launched in The Netherlands in the late 18th century. Height to 180 cm (6 ft). Good scent.

A detail of a Roman garden fresco in Casa del Bracciale d'Oro, Pompeii.

BELLE AMOUR An Alba. Leaves are uncharacteristic. Found by Nancy Lindsay on the wall of an old convent at Elboeuf in Normandy, introduced 1950. Summer flowering. Height to 180 cm (6 ft). Myrrh scented.

while drunk or sober, would be considered confidential. Hence the expression *sub rosa*, 'under the rose', which means secretly or in strictest confidence. The origin of this is obscure, but according to one legend Cupid bribed Harpocrates (the god of silence) with a rose not to betray the amours of Venus. The habit of sculpting roses on the ceilings of banqueting halls and dining-rooms sprang from this.

Rose Cultivation in Roman Times

The Romans' incessant demand for roses had to be met by a constantly increasing supply and much information and advice about cultivating roses at all sorts of levels can be found in Roman writings, from tips to individual gardeners to treatises on the various methods of propagation and information on commercial rose growing and rose importation from Egypt.

The cultivation of private rose gardens, roof gardens and balcony gardens was popular, as can be seen in frescos and in peristyle gardens excavated at Pompeii. It enabled individuals to have a constant supply of roses for wreaths and a wonderful fragrance to counteract the smells of the city and keep disease at bay. It probably also allowed them to use roses, in a small way, for cosmetic or culinary purposes. Both Varro (117–28 BC) in *De re rustica* and Pliny the Younger (AD 62–113) in his letters give advice on rose planting and rose propagation for individual gardeners. In *An Enquiry into the Natural Sciences* Seneca (3 BC–AD 65), the Roman philosopher who taught Nero, describes how roses were cultivated in 'forcing houses' and brought on by watering with warm water. Pliny the Elder (AD 23–79) in his encyclopaedic *Naturalis Historia* also wrote about the advantages of heat in forcing roses to flower early. The Romans were desperate for roses all year round so there is much advice on pruning in *De re rustica* by Columella (first century AD), a Roman landowner, and later, in the fourth century, in Palladius' *De re rustica* – fourteen volumes on agriculture and horticulture. Palladius also advocated the warm water method for bringing on early blooms.

THE ROSES OF HELIOGABALUS BY SIR LAWRENCE ALMA-TADEMA (1836–1912) Although the revellers reclining on their couches look very relaxed they are about to suffocate under a deluge of roses.

AGATHE FATIMA A Gallica. Known since 1820. Summer flowering. Height to 150 cm (5 ft). Good scent. Photographed at Malmaison near Paris with a reconstruction of Josephine's summer-house in the background.

GALLICA ROSES are some of the most ancient of garden roses. They were bred from the wild *Rosa gallica* and grown by the Greeks and Romans, and probably in earlier civilizations. Rather narrow, rough leaflets with impressed veins, and red to purplish flowers are characteristic of the group. If grown on their own roots they will sucker widely. They flower only in midsummer. The variety Officinalis is thought to have been brought back to Europe by Thibault IV (1201–53). From 1300, it was cultivated for petals, which keep their scent when dried, and became a great speciality of the town of Provins in France. Most of the sumptuous Gallica Roses with huge, flat, very double flowers were raised in France in the early 19th century. The Empress Josephine is said to have grown over 160 varieties at Malmaison.

A mural in the House of the Vettii, Pompeii.

LE ROSIER EVÊQUE, L'EVÊQUE, THE BISHOP A Gallica with purple flowers that fade to greyish-violet. An old French variety illustrated by Redouté in 1821. Summer flowering. Height to 130 cm (4½ ft). Good scent.

To supply the vast number of roses required by emperors like Nero and Heliogabalus there had to be large-scale rose production. This took place at Paestum, Praeneste (modern Palestrina, south-east of Rome) and Leporia (20 kilometres/12½ miles north of Naples in Italy), around Egypt's Nile Delta and at Carthage in North Africa. Paestum was a flourishing town in southern Italy, on the gulf of Salerno. It had been founded in *c*.600 BC by the Greeks who called it Poseidonia. In about 270 BC it was taken over by the Romans and developed into a profitable rose growing area. It also became a popular holiday resort when the roses were at their best – rather like tulips in Holland today.

Because of a reference in Virgil's *Georgics* (37–30 BC) to the rose gardens of twice-bearing Paestum, early rosarians were under the impression that a special and particular rose grew there. However, Pliny the Elder makes no mention of it in *Naturalis Historia*, although he lists all the other roses known at the time, and it has now been concluded that there was no particular rose specific to Paestum, but that it was a famous area for growing roses – perhaps several different kinds. The 'twice bearing' reference probably means that there was one rose that flowered twice in the year, i.e. *Rosa damascena*, the Autumn Damask, or that there were two roses – one that grew early in the season and was forced in greenhouses or with warm water and another that flowered later thus increasing the length of the season for blooms. Alternatively, the same type of rose could have been planted at slightly different times of year, with some plants forced and some held back to prolong the season. It would be another fifteen centuries before the arrival of the true repeat-flowering rose from China, in Josephine's era. Some of the roses mentioned by Pliny the Elder are the *Rosa gallica* grown at Praeneste, which flowered late in the season and was most sought after; and a form of *Rosa alba* with white, scented flowers which was known as the Rose of Campania and grew around Leporia. The 'hundred-petalled' rose, previously misnamed as *Rosa centifolia* and now recognized as *Rosa damascena*, also came from the same area. Despite these major rose-growing areas in Italy and the various methods used to force roses to bloom in winter, demand still outstripped supply so the Romans imported roses from Egypt and Carthage. How they remained fresh and intact after the six-day journey by ship from Egypt is unknown. In the winter of AD 89–90 Paestum produced so many of its own roses that there was no need that year for any to be imported from the Nile Delta. However, the massive Roman cultivation of roses had meant a decrease in their production of corn (already commented on by Horace (65–8 BC) in his *Odes*) and the problem was emphasized again by Montial (AD 41–100) in these lines:

> O Nile, the Roman Roses are now much finer than thine!
> Your Roses we no longer need, but send us your corn.

The Rose in Egypt

Although Egypt is the source of the earliest pictures of gardens, dating back to 2600 BC, and although much has been learned from papyrus scrolls and the stone reliefs in ancient temples about the plants grown in the gardens, there is no concrete evidence that the rose existed there in pre-Roman times. The oldest Egyptian 'catalogue of plants' is the one that was recorded in stone relief at Karnak in the second millennium BC at the instigation of Tuthmosis III. He collected all kinds of different specimens during his campaigns in Syria and Palestine (*c.* 1450 BC), which were carved in relief at Karnak in the side chamber now known as the Botanical Room, off the feasting chamber in the temple of Ammon. Information about these plants was recorded in hieroglyphics at Thebes and in the late nineteenth and early twentieth centuries Georges Schweinfurth and others attempted a systematic identification of them. Positive identification was difficult in many instances and no roses were found.

Controversy abounds as to when roses were first introduced into Egypt. Some experts believe that the Coptic word *ouert* or *werd* relates to the Arabic *ward* for rose and dates back to the fourteenth century BC; others believe the rose was introduced into Egypt by the Greeks in the fourth century BC. Exactly where these early roses were grown is unclear. Sources mention the area around the Nile Delta but Pierre-Simon Girard (1765–1836), who led a scientific mission into Egypt after its conquest by Napoleon, discovered hundreds of rose fields and numerous ovens for rose water distillation in the Medin-el-Faiyum area.

Were these a survival from the Roman Empire, when huge quantities of roses were exported to Italy (page 21) and when, according to Pliny the Elder, the Egyptians made artificial roses from wood shavings scented with rose balm? Stories of Cleopatra VII (69–30 BC) carpeting the floor of the banqueting hall or throne room with roses to a depth of 60 centimetres (2 feet) when Mark Anthony (*c.* 81–30 BC) visited her (at a reputed cost of £325 in gold) verify that roses were grown in abundance in Egypt at that period. It may have been accounts of this occasion that gave rise to the Romans' predilection for using masses of roses at their feasts and festivals.

Rose growing in Egypt later declined in favour of corn production, but evidence from Egyptian tombs of the second and third centuries AD affirms that roses were used in funeral wreaths. The Holy Rose identified as *Rosa sancta* (*Rosa × richardii*) can still, apparently, be found at Mau-Tsada, a mountain village in northern Ethiopia; if the goats haven't eaten all the bushes!

The Rose in Chinese Medicine

There is no doubt that the rose has existed in China for thousands of years. Numerous books record its very early use in medicine and written records list the large numbers of roses planted in the Imperial Gardens. The history of Chinese pharmacology (plant medicine) is a fascinating but difficult subject for the botanist. Apart from the problem the average, non-Chinese-speaking Westerner has in finding works in translation, information about quite recent archaeological discoveries is difficult to obtain.

The Chinese were brilliant and copious preservers of information on a vast range of subjects. We know this in the botanical/medicinal field because

TUSCANY The Old Velvet Rose. A Gallica known since 1820, possibly the 16th century. Summer flowering. Height to 120 cm (4 ft). Good scent.

TUSCANY SUPERB A Gallica. Like a larger version of Tuscany. Known since 1837. Probably a sport or seedling of Tuscany. Summer flowering. Height to 120 cm (4 ft). Good scent.

LOUIS PHILIPPE A Gallica. Raised by Hardy in France, launched 1824. Summer flowering. Height to 150 cm (5 ft). Good scent.

of the numerous herbals written since the sixteenth century that constantly update, and expand, knowledge already recorded in previous books. These in turn refer to yet more ancient books that have not been preserved. One of the reasons why so much of China's history has been passed on only by oral tradition and then recorded in the centuries after Christ is because in 213 BC the Emperor Ts'in Shi Huang Ti (246–209 BC), the builder of the Great Wall of China, ordered all books except those on medicine, divination and husbandry to be burnt.

Despite the fact that medical books were spared, no copies exist today of the most famous book on Chinese *Materia Medica*: the *Shên-Nung pên-ts'ao ching* (Shen Nung's classic *Materia Medica*). It dates back to between the fifth and second centuries BC and we learn of its existence and contents from references in later *Pen-ts'ao* books and other literary fragments. We do not, of course, know its exact contents, but we do know that it formed the basis for a very famous herbal of the sixteenth century that does exist: Li Shih-Chen's *Pen-ts'ao kang mu*. Scholars have realized that the oral and written tradition in China is so strong that when a new *Pen-ts'ao* is written it is not a totally original piece of work that throws out all the old and traditional theories and comes up with a whole new set of plants and suggested uses; rather, each new herbal is a reaffirmation of the known remedies of the past, merely a new edition of the same original work that is continuously improved upon over the centuries. Bernard Read's translation (1936) of Li Shi-Chen's *Pen-ts'ao kang mu* (1596) lists four kinds of roses as being used in various ways for medicinal purposes – *Rosa banksiae*, *Rosa multiflora*, *Rosa laevigata* and *Rosa indica* (*chinensis*) – and he claims the first two were passed down from the earliest *Pen-ts'ao* of Shen Nung. In other words, roses were almost certainly used in China several hundred years before the birth of Christ, and quite probably many hundreds of years before then.

Two recent archaeological discoveries in China confirm the existence of a body of pharmaceutical knowledge that was listed and recorded in ancient times. The oldest written evidence for the Chinese use of plants in medicine dates back to the third century BC. In 1972 an archaeological dig in a Han grave in Wu-wei country in Kansu Province unearthed 92 medical texts written on bamboo and wooden slates which contemporary experts date to *c.*220 BC. These texts list over one hundred drugs, 69 per cent of which also appear in the *Shên Nung pên-ts'ao ching*. I have been unable to find out whether roses *per se* are mentioned as my knowledge of ancient Chinese is non-existent and there is no English translation of these texts. In 1973 silk fragments dating back to the second century BC were found in the Han Grave No. 3 of the Ma-wang-tui site near Ch'ang-sha. One of them, the *Wu-shi-erh ping fang* (Prescriptions against fifty-two illnessess), mentions 247 drugs, from mineral,

DUCHESSE D'ANGOULÊME A Gallica with stems that arch outwards. Raised by Vibert in France, launched before 1827. Possibly a hybrid with *Rosa centifolia*. Summer flowering. Height to 90 cm (3 ft). Good scent.

DUCHESSE DE MONTEBELLO A Gallica. Raised by Laffay in France before 1829. Summer flowering. Height to 150 cm (5 ft). Good scent.

A view of the ancient Moorish gardens of the Alhambra in Granada, looking towards the Generalife. The gardens and waterworks are wonderfully preserved; what a shame we find only modern roses in the beds.

TRICOLORE, REINE MARGUERITE A Gallica. Raised by Lahaye (père) in France, launched 1827. Summer flowering. To 120 cm (4 ft). Good scent.

animal and human sources as well as plant ones, in 170 different prescriptions. About half these substances are in the earliest *Pen-ts'ao* although roses are not among them.

This recent evidence suggests that the Chinese had a kind of 'databank' of pharmaceutical knowledge that had been gleaned over the centuries and passed on both orally and in written records; and this databank was the foundation for the specialized literary genre of *Pen-ts'ao* that continues to this day.

The Rose in Persia

Persian carpets, paintings, miniatures and poetry are riddled with roses. The production of roses and attar of roses and the association of the rose with all aspects of spiritual, cultural and commercial life had been part of the Persian tradition for centuries. Yet strangely, although many botanists believe that the roses cultivated in the West since Greek and Roman times originated in Persia, very little is actually known about the region before the seventh century AD when the Arab religion of Islam swept through the country and most of the ancient texts which recounted the earliest history of the Persian people were destroyed. From the ninth century onwards there are numerous references to roses in every aspect of Persian life. Many records tell of rose fields for producing the finest attar of roses in and around Nishapur, Teheran, Isfahan, Shiraz and Kashan – areas which are still famed for their roses and attar. Time and time again, Persian poetry uses the symbolism of the rose to express the complexity of life. For example, Sa'di (1194–1296), born in Shiraz, is the author of two books in which the rose symbol is paramount – *Bustan* (Garden of Perfume) and *Gulistan* (Rose Garden) – and Shabistari (c.1250–c.1320) wrote the *Gulshan i Raz* (The Secret Rose Garden). And of course, there is the *Rubaiyat* of Omar Khayyám (1020–1123). The translation of this work by Edward Fitzgerald (1809–1883) almost single-handedly created the European concept of eleventh-century Persia. According to Shirazi, who wrote a biography of Omar Khayyám in 1905, the reason why many poets used the rose as a symbol was because they were Sufis: Sufism contains elements of Vedantism, Muhammedanism, Christianity and pantheism and was disapproved of by the religious authorities. Writing symbolically provided the opportunity to say things both metaphorically and literally, and the symbol of the rose had so many associations for literate Persians that no further explanation was necessary. In Sufism the rose symbolized achieving perfect understanding and union with God. It was also a symbol for life itself. Its beauty represents the perfection we should all seek to achieve. Its thorns symbolize the difficulties we all face in attempting to reach our ideal, and the fact that the bushes bloom again show us that our efforts must be continuous and will, in the end, succeed.

OMAR KHAYYÁM A Damask. Plants are stiffly upright with small leaves. Raised at Kew Gardens, London from seed collected from Omar Khayyám's grave at Nishapur (page 25) and launched 1893. Summer flowering. Height to 200 cm (7 ft). Very good scent.

ISPAHAN, ISFAHAN, POMPOM DES PRINCES A rather upright-growing Damask. Known since 1832. Summer flowering, over a long period. Height to 200 cm (7 ft). Good scent.

ROSA HEMISPHAERICA, ROSE DE TURCS An old garden rose from Turkey. Thin, bluish-grey leaves distinguish it from *Rosa foetida* Persiana. Needs a hot climate for flowers to open properly. Introduced before 1625. A sport of *Rosa hemisphaerica*. Summer flowering. Liable to blackspot. Little scent. Photographed at the Roseraie de l'Haÿ, Paris.

The grave of Edward Fitzgerald in the tiny church at Boulge, Suffolk.

As the stricter tenets of Islam took hold on Persian society, so the symbolism of the rose became increasingly central to Islam, just as in Europe its pagan symbolism gradually changed and was incorporated in the Christian symbolism of the Middle Ages.

The Rose of Omar Khayyám

In 1884 William Simpson, an artist-illustrator for the *Illustrated London News* happened to visit Nishapur, the Persian city where Omar Khayyám was buried (near modern-day Mashhad in northern Iran). Simpson was an admirer of the *Rubaiyat* and, remembering that Khayyám was reputed to have predicted that his tomb would be 'on a spot where the north wind may blow roses on it', he visited the cemetery at Hira and collected seeds from the rose bushes which he did, indeed, find growing on Khayyám's grave. The seeds were brought back to England and sent to Kew Gardens in London where a bush was eventually reared. In 1893 members of the Omar Khayyám Club made a pilgrimage to the tomb of Edward Fitzgerald at Boulge graveyard in Suffolk to plant a graft from the rose found by Omar Khayyam's tomb on the grave of his greatest translator. The following verses, by the poet Edmund Gosse, were recited at the little ceremony:

> Reign here, triumphant rose, from Omar's grave,
> Borne by a dervish o'er the Persian wave;
> Reign with fresh pride, since here a heart is sleeping
> That double glory to your Master gave.
>
> Hither let many a pilgrim step be bent
> To greet the Rose re-risen in banishment;
> Here richer crimsons may its cup be keeping
> Than brimmed it ere from Naishápur it went.

The rose, a Damask now called Omar Khayyám, still grows at the foot of Fitzgerald's grave.

LA BELLE SULTANE, *ROSA GALLICA* VIOLACEA, GALLICA MAHEKA, CUMBERLAND A tall-growing, almost single Gallica of rich colour. Known since 1795. (Possibly a Gallica × a Damask.) Summer flowering. Height to 180 cm (6 ft). Good scent.

Tradition tells of Josephine's youthful friendship on Martinique with a distant cousin, Aimée du Buc de Rivery, whose father had a plantation. Sent to France for her education, Aimée was returning to Martinique in 1784 when her ship disappeared. She is supposed to have been captured by Barbary corsairs and taken to Algiers where she was sold to the Bey. From here she was sent as a gift to Sultan Selim III (d. 1807) in Constantinople where she entered his harem and became the mother of Mahmud II (b. 1785). Known as La Sultane Validée, she wielded considerable influence. An embroidery of the story has the girls visiting an old woman who prophesied that they would both become queens.

ROSE DE RESCHT A Damask with flowers that are typically on short stalks. Introduced by Nancy Lindsay from Iran in the late 1940s. Repeat flowers well. Very resistant to disease. Height to 120 cm (4 ft). Very good scent.

Quatrain XV from the *Rubaiyat* of Omar Khayyám, illustrated by Edmund Dulac: 'Look the blowing rose about us.'

ROSA MUNDI, *ROSA GALLICA* VERSICOLOR A suckering shrub that often reverts to the Apothecary's Rose (below). An ancient variety known since at least 1581. Legend says it was named Rosa Mundi after Fair Rosamund, mistress of Henry II. A striped sport of the Apothecary's Rose. Suffers from mildew but well worth a place in any garden. Summer flowering. Height to 150 cm (5 ft). Good scent.

APOTHECARY'S ROSE, ROSE DE PROVINS, RED ROSE OF LANCASTER, *ROSA GALLICA* OFFICINALIS A Gallica. Known in northern Europe since before 1400. Summer flowering. Height to 150 cm (5 ft). Good scent.

Thought to be the rose that Thibault IV (1201–53) brought back from the Seventh Crusade in 1250 and grew at his château in Provins. Later grown in vast quantities in the area where it was used to make a preserve that was popular for its medicinal properties.

The Rosa Mundi border at Hidcote Manor, Gloucestershire.

EMILIA IN HER LITTLE MARY GARDEN By the Master of the Hours of the Duke of Burgundy.

A double border of the Apothecary's Rose at Kiftsgate House, Gloucestershire.

The Rose in the Dark Ages

With the fall of the Roman Empire in the fifth century AD, one of its major cultural symbols, the rose, also suffered a decline. For several centuries it underwent a period of relative obscurity after its excessive exposure under the Romans. The main reason was the rising influence of Christianity and its initial rejection of the pagan gods and rituals connected with the Romans who had tried so hard, albeit unsuccessfully, to wipe out the irrepressible tide of the Christian belief in one God.

However, in its early ascetic phase the Christian Church had something of a problem establishing emotional and symbolic alternatives for the numerous Roman deities that had been replaced by the Christian concept of one God. Although the fact that He was a threefold godhead – God the Father, God the Son and God the Holy Spirit – helped satisfy several aspects of man's spiritual needs that had been met by numerous gods in the pre-Christian religions, the basic problem was that He did not incorporate dual sexuality. The lack of a symbol representing the different aspects of femininity – innocence, purity, sexuality, fecundity and motherhood – manifested in the ancient religions by Aphrodite, Athene, Artemis and Hera was an issue that had to be addressed.

Eventually, as Teresa McLean explains in her excellent book *Medieval English Gardens*, the problem was resolved by the birth of 'the Cult of Mary, the Mother of God, and the rose as her symbol.' McLean argues that the rose itself was so irresistible, and such a perfect symbol of love, beauty, pain, martyrdom and death (as the Romans and Greeks had recognized) that it was crazy not to incorporate it into Marianism – the Mary cult. The rose of love, once praised in pagan poems, became the Christian rose of numerous paintings and works of literature, perhaps the most famous of which was Guillaume de Lorris' allegorical romance *Roman de la Rose*. The Mary cult which the Church promulgated operated on various levels: she was simultaneously the symbol of purity and the symbol of motherhood and the heart of this paradox lay in the mystery of the virgin birth of Christ.

The Hortus Conclusus

After the decline of Rome's influence throughout Europe and before the advent of a greater stability from the eleventh century onwards, monks were the guardians of much of the knowledge about horticulture, botany and medicine (among many other subjects). In the centuries when growing and using roses for pleasure was frowned on, they continued to plant them in their monastery gardens for medicinal purposes and when the rose again became an approved flower it was readily available for widespread cultivation. In addition roses were highly prized and loved among the Persians, and among the Muslim Arabs who cultivated them in their palaces and gardens in Sicily and Spain. Roses and eastern ideas were also brought back to Europe by the Crusaders. As a result, they were easily found to be grown in what became known as the *Hortus Conclusus*: the enclosed garden.

The historical background to the *Hortus Conclusus* is complex. It combines elements of the biblical Garden of Eden and the Persian Paradise Garden as idealized by writers and poets, and has its origins in the *Song of Songs* traditionally attributed to King Solomon. This poem likens the lover's beloved to a garden: 'a garden enclosed; a sealed fountain'. The only person allowed access to this private, enclosed place, to 'taste its rarest fruits' is the lover. As McLean says, the Church was quick to draw the allegorical analogy between 'Mary's inviolate womb [and] the sealed garden of the *Song of Solomon*, penetrated only by God. A closed gate, through which only Christ could enter ...'

TRICOLORE DE FLANDRE A Gallica. The ground colour of the flowers is white. Raised by Van Houtte in Belgium, launched 1846. Summer flowering. Height to 100 cm (3½ ft). Good scent.

BELLE SANS FLATTERIE A Gallica. Raised by Godefroy in France, launched 1829. Summer flowering. Height to 120 cm (4 ft). Good scent.

PANACHÉE SUPERBE A Gallica hybrid. Probably a Gallica-China hybrid.) Summer flowering. Height to 150 cm (5 ft). Good scent.

The Renaissance Rose

The symbolism of the rose was associated not only with Mary but also with her son, Jesus, who shed His blood for mankind and whose five wounds on the Cross are symbolized by the five petals of the rose. The oldest meaning of the word 'rosary' was a rose garden (*rosarium*), the enclosed rose garden of Marianism. Later it came to refer to the strings of beads (possibly themselves made of dried rose hips or carved from rose wood) that monks used for counting their prayers, originally paternosters, but Hail Marys by the twelfth century. Gradually the enclosed rose garden dedicated to Mary and used for spiritual contemplation became a garden associated more with the courtly ideas of chivalric love and, later still, a garden where earthly lovers would meet.

By the fourteenth century roses were widely cultivated once again and were used for personal adornment, cosmetics and in cooking. The Rose of Provins, the Apothecary's Rose, brought back from the Crusades by Thibault IV (1201–53) was cultivated extensively by him at his château in Provins and was much admired for its wonderful strong smell.

The religious symbolism of the rose became increasingly secularized. It became a symbol of human love and also of kingly power: in England the white rose was associated with the House of York and the red rose with the House of Lancaster. When the Wars of the Roses ended in 1485 the heraldic badge of the Tudor Rose, which Henry VII inaugurated to symbolize the merging of the two dynastic families, was a small white rose upon a red one. It is still the badge of the royal house of England.

For the next two centuries roses appeared everywhere: in painting, poetry, sculpture, stained-glass windows, coats of arms, seals, coins and badges. Roses were back in fashion again, with a vengeance.

FEUX AMOUREUX A Centifolia. Known since 1810. Summer flowering. Height to 120 cm (4 ft). Good scent.

CENTIFOLIA ROSES are the most recent of the groups of ancient Europe. They originated in Holland in the late 16th century from hybrids between Autumn Damasks and Albas. Centifolias have wonderfully scented, pale pink, fully double flowers that hang downwards and were especially prized by the Dutch flower painters. Most are sterile, but the basic type has produced several mutations or sports including Mosses, Chapeau de Napoléon with its crested sepals, and Miniatures. In *Rosa centifolia* and its sports the leaflets are large and rounded, producing a very lush effect on a large and rather floppy shrub.

MADONNA OF THE ROSE BOWER BY MARTIN SCHONGAUER (1440–91) The red roses definitely look like Gallicas, the white one must be an Alba. The large, red flower on the left is a peony.

FANTIN LATOUR A Centifolia-like hybrid. A spreading shrub. Known since the late 19th century. (Centifolia × China or Gallica × Hybrid Tea.) Summer flowering. Height to 180 cm (6 ft). Good scent.

CHAPTER TWO

Dutch Flower Painting

The Dutch and Flemish still-life painters and the Centifolia Roses they loved to paint are described in this chapter.

OLD CABBAGE ROSE, PROVENCE ROSE, ROSE DES PEINTRES, ROSA CENTIFOLIA A Centifolia with loose, spreading stems and coarse leaves. Known since the 16th century. Summer flowering. Height to 150 cm (5 ft). Very good scent.

FLOWERS IN A GLASS VASE BY JACOB VAN WALSCAPELLE (1644–1727) Painted when the artist was only 23. The rose was the great favourite of the Dutch still-life masters. This painting shows the Old Cabbage Rose, *Rosa centifolia*.

ROSA CENTIFOLIA MUSCOSA, OLD PINK MOSS A Centifolia Moss with mossy buds and flower stalks. Known since 1700. A sport of Centifolia. Summer flowering. Height to 120 cm (4 ft). Very good scent.

UNIQUE PROVENCE A Centifolia that was, and still is, grown at Malmaison. Good scent.

Paintings of flowers are among the best sources of knowledge of the roses cultivated in early gardens. They attained their highest levels of perfection during the seventeenth and eighteenth centuries in Holland and Flanders. Before this, flowers were usually decorations in Books of Hours and other manuscripts, or incidentals in larger paintings. Roses are commonly used in these contexts and the varieties depicted show which ones were familiar at the time. One of the side panels of the great altar-piece in Ghent Cathedral, by the Flemish artists Hubert and Jan van Eyck in *c.* 1430, depicts a garden; growing among the grapes, figs and pomegranates is a rose bush covered with large red flowers. This is certainly *Rosa gallica* Officinalis, for the typical poise of the leaves is accurately shown.

Many of the roses that appeared in gardens during the sixteenth century were introduced from Constantinople, where they were grown by the great French botanist and gardener Clusius (1526–1609). *Rosa foetida*, the Austrian Briar, and its scarlet variety Bicolor, came into gardens around this time and both were depicted in flower paintings alongside the Gallicas and Damasks which had been grown earlier. The double yellow that soon appeared seems to be *Rosa hemisphaerica*, not the Persian double, which was introduced to Europe only in 1838. By 1614, the *Hortus Floridus* of Crispin de Passe, published in Utrecht, contained five roses, much the same as the ones that appear in contemporary Dutch flower paintings.

The reasons for the popularity of the large flower painting in Holland at this time are complex, but the rise of a respectable bourgeoisie seems to have been the catalyst. The wealthy merchants who wished to have their portraits painted also developed an interest in flowers, an interest that in the case of tulips became an obsession. Soon painters began to include what we now call 'florist's flowers' – highly bred cultivars of plants such as the hyacinth, tulip, auricula, poppy, fritillary and, of course, the rose. It is interesting that only a very limited selection of roses was generally depicted. *Rosa centifolia* is by far

BULLATA, ROSIER À FEUILLES DE LAITUE A Centifolia with crinkled and almost savoyed leaves. Launched 1801. A sport of *Rosa centifolia*. Summer flowering. Height to 150 cm (5 ft). Very good scent.

BURGUNDY ROSE, POMPOM DE BOURGOGNE, *ROSA CENTIFOLIA* PARVIFOLIA A Centifolia. Small foliage; suckering plant with crowded, upright shoots. Known since 1664. Summer flowering, can be shy with its flowers. Height to 45 cm ($1\frac{1}{2}$ ft). Little scent.

PETITE DE HOLLANDE, PETITE JUNON DE HOLLANDE, POMPOM DES DAMES NORMANDICA A dwarf Centifolia sport with small leaves and flowers. From The Netherlands *c.* 1800. Summer flowering. Height to 120 cm (4 ft). Good scent.

CHARLES DE MILLS, BIZARRE TRIOMPHANT A Gallica with flowers that open crimson and fade to purple. Of uncertain origin. Summer flowering. Height up to 150 cm (5 ft) but with floppy stems. Little scent.

ROSE DE MEAUX, *ROSA CENTIFOLIA* POMPONIANA A Centifolia. Illustrated by Sweet in 1789. Summer flowering. Height to 100 cm (3½ ft). Little scent.

HENRI MARTIN, RED MOSS A Centifolia Moss. Raised by Laffay in France, launched 1863. Summer flowering. Height to 180 cm (6 ft). Good scent.

PAUL RICAULT A Bourbon hybrid or possibly a Centifolia hybrid. Very like a Centifolia in habit. Raised by Portemer in France, launched 1845. Summer flowering. Height to 150 cm (5 ft). Very good scent.

TOUR DE MALAKOFF A Centifolia with nodding stems and purplish-pink flowers. Raised by Soupert & Notting in Luxemburg, launched 1856. Summer flowering. Height to 180 cm (6 ft), may be trained as a climber. Good scent.

the most commonly represented, with only occasionally another species such as *Rosa alba maxima*, *Rosa foetida* and *Rosa foetida* Bicolor or *Rosa moschata* Autumnalis. In England, on the other hand, Tradescant was able to list no less than thirty-two different species and cultivars in his collection at Lambeth in London by 1656. He also lists Mensalis, Monthly Rose, which sounds suspiciously like the Chinese Monthly Rose. Although this is generally thought to have been introduced only in 1793, an early sixteenth-century painting in the National Gallery in London by the Florentine Angelo Bronzino seems to show this pink China.

Of the many great painters of the Dutch and Flemish schools of flower painting, the Brueghel family dominate the early, sometimes called primitive, period. Jan (Velvet) Brueghel (1568–1625) was born in Brussels; his technique is wonderfully clear cut and depicts large numbers of different flowers, sometimes arranged in vases, sometimes as garlands framing figures such as the Virgin and Child. This technique was also employed by Jan Brueghel (1601–78), his pupil and his son. In their large and complex pictures not only is every flower delineated with great technical accuracy, but art historians have also interpreted the various flowers as having multiple layers of religious symbolic meaning. A number of other painters either studied with, or were influenced by, Brueghel's work, among them Ambrose Bosschaert the Elder and Daniel Seghers. In later paintings, roughly dating from 1650, artists like William van Aelst, Jan Davidsz de Heem, Simon Verelst, Jacob van Walscapelle and Rachel Ruysch employed a freer, more self-confident style. Fewer flowers are shown, but they are larger and more naturally depicted.

Jan van Huysum (1682–1749) was the consummate master of the genre. Born in Amsterdam, he was taught by his father Justus (1659–1716), also a successful flower painter. Jan's greatest asset was the ability to arrange the flowers he depicted in the most elegant and satisfying way, and Centifolia Roses together with double opium poppies provided him with the lavish flowers he needed. Later painters such as Jan van Os and Gerard van Spaëndonck (the teacher of Redouté, see page 38) tried to emulate his style. Of these Jan Frans van Dael (1764–1840) was perhaps one of the nearest in ability and style to his mentor. It is interesting that one of his paintings, depicting large numbers of roses, poppies, irises and tulips and entitled *Le Tombeau de Julie*, hangs at Malmaison today.

EUPHROSYNE L'ÉLÉGANTE A Gallica.
Raised by Descemet. Summer flowering.
Height to 120 cm (4 ft). Good scent.

BELLE HERMINIE A Gallica. Raised by
Coquereau in France, known since 1848.
Summer flowering. Height to 120 cm
(4 ft). Good scent.

PERLE DES PANACHÉES, PANACHÉE
DOUBLE, COTTAGE MAID An upright
Gallica. Raised by Vibert in France,
launched 1845. Summer flowering.
Height to 90 cm (3 ft). Good scent.

CHAPTER THREE

The Empress Josephine

This chapter picks up the quest for the rose with Josephine Bonaparte and the revolution in rose growing that she inspired and concludes with Redouté, the great rose illustrator. The appropriate groups illustrated are the later Gallicas and early Bourbons.

LA ROSE DE LA MALMAISON BY HECTOR VIGER DU VIGNEAU The painting features Josephine, Napoleon, Emilie de Beauharnais, Julie Cléry (wife of Joseph Bonaparte), Pauline (widow of General Leclerc), Mme Devaux, Mme de L'Orsay, Hortense, Caroline and Mlle d'Arberg. Everywhere you look in this picture there are roses, showing the passion shared by Josephine and the painter.

Of all the many patrons of horticulture and the arts over the years, Josephine must have been one of the most charismatic. She enjoyed the luxury of popularity in her own lifetime. As mistress, and later wife, of Napoleon, she had power and influence, yet was able to retain the affection of the common people – a rare attribute in the aftermath of the French Revolution. Indeed, it was only by an extraordinary stroke of luck that she survived at all; she had been held a prisoner and escaped the guillotine only because of the timely death of Robespierre, architect of the Terror.

Josephine was born Marie Josèphe Rose Tascher de La Pagerie on 23 June 1763 and was brought up on the Windward Island of Martinique in the West Indies, where her father was an impecunious landowner and sugar planter. Josephine (as she was later to be called by Napoleon) seems to have enjoyed her childhood in this wonderfully beautiful place and it was probably here that she acquired her taste for luxury, extravagance and exotic plants. Her first marriage, in December 1779, to the wealthy Vicomte Alexandre de Beauharnais, a French army officer who was also born in Martinique, failed. The union, however, produced two children: Hortense (who married Napoleon's brother Louis and became for a short time queen of Holland) and Eugène (later the duke of Leuchtenberg). Both seem to have been a constant source of support to their mother. The unfortunate Alexandre was guillotined in 1794 despite his early support of the revolutionaries, and his estranged wife was left to fend for herself and her children. She became the friend and mistress of a number of well-known men, among them Paul Barras, one of the five members of the Directory that ruled France from 1795 to 1799, and her name was even linked with that of the notorious Marquis de Sade.

Josephine met Napoleon through her son, who was a soldier, and on 9 March 1796 they were married in a small private ceremony. Within a few days Napoleon had set off to take command of the French army in Italy, from whence he fired off a succession of passionate, jealous letters to his new wife, exhorting her to write more frequently and to think only of him.

The Garden at Malmaison

Napoleon became first Consul of France in 1799 and was proclaimed emperor on 18 May 1804. While he busied himself with military matters his empress organized a busy social life with a salon composed of many of the most famous people of the time. The couple had acquired the Château de Malmaison in the pretty village of Reuil (now a suburb of Paris) in 1799, as a country retreat, and Josephine now set out to transform the dilapidated house and garden into a residence fit for the imperial household. Her extravagance was quite remarkable, and Napoleon was frequently required to pay off his wife's debts. Although he occasionally tried to curb her expenses, he also enjoyed the improvements being undertaken at Malmaison.

Napoleon wrote regularly while away from home, and one comes across touching domestic details such as the following, dated 16 July 1801, and written in Paris while Josephine was taking the waters at Plombières: 'It has been such awful weather that I have stayed in Paris. Malmaison without you is too sad … I have received for you, from London, some plants which I sent on to your gardener.' Unfortunately, Napoleon does not appear to have kept Josephine's letters, in fact, very little written by her survives at all – a pity, as it would provide a fascinating insight into life at Malmaison. Napoleon was away so much that the house and garden were almost entirely arranged

THALIE LA GENTILLE A Gallica hybrid. (Possibly Gallica × Damask.) Summer flowering. Height to 120 cm (4 ft). Good scent.

IPSILANTÉ A Gallica with very large, flat flowers. Summer flowering. Very resistant to disease. Height to 130 cm ($4\frac{1}{2}$ ft). Very good scent.

PRÉSIDENT DE SÈZE, MME HÉBERT A Gallica. Branches arch to the ground and flowers have a crimson centre and lilac edges. Raised by Hébert in France, launched 1836. Height to 130 cm ($4\frac{1}{2}$ ft). Good scent.

GROS PROVINS PANACHÉE A Gallica hybrid with purplish flowers streaked with white. Raised by Fontaine in France, launched 1866. (Gallica × a China hybrid.) Summer flowering. Height to 150 cm (5 ft). Good scent. Photographed at the Roseraie de l'Haÿ, Paris.

AIMABLE AMIE A Gallica, an old variety now grown at Malmaison near Paris. Known since 1860. Summer flowering. Height to 150 cm (5 ft). Good scent.

SISSINGHURST CASTLE, ROSE DES MAURES An ancient, low-growing Gallica found at Sissinghurst Castle by Vita Sackville-West when she started to clear the garden. Summer flowering. Height to 100 cm (3½ ft). Good scent.

LA BIEN AIMÉE A Gallica hybrid, possibly with a China. Its smooth leaves are unlike those of a Gallica. Summer flowering. Height to 120 cm (4 ft). Good scent.

by Josephine, who nevertheless kept him informed of progress. He quite often refers to the developments in his letters.

Josephine's extravagance and enthusiasm ensured that her garden became one of the finest in France. A well-known botanist, Charles-François Brisseau de Mirbel, was its supervisor. He compiled a catalogue of the plants grown at Malmaison and, through his friendship with another distinguished botanist, Felix Delahaye, ensured the acquisition of many unusual plants. Josephine's family sent seeds from the West Indies and Napoleon himself contributed by sending back seeds and plants from the great botanic garden at Schoenbrunn Palace in Vienna. Famous botanists like Aimé Bonpland were delighted to offer their advice and help. Bonpland gave her seeds and plants collected on his expedition to Central and South America (1799–1804) and later wrote for her *Descriptions des plantes rares cultivées à Malmaison et à Navarre* which was illustrated by Redouté (page 38). Étienne-Pierre Ventenat, a respected botanist employed by Josephine to identify some of the many plants she received from abroad, was given the title Botanist to Her Majesty. He it was who wrote the text of the *Jardin de la Malmaison*, a two-volume work describing over 200 plants.

Josephine happily spent all Napoleon's money (and more!) on beautifying Malmaison. In 1805 she constructed 'la grande serre', an enormous greenhouse for the cultivation of tender and exotic plants. This extravagance does not seem to have displeased her husband, despite the fact that the cost amounted to nearly five times the original estimate. In April 1807 he wrote, '… I have ordered for Malmaison everything you desire,' and a month later was pleased that '… you are quite well and always adore Malmaison'. In a single year during this period Josephine spent £2600 on plants from Kennedy and Lee's nursery at Hammersmith, then west of London.

Napoleon and Josephine were divorced in December 1809 because of their inability to produce the son and heir for which Napoleon was desperate. Although Josephine was humiliated and upset by the dissolution of their marriage, they seem to have remained on friendly terms for the rest of their lives. Indeed, on 21 December 1809, less than a week after the divorce, Napoleon wrote, 'Hortense whom I have seen this afternoon has given me, my friend, all your news. I hope you have been to see your plants today; it has been a lovely day … goodbye, my dear, sleep well.'

Josephine was allowed to retain the title of empress, and Napoleon bought her the Château de Navarre in the Eure valley west of Paris, in the hope that she would stay away from the city and out of the way of his new wife, the Archduchess Marie Louise of Austria. Although Josephine did not at first like Navarre, she inevitably started to make a garden there and became fond of it. She also kept Malmaison. It seems fair to suggest that she threw herself into gardening at least partly as a compensation for the loss of Napoleon.

Roses Break the English Blockade

In 1810, at the height of the Napoleonic Wars, extraordinary arrangements were made by the French and British admiralties to ensure the safe passage of a new China Rose *Rosa indica* Fragans, known as Hume's Blush Tea-scented China, from England to Malmaison; it was illustrated by Redouté in 1817. The nurseryman John Kennedy received a special passport to take this rose and other plants from the Vineyard Nursery, Hammersmith to Malmaison. Her bill in 1811 was £700 – less than the £2600 she had paid in 1803, but still a considerable sum.

In a letter dated 7 January 1810, Napoleon had written, 'I was pleased to see you yesterday. I feel how much your company delights me … I worked today with Estève (the financial administrator). I have allotted 100 000 francs for 1810, as a special sum for Malmaison. So you can plant anything you want and spend the money as you like … You should still find 5 or 600 000 francs

COMPLICATA A Gallica. A strong-growing shrub with flowers about 12 cm (4 in) across. Possibly a cross between *Rosa gallica* and *Rosa canina*. Summer flowering. Height to 300 cm (10 ft) if supported.

ALEXANDRE LAQUEMENT, ALEXANDER LAQUEMONT A Gallica. Known since 1906. Summer flowering. Height to 130 cm (4½ ft). Good scent. Photographed at Mottisfont Abbey, Hampshire.

DUC DE GUICHE, SERAT ROMAIN A Gallica. Flowers fade to purple. Raised by Prévost in France, launched 1929. Summer flowering. Height to 150 cm (5 ft). Good scent. Photographed in the old rose garden at Malmaison near Paris.

ROSA SUBLAEVIS A large shrub or climber, a Gallica hybrid usually called *Rosa × polliniana*. First found near Mont Baldo in Italy by Pollini. (*Rosa gallica × Rosa arvensis*.) Summer flowering. Height to 250 cm (8 ft). Good scent. Photographed at the Roseto di Cavriglia, Italy.

Malmaison as it is today, seen through the cedars that have grown up since it was painted by Petit Pierre Joseph.

PORTLAND ROSE, SCARLET FOUR SEASONS, ROSA × PORTLANDICA Named after the second duchess of Portland who was one of the first people to grow it in England. Of uncertain origin, known since 1775. (Possibly *Rosa gallica × Autumn Damask*.) Repeat flowering. Height to 60 cm (2 ft). Good scent.

in the chest at Malmaison.' By 1813 Josephine was able to announce proudly that, 'My garden is the prettiest in the world. It is more popular than my salon.'

She suddenly fell ill, and died on 29 May 1814 at Malmaison. Aimé Bonpland was at her bedside, and Redouté visited her shortly before her death. Her funeral was attended by thousands from all backgrounds, who mourned her not only as an exceptional person but also as the symbol of the Empire, an era that had ended with Napoleon's abdication and exile to Elba just over a month earlier.

Throughout her life she had delighted not only in acquiring plants but also in sharing them with as many other people as possible. She exchanged plants with botanic gardens and was generous in sharing discoveries with nurserymen like Jacques-Martin Cels. As a result, numerous plants found their way into general cultivation in France. A number of plants were named after her – *Amaryllis josephinae* now *Brunsvigia josephinae*, *Lapageria rosea* (after her maiden name de La Pagerie) and *Josephinia imperatricis*, all of which were illustrated by Redouté (page 38). She also took a keen interest in plant breeding, and encouraged her gardeners to experiment with geraniums, pelargoniums and dahlias. However, the plant with which her name is most closely associated is, of course, the rose.

CUISSE DE NYMPHE EMUÉ Detail.

CUISSE DE NYMPHE EMUÉ An Alba. This is just a deeper pink variety of Great Maiden's Blush. Raised by Vibert in France. Summer flowering. Height to 150 cm (5 ft). Very good scent. Photographed at Malmaison near Paris.

The front of the Château de Malmaison painted by Petit Pierre Joseph *c*.1805.

The Greatest Rose Collection in the World

In its heyday, Malmaison boasted a huge collection of different rose species and cultivars. Many are still popular today, although the naming of several are uncertain; John Kennedy, who supplied Josephine with various plants including heathers and roses, declared in a letter in 1808 that the names were 'unbotanical'. Her collection formed the basis for the great monograph written by Claude-Antoine Thory and illustrated by Redouté. It is still the most famous and valuable of all rose books and owes much to her enthusiasm, although the first part of *Les Roses* was published in 1817, three years after her death, and the work was not completed until 1827. Likewise, the beautiful white Bourbon Rose, Souvenir de la Malmaison, was not raised until more than twenty years after she had died.

The Fate of Malmaison

Napoleon escaped from Elba in 1815 and re-entered France where he visited Malmaison for the last time. After his defeat at Waterloo in June 1815, he was banished by the British to St Helena, where he died in 1821.

After Josephine's death she was found to have amassed huge debts, and much of her property was sold. The house and garden at Malmaison passed to her son and daughter, but they were exiled by the ruling Bourbons who were afraid of the interest and support excited by all things Napoleonic. Bonpland stayed on at Malmaison until 1817, but after Eugène's death in 1824 the château was sold. It fell into a state of disrepair and was sacked in 1871 during the Franco-Prussian War. Finally, in 1904, it was given to the state and is now a museum. In 1912 Jules Gravereux, the rosarian and owner of the famous rose garden at l'Haÿ, attempted to track down all the roses that were supposed to have been grown at Malmaison in Josephine's day, and gave a selection of those he was able to find to help restore the garden there.

LA BELLE DISTINGUÉE, LA PETITE DUCHESSE, LEE'S DUCHESS A hybrid of *Rosa rubiginosa*, the Sweet Briar. Summer flowering. Height to 130 cm (4½ ft). Good scent. Photographed at Mottisfont Abbey, Hampshire.

Josephine's influence on rose growing in France lasted long after her death. Because of her love for roses, numerous breeders vied with one another to produce new ones, mainly Gallicas, Damasks and Albas at first, then Mosses, Hybrid Perpetuals and Teas. Throughout the nineteenth century France reigned supreme as the home of the best roses, which were exported and grown all over the world. It was only after the First World War that English, Irish and German breeders became as important.

Redouté, the Greatest Flower Painter

It is largely due to the influence and patronage of the Empress Josephine that Pierre-Joseph Redouté (1759–1840) is probably the best known of all flower painters. Countless reproductions of his work adorn bedroom walls, table-mats, and waste-paper baskets all over the world, yet he was born in humble surroundings in an obscure village in the Belgian Ardennes. Pierre-Joseph was one of five children of a painter and decorator employed by the ancient abbey of St Hubert, and one of the monks taught the boy to recognize the wild plants used for their medicinal properties. This early familiarity with plants must have been of use to him later in his career.

DUCHESSE D'ORLÉANS A Gallica. Illustrated in *Les Roses* by Redouté. Marie Amélie, duchesse d'Orléans, was the wife of Louis-Philippe who became king of France in 1830. Adélaïde d'Orléans, their daughter, was one of Redouté's pupils, and a Rambler was named after her.

Redouté left home at thirteen to seek work and started by painting portraits of rich merchants and decorating their houses for them. He visited Amsterdam in order to study the work of the great Dutch masters, notably Jan van Huysum, one of the most talented of all flower painters, and began to sketch flowers and include plants in his other paintings. In 1782 he arrived in Paris where he helped his brother Antoine-Ferdinand (also a painter who, incidentally, worked on the château at Malmaison) to decorate a new theatre. In his spare time, Redouté visited the Jardin des Plantes (then known as the Jardin du Roi) where he drew and painted flowers; he also attended lectures given by the Royal Professor of Painting, Gerard van Spaëndonck, and became his pupil. Van Spaëndonck (1746–1822) was Dutch – a follower of van Huysum, and considerably influenced Redouté's painting. He contributed to the royal collection of *vélins* (paintings on vellum) and Redouté later continued his work.

It was at the Jardin des Plantes, in *c*.1783, that Redouté met an art dealer who engaged him to paint a series of flowers which were engraved and published as models for students interested in botanical art. More importantly, he also met the botanist Charles-Louis L'Héritier de Brutelle who commissioned him to illustrate *Stirpes Novae aut Minus Cognitae*, a book that described new and little known plants. L'Héritier was to prove a formative influence on, and a benevolent patron to, Redouté. In 1787 he invited the young artist to London where he was able to meet such luminaries as the artist James Sowerby and Sir Joseph Banks, the botanist and explorer (after whose wife *Rosa banksiae* was named). In the following year, Redouté and L'Héritier collaborated on two more books: *Geraniologia* and *Cornus*. Also in 1787, Redouté was appointed flower painter to Queen Marie-Antoinette, a post which he occupied until her death in 1793.

In 1799 Redouté published the first part of his book on cacti and succulents, *Histoire Naturelle des Plantes Grasses*, which was such a success that he decided to start work on one illustrating the lily family. By this time he was prospering, receiving a salary for illustrating books at the Museum National d'Histoire Naturelle (formerly the Jardin du Roi). He made the acquaintance of Jacques-Martin Cels, who had a famous nursery and garden in Paris, and through him met Ventenat, who was at that time describing some of the rare and unusual plants growing in Cels' garden. Redouté illustrated Ventenat's *Description des Plantes nouvelles et peu connues, cultivées dans le Jardin de J.M. Cels* (published in 1800) and a later work on the same subject. It was through this that he came to know Josephine: Ventenat was appointed official botanist at Malmaison, and Redouté was asked to paint the flowers in its garden. So began a long and fruitful partnership that lasted until Josephine's death.

Although they made an unlikely pair – the urbane and influential wife of

Rosa Indica.

P. J. Redouté pinx.

La Bengale bichonne.

Imprimerie de Rémond.

Langlois sculp.

SLATER'S CRIMSON CHINA, SEMPERFLORENS, *ROSA INDICA,* LA BENGALE Illustrated by Redouté in *Les Roses.* We have photographed fresh roses with the drawing to compare the rose as grown today with Redouté's painting of 1821.

EMPRESS JOSEPHINE, IMPÉRATRICE JOSÉPHINE A Gallica hybrid, probably with *Rosa majalis*; the wide stipules suggest this. Large leaves with impressed veins. Known since 1820. Summer flowering. Height to 160 cm (5½ ft). Scent slight.

SOUVENIR DE LA MALMAISON A Bourbon. A magnificent rose in hot dry conditions but in wet weather it fails to open or gets very spotted. Introduced by Béluze in France, 1843. (Mme Desprez × a Tea.) Summer flowering. Height to 180 cm (6 ft), double that as a climber. Very fragrant.

Napoleon and the ugly, unsophisticated artist – Redouté appears to have formed a remarkable friendship with Josephine. By giving Redouté free access to the gardens and hothouses of Malmaison, she enabled him to produce ever finer work which still stands comparison with that of any other botanical artist. The first instalment of *Les Liliacées*, published by Redouté himself, appeared in 1802, and Josephine ensured that it was well subscribed, as indeed it needed to be: another seventy-nine parts followed over a period of fourteen years. Many consider this to be one of the greatest illustrated botanical works ever published; it is certainly one of the best known. Josephine bought the original paintings, executed on vellum, and these, together with a special copy of the text, also on vellum, were bound in sixteen volumes.

In 1804 Josephine assumed the title of empress and at about this time started to pay Redouté a salary for his work at Malmaison. This enabled him to buy himself a small estate at Fleury-Medon, south of Paris, where he was at last able to grow plants himself. After Josephine's divorce in 1809 he occasionally travelled to her Château de Navarre in Normandy to paint. The *Description des plantes rares cultivées à Malmaison et à Navarre*, published in 1813, has fifty-four plates by Redouté.

Ironically, Josephine had died by the time Redouté started to publish his most famous project, *Les Roses*, although it is certain that many of the roses illustrated were drawn from specimens at Malmaison. *Les Roses, décrites et classées selon leur ordre naturel par Claude-Antoine Thory*, to give it its full title, was published in three volumes between 1817 and 1824. It contains 167 engravings, with text by Claude-Antoine Thory, a lawyer, friend of Redouté and amateur botanist. It set out to illustrate every variety of rose that grew in France and was such a success that three editions were published – the last between 1828 and 1830. In the meantime, Redouté's finances had become less satisfactory than previously. Deprived of his salary from Josephine, and with all the expense of publishing his own books, he sought ways of earning extra money. One of his efforts was the publication of what we would nowadays call a 'coffee table book': *Choix des plus belles fleurs et des plus beaux fruits*, in effect a selection of paintings chosen for their artistic merit rather than for strictly botanical reasons. Of the 144 paintings contained in this work, no fewer than forty-four were of roses, an indication not only of Redouté's special affection for them, but also, presumably, of the public's taste.

In 1830 Louis-Philippe became king of France, and his queen, Marie Amélie, appointed Redouté 'Peintre de Fleurs du Cabinet de la Reine', a post which seems to have carried some form of remuneration. In spite of this, he was dogged by money worries and worked feverishly to the end of his life. On 19 June 1840, while working on a painting of a lily, he died suddenly of a cerebral haemorrhage – he was eighty-one. L'Héritier, his early friend and patron, prophesied truly when he wrote some forty years earlier: 'Dear Redouté, the truth of your brush, even more than its magic, will make me share, perhaps, the celebrity that our work together will one day earn for us both.'

Gallicas in the old rose walk at Hidcote Manor, Gloucestershire.

CHAPTER FOUR

The Rose Quest in China

This chapter is a diary of our journeys through the foothills of the Himalayas in western China. We were searching for wild roses and the old cultivated ones that are still to be found in temples, farms and gardens.

THE MACARTNEY ROSE, *ROSA BRACTEATA* An evergreen climber. Introduced into Britain in 1793 on the return of Lord Macartney from China. Tender, needing a warm wall in frosty areas. Flowers for a long period from midsummer to autumn. Height to 240 cm (8 ft). Scented.

The Chinese were always obsessively suspicious of foreigners, and for many centuries allowed only a handful of Europeans to visit the interior of their country. The Portuguese were the earliest Westerners to establish a permanent base there when they set up a tea trading-post in Macao in around 1540 and until 1699, when the English East India Company first established its factory, they had a complete monopoly of the trade from the ports of Macao and Canton.

Although foreigners were allowed to trade in the ports they could not travel inland, learn to speak Chinese or employ Chinese servants other than official licensed interpreters. Large bribes were needed before any business could be done. In the late eighteenth century the British government and traders decided to send an embassy to the Chinese emperor in Peking (now Beijing) to try and get some of these restrictions lifted and make trade easier and more profitable. The large party that left London in 1792 under the leadership of Lord Macartney took £15 000 worth of presents for the emperor and his court – and included two professional gardeners. Lord Macartney's secretary was Sir George Staunton, a keen amateur botanist and gardener. On their return journey the party travelled overland from Peking to Canton which gave Sir George the opportunity to collect many plants including two roses. One was a large-flowered, single, white Climber, *Rosa bracteata*, now known as The Macartney Rose and famous as a parent of the yellow Climber, Mermaid; the other was a small, double-flowered, pink China Rose collected in a garden near Canton.

Sir George was not the first person to bring this rose to Europe. It had been collected in the garden of the customs house in Canton in 1751 by Peter Osbeck, a pupil of Linnaeus, the great Swedish botanist. In England this small, pink rose became known as Parson's Pink China after the garden in Rickmansworth where it was reported in 1793. It caused little interest at the time, except for its ability to go on flowering throughout summer – its flowers were small and poorly scented compared with the European Damask and Gallica Roses which were then fashionable and being raised in large numbers. It was, however, propagated and sold by James Colville's famous nursery in the King's Road, London as the Pale China Rose, and is still popular in gardens today where it is usually called Old Blush. A year or two earlier another China Rose had arrived in London, imported by Gilbert Slater of Low Leyton in Essex who was involved in the East India trade in 1791. It had even smaller flowers than Parson's Pink China, but they were a rich, bright crimson. It is sometimes called Slater's Crimson China but also Semperflorens because of its almost continuous flowering.

Parson's Pink China and Slater's Crimson China were sent to Paris – gardeners in France remained active during the Revolution – and by 1798 their seeds were being sown by Thory and Redouté and new hybrids were raised, many, from 1800 onwards, on Josephine Bonaparte's estate at Malmaison. New plants continued to trickle back to Europe from Canton and Macao and, in 1809, a large-flowered, pale pink, repeat-flowering rose was introduced by Sir Abraham Hume of Wormley Bury, Hertfordshire, a specialist in chrysanthemums. It came to be called Hume's Blush Tea-scented China and was then unique for its large, elegant flowers. This, too, reached Josephine, in 1810, despite the English blockade of French ports. It was said that only

HUME'S BLUSH TEA-SCENTED CHINA (A STUD CHINA) Normally considered a Tea. The British Admiralty allowed it through their blockade of France to Josephine at Malmaison in 1810. Brought from Canton in 1809 by Sir Abraham Hume. Repeat flowering. Height to 150 cm (5 ft), more as a climber. Fragrant.

PARKS' YELLOW TEA-SCENTED CHINA (A STUD CHINA) A Climber. Although known as a China, it is much closer to the wild Tea Rose and is thus really a Tea. An important stud China because it introduced yellow into the breeding lines. Brought to the (Royal) Horticultural Society in England from China by Parks in 1824; by the next year Hardy had it in Paris. It is an important ancestor of Hybrid Teas. Spring flowering. Height to 180 cm (6 ft). Scented; the leaves are said to have a tea scent.

OLD BLUSH, PARSON'S PINK CHINA (A STUD CHINA) Originally introduced in Sweden 1752. Arrived in USA *c.* 1800 where Champney used it to breed Noisettes. Also thought to be one parent of the Bourbons. Flowers continuously. Height to 180 cm (6 ft). Well scented, of apple blossom.

A rose we found on the Boaxing road. Looking very similar to Old Blush as cultivated in the West.

SLATER'S CRIMSON CHINA, SEMPERFLORENS (A STUD CHINA) A low-growing China. Imported to Britain from China by Slater *c.* 1792 and soon dispersed all over Europe. It was a parent of the Portland rose and thus a grandparent of the Hybrid Perpetuals. Flowers continuously. Height to 90 cm (3 ft). Little scent.

one in a thousand plants sent back from China survived the precarious voyage. They were packed in open-sided crates and travelled on deck. Because there were still restrictions on foreigners travelling inland in China most of these roses were garden plants, often very ancient cultivars or complex hybrids bought from nurseries in Canton or Macao.

The most important figure in the introduction of Chinese plants to Europe was John Reeves, the chief inspector of tea for the East India Company at Canton between 1812 and 1831. Through him, such familiar plants as wisteria came to England. One which failed to survive was a yellow-flowered China Rose which has never, as far as we can tell, been in cultivation in the West. Its portrait can be seen among Reeves' paintings of plants in his collection, now in the Lindley Library in London.

It was probably also through Reeves that two yellow, climbing roses were finally introduced. In 1823 the Horticultural Society sent John Parks to China with an introduction to Reeves. Parks brought back to Europe a tall, yellow-flowered, climbing Tea Rose usually called Parks' Yellow Tea-scented China, and the yellow, double Banksian rose; both were slightly too tender to grow and flower well in any but the warmest parts of England, but the Banksian rose is wonderful in southern France, California and the USA's southern states.

Other China Roses were certainly introduced at about this time, sometimes through India – the so-called Bengal roses. However, Slater's Crimson China, Parson's Pink China, Hume's Blush Tea-scented China and Parks' Yellow Tea-scented China seem to have been the important ancestors of the modern Hybrid Teas and most other modern roses. They are therefore known as the 'four stud Chinas'. They came to be the ancestors of the modern roses both by design, and even more by chance, but the complicated story of how this happened belongs in a later chapter.

The detective work to identify the four stud Chinas was done in the 1930s by Dr C.C. Hurst. He used the then new science of genetics, and his theories have never been challenged. By then, only Parson's Pink China had survived in European gardens. Slater's Crimson had recently been rediscovered and reintroduced from Bermuda but the two tea-scented Chinas had disappeared altogether. (Plants grown in greenhouses had probably been superseded by better, newer roses such as Maréchal Niel, while those growing outdoors were probably killed in a series of hard winters in the later nineteenth century such as those of 1874 and 1895 when the Thames froze over in London.) Hurst, however, deduced from the tea-scented Chinas' progeny and from old paintings that they were probably hybrids between the Tea Rose *Rosa gigantea* and the wild China *Rosa chinensis* var. *spontanea*. Recently the two lost tea roses are said to have been refound, although there is some doubt as to whether they are exactly the same plants as were originally introduced.

It was about 1870 before the first European botanists were really able to visit the wilds of China and collect seeds in the mountains and gorges of the Himalayan foothills that border Tibet. In these mountains in western China the European plant hunters found the wild ancestors of garden flowers long grown and treasured by the Chinese who lived along the country's eastern coast. The wild tree peony was found by the American anthropologist and botanist Joseph Rock in 1925 and the plant collector George Forrest found the wild *Camellia reticulata* in 1924; in its cultivated form, Captain Rawes, it had been introduced from Canton in 1821. He also collected the ancestors of the wild Tea Rose, *Rosa gigantea*, and the Banksian rose in Yunnan Province. Earlier, in 1884, the Irish plant collector Augustine Henry had reported seeing wild *Rosa chinensis* in the mountains of Hubei beyond the Ichang gorges. However, these wild China Roses remained something of a mystery because they were never brought into cultivation. Only in 1983 were they sighted again, and photographed and studied, in a remote part of southern Sichuan by the Japanese botanist Mikinori Ogisu. He had been inspired in the search by Graham Thomas while a student at the Royal Horticultural Society gardens at Wisley.

Our first find in China was overwhelming – a lovely bush of the Tea-scented Rose, *Rosa gigantea,* growing in a ditch about half a mile from the Burma Road 50 miles west of Kunming. It was well scented but we all fell out over whether the scent actually was in any way reminiscent of tea.

THE TEA-SCENTED ROSE, *ROSA GIGANTEA* Previously known as *Rosa odorata* var. *gigantea.* The specimens we found are typical of the Chinese form, around 200 cm (7 ft) high with pure white flowers 7 cm (2½ in) across. In Burma, where it was originally found in 1882, it grows to an enormous size with flowers up to 14 cm (5½ in) across. The Tea-scented Rose is too tender to flower well in northern climates but does well in California and the Mediterranean. Summer flowering. One of the most important roses of China and, with the China Rose, the main parent of our modern Hybrid Teas.

Our Quest in China

Our aim in visiting China was to try to tie in some of the threads of this story; to visit the area where the China Roses originated and from which they came to Canton; to photograph them growing wild; and to see if any old Chinese garden roses had survived the Cultural Revolution, saved from the Red Guards by the remoteness of a mountain monastery or village. Perhaps we could rediscover, in China, Hume's Blush Tea-scented China or Parks' Yellow Tea-scented China. Perhaps we could find some exciting rose not known in the West, or even see Reeves' dwarf, perpetual-flowering, yellow rose, so beautifully painted by a Chinese artist in Canton nearly 200 years ago.

THE MYSTERY

Were the old China Roses originally from the interior? Were there other cultivated roses that had not been imported into Europe? Where in China had the breeding of cultivated roses taken place? While these questions were too gigantic to answer conclusively, we were determined to see if we could dig out any clues.

THE PLAN

Our plan was to spend some days in Yunnan Province, known to be home to the wild tea-scented China Rose, *Rosa gigantea,* then to fly to Sichuan where Mikinori Ogisu had recently found a key wild rose, the wild red China *Rosa chinensis* var. *spontanea.* We would also study all the wild roses we could find and any cultivated ones we came across in farms and temples.

PINK TEA-SCENTED ROSE, *ROSA GIGANTEA* We found this plant growing up trees at the edge of a farmyard north of Dali in Yunnan. The flowers are up to 12 cm (5 in) across and the plant was at least 750 cm (25 ft) high. Although it is possible for the wild plant to have pink flowers this is more probably a primitive hybrid. I think it can well be compared with Cooper's Burmese (page 76). Scented.

As we walked round Kunming on our first morning we saw roses in pots outside houses, roses on balconies, roofs and terraces. This one looks like a primitive China hybrid.

A double *Rosa multiflora* Rambler that grew to a width of 550 cm (18 ft) over the back wall of a house in Dali.

PREPARATION

The simplest way to travel in China is through one of the Chinese tourist agencies. You plan the trip and they provide a guide, car and driver to take you wherever you want to go, and organize meals and accommodation. You will be quoted an all-in price for air fares, car hire, etc. Ours came to just under £3000 each for twelve days, but this even included beer for lunch and dinner!

What follows are notes from the diary we kept during the trip.

DAY ONE

Left London … flew direct to Hong Kong then changed flights A five-hour gap and on to Kunming. There are three of us: Martyn Rix, Roger Phillips (myself) with Ian Keill who has come along for the ride to see what we get up to, with a view to turning it into a television spectacular. Ian totes a home video camcorder with him and videos every step. Martyn and I are replete with Nikons and loads and loads of film.

DAY TWO

Kunming, trying to sort out various disasters, including having lost all our baggage. In losing the bags we've lost the tape for the video camera and, of course, all our medicines. At last we are on the road without them. We've managed to get ourselves a mini-van so at least there's room for everybody. Before leaving Kunming we walk around the town a little and discover a Peace rose in a window-box! Did we come half-way across the world for this? However, the next house along has some pretty China Roses which very much resemble Old Blush.

As we drive along we keep seeing *Rosa banksiae*, Lady Banks' White Rose, in ditches between the paddy fields. We stop when we see a much bigger white rose in a ditch and run excitedly across the fields to discover that we have found the beautiful, large, white Tea Scented Rose, *Rosa gigantea*; the buds are really elegant, long and very narrow. This is thought to have been the rose from which the Tea Roses of cultivation were bred.

Tiny fields filled with young rice plants ready to be transferred to the paddy fields. The lake features masses of fish farms.

ROSA LONGICUSPIS This rose spreads into enormous thickets.

This first day's drive into China from Kunming up to Dali (300 or 400 miles) is really fascinating because the whole gamut of Chinese agriculture can be seen. The young rice is growing in nursery beds ready for planting out. The water buffalo are ploughing the paddy fields. Crops of oil-seed rape are being gathered by farmers armed only with sickles. The rape is dried on the roadside to prepare it for the extraction of the oil. As we approach one village, we see fields of broad beans. Cabbages and even asparagus are growing in small family plots. Sometimes we see banana trees sprouting up in a row. At the moment the main crop that is being harvested is wheat which has been growing on the rice terraces through the winter. Every single field, every single piece of land is terraced. All the work is being done by hand: people carrying water; people carrying ducks; people carrying apples on yokes; people flailing corn at the side of the road. Sometimes the corn or rape is laid on the road surface so that passing trucks do the actual threshing. Other people are winnowing out the husks from the corn with gigantic sieves. Again, wherever you look, people with mattocks are breaking up the soil, getting ready for the new planting. Everybody wears a sun hat; old-fashioned straw ones or much more modern white plastic hats, a complete variety. Transportation is on tiny carts pulled by donkeys or very small ponies. Water is stored everywhere, always on higher ground so it can be run down to flood the paddy fields. The buildings in the villages are made of adobe bricks with roofs that are sometimes tiled and sometimes thatched. All the houses are the colour of the surrounding soil so they match and blend in perfectly. We've just passed a pottery. The potter was firing pots in a dusty black kiln, where obviously he also made roof tiles as there were vast heaps all around his compound.

ROSA LONGICUSPIS The rose sometimes sold as this is really *Rosa mulliganii*. We found the real thing growing in profusion as a very large, free-standing shrub with evergreen, shining leaves and red thorns. It can be grown as a climber to a height of 200 cm (7 ft) or more. Not much grown in gardens, but well worthwhile as it flowers profusely in tight bunches of up to 15 flowers. It has a delicate sweet scent. Summer flowering. In northern climates it needs a hot position to flower well, but would do perfectly well in California or the southern states of America.

This Reeves' drawing of *Rosa multiflora* shows a double form.

In this close-up of *Rosa multiflora* you can see the saw-toothed leaflet at the stem base (divided stipule) that distinguishes this species.

The second rose we stop for and take shots of is *Rosa longicuspis*, white with thin stems, and tall styles in the centre of the flower. The foliage is a superb, fresh bright green. It's not much used as a garden rose in cool climates, but would do well in southern Europe and California.

We lunch very late in a little café. Martyn investigates a bowl of 100-year-old eggs and the family promptly cook a great big plate of them for us. We make a valiant effort but fail to finish them.

DAY THREE

Martyn and I go out before breakfast into the city of Dali and wander into someone's little yard – having got past the resident mastiff – and find a superb, climbing China hybrid, a huge plant with rather small, double, pink, cupped flowers.

After that we go to the beggars' market which is held only once a year, on the road leading up to a little Buddhist temple. All the way to the temple there are blind people and beggars of all kinds. In the middle of the road lie small pieces of cloth on to which passers-by throw rice and small coins. At the end of the day the beggars presumably divide this all up, eat the rice and keep the money. When we arrive at the temple we find people writing fortunes. You can sit down, have someone write your good wishes on an inscribed prayer, then take it into the temple and burn it on a gigantic bonfire of prayers.

Back on the road, we scream to a halt again yelling: 'Stop! Halt! Look, rose.' Down by a little ditch a wonderful pink rose is growing against a background of rice fields. It turns out to be an odd form of *Rosa multiflora*. In fact, we discover that it is just starting to turn into a double form by growing a secondary row of petals which makes it look even pinker, stronger and better than the cultivated forms found in the West. *Rosa multiflora* is recognized by its laciniate stipule at the base of the leaf stem, a little green 'sheath' cut into a row of small teeth. By looking for this character it is easy to spot a *Rosa multiflora* or a hybrid with *multiflora* blood.

Martyn Rix finds yet more *Rosa multiflora* by the river bank.

ROSA MULTIFLORA Has no common name but certainly deserves one, for it is the parent of a very great many roses including the Hybrid Musk shrubs and many famous Ramblers including Blush Rambler, Rambling Rector and Seagull. It is known in cultivation as a creamy-white-flowered rose but we found it in a great many localities in China, growing on the narrow banks between paddy fields. All the plants we found were pink, very often a good strong pink. Summer flowering. It grows as a shrub to 180 cm (6 ft) square, but as a Rambler it may attain more than twice that height. It has been much used as an understock for growing cultivated roses in the past. In eastern North America the white form has become naturalized in hedgerows. The scent is slight, but is carried on the wind.

The beggars' market, held once a year in Dali.

A view of our Lijiang Road Climber with the white, single Lady Banks' Rose growing through it.

THE LIJIANG ROAD CLIMBER This was certainly one of our most exciting finds in China, growing in a sort of hedge with the white, single Lady Banks' Rose. An extremely free-flowering, pink, scented, loosely double Climber, it was quite common on the way up through the mountains to Lijiang in Yunnan. The nearest named rose to it in cultivation in the west is Belle Portugaise.

We are about 600 metres (2000 feet) above Dali on our way to Lijiang, on a high plateau. Passing an area where lime-firing is an important local trade, we see hundreds of kilns looking like some amazing prehistoric village. Everywhere the hedgerows are lined with wild *Rosa banksiae*, all in flower and hanging down over absolutely everything. I am now debating whether the rose was called after Lady Banks, or Banks himself, or whether it got its name because it grows on every bank between every field. Two more new crops occur at this level: fields of peas and fields of lentils.

The village we are now in is Kien Twan and we have just had the most exciting stop. We saw a bright red rose fading to a sort of magenta in someone's garden and photographed it. It had lots of Old Rose characteristics and very good scent. Then, at the end of the farmyard, Martyn spotted a great big rose 6–9 metres (20–30 feet) up a tree. At first we couldn't find any flowers but we found one hip: a big, round, beautiful, bright orange one. Round the back of the farmyard we found a couple of flowers. It was a pink *Rosa gigantea*, the very rose we'd been looking for when we spotted the one in the ditch; only much bigger, with flowers about 10 centimetres (4 inches) across and big, floppy petals with quite distinct markings. What we found may have been one of the original parents of the Teas that were used to breed the roses in China and Hybrid Teas in Europe that have given us many thousands – tens of thousands – of roses over the last 150 years.

Evening. A fantastic day to look back on. We started by getting stuck in the most awful traffic jam. The road on the top of a pass between Dali and Lijiang was being mended; a truck had broken down and behind it were about 50 more trucks all stuck across the road, which was only one lane wide. Martyn and I walked on about two miles ahead, botanizing the while and trying to collect rose hips and so on, and suddenly came round a bend and looked down into a valley. Behind some small trees we could see a bright pink rose. We ran down the road to it in high excitement and it was, indeed, a Tea China Rose. It looked very closely related to *Rosa gigantea* but was a really strong pink, double but not fully double, with bright yellow stamens in the centre. The petals faded slightly towards the centre. The long, pointed buds were also a bright, strong pink.

We arrived in Lijiang and one of the things we wanted to do, apart from

White Lady Banks' Rose, *Rosa banksiae* var. *normalis* This is the wild form of the Banksian rose which is usually seen in the double yellow or double white form. It can be found in much of China, but in Yunnan it is often the dominant wild plant of roadsides and field edges growing as a rampant shrub or clambering over trees to a height of 450 cm (15 ft). Spring flowering. Scented with a pleasant, violet-like odour. Although this rose was only properly described in 1902 it had actually been brought to Britain as early as 1796 by Robert Drummond who planted it at his home, Megginch Castle, on Tayside; here it hardly flowered and barely survived because the climate was too cold for it. However, in 1902 E.H. Woodall, the plantsman, took cuttings and grew them near Nice in southern France where they prospered and flowered well, enabling a definite identification to be made.

Roger Phillips: 'I wanted to be photographed finding this rose, it makes the whole trip worthwhile.'

A view of the white Lady Banks' Rose, showing how it forms hedges around every field.

ROSA SERICEA This was growing in the dry limestone mountains west of Lijiang, where it makes only a tiny low shrub, partly due to animal grazing. In better conditions it will make a shrub up to 300 cm (10 ft) high. Spring flowering. Well known in specialist gardens where the variety *pteracantha* (opposite) is grown for its huge red thorns on young shoots.

looking at the village in which George Forrest had lived in the early part of the century, was find out about Joseph Rock, the American botanist who had lived near there in the 1940s. We finally discovered that a man whose father had been Rock's assistant was a member of an orchestra that played ancient Taoist music. Unfortunately, we only arrived in time to hear the last three or four numbers. The orchestra consisted of about 25 musicians, most of them very old with long, white beards, dressed in traditional Chinese costume. After the performance we approached the leader of the orchestra only to find that it was he who was the son of Rock's assistant. He was delighted to see us and to find out that we were interested in botany, and told us he had some of Rock's papers and his desk, which had been left to his father. He lived not far away, in the very room in which Joseph Rock had worked when in Lijiang, and invited us to visit him. It was wonderful to meet this man and he was so excited to meet us. We all felt that we had made a real contact with the botanists of the past. A great experience.

DAY FOUR

In the morning we visit the Monastery of 10 000 Camellias. A very old man, one of the priests, looks after its plants. He speaks the Nassi dialect. Nearby is the village George Forrest worked from when he was collecting in the region. Joseph Rock must also have worked from there because he is remembered wherever we go. A big eucalyptus in the middle of the village was planted by him fifty years ago. Apart from that we find other signs of the presence of foreign botanists. For instance, there is a fully grown olive and a Japanese willow, *Salix matsudana tortuosa*. Neither is a native Chinese plant and they could only have been introduced by a visitor.

YELLOW *ROSA GIGANTEA* This rose was growing in the public park in Lijiang together with yellow Lady Banks' Rose. It seems to be another hybrid unknown in the West. This habit of growing two Climbers, one small and the other large, which flower together is something that I shall emulate in my garden at home.

THE ROSE QUEST IN CHINA

10,000 CAMELLIAS RED CHINA ROSE
We found this superb, deep red, semi-double China Rose growing in the temple in the foothills a few miles outside Lijiang. It shows that there certainly are China Roses way up in the mountains of Yunnan that are not in cultivation in the West. It was just coming into flower as the season is quite a bit later at this altitude.

The ancient *Camellia reticulata* known as 'the camellia of 10 000 blooms'.

ROSA SERICEA FORMA *PTERACANTHA*
Photographed in the garden at Rose Acres, California. This form is grown as a curiosity, for its enormous winged thorns, but it is also very pretty for about a week in spring when it is covered with small, white flowers.

The Buddhist priest who was in charge of the garden at the Monastery of 10 000 Camellias.

Lime kilns on the roadside, looking like ancient ruins.

We found this interesting rose in the tiny village near Lijiang where Joseph Rock, the American botanist, worked.

There is a great love of roses in China. Here the family pose in front of their wonderful red Climber on the road outside Emei in Sichuan.

A new section of hybrids altogether? It certainly looks like it. This rose has some *Rosa multiflora* and some China characteristics.

A double Multiflora/China hybrid, from the Reeves' drawings, similar to the rose shown above.

DAY FIVE

In the flower market back in Kunming, after a horrendous overnight drive, we find a man with just one rose in a little pot. He says it is a 'monthly rose' – the very name that was given to the first repeat-flowering rose to come to Europe from China. It's interesting that the name is still in common usage!

DAY SIX

We have just arrived at the Jing Jang Hotel in Chengdu, capital of Sichuan, and disasters are piling up one on top of the other. Having lost our bags on China Airlines coming to China, the travel service had arranged for them to be sent on to us. Customs wouldn't release them and as a result, when we arrived at the hotel where we were to meet Mikinori Ogisu, we found a message that he had given up waiting and gone up country.

DAY SEVEN

We move on to Mount Emei, the holy mountain, in a Toyota Land Cruiser, known locally as Jeepo, with a new guide, Cai Ming, whose name he told us could roughly be translated into English as Vegetable.

Sichuan has been known as the land of abundance since ancient times because of its enormous, incredibly fertile central plain. The journey from Chengdu to Mount Emei takes five hours but with quite long stops on the way. We find masses of beautiful *Rosa roxburghii*, the Chestnut Rose, so-called because of the spines that cover its buds and fruit. The leaflets are very tiny, about twelve to a leaf.

Our hotel is at the bottom of Mount Emei. The hills around us rise out of the mist like giant, pine-covered spear-heads. Tall, narrow and rocky they look exactly like a Chinese watercolour.

DAY EIGHT

Mikinori Ogisu had left Martyn a little pencil map, consisting of three lines, and with it we try to find the missing China Rose he had rediscovered. As far as we know he was the first modern botanist ever to see it! We rush up and down passes and explore river valleys and rocky gulches until we spot what we think must be the rose on the other side of a deep ravine. We then go miles down the valley, cross it at a bridge and walk back along the other

Misty hills behind the first temple we visited on Mount Emei.

The map of Mount Emei is a wonderful Chinese watercolour.

A nursery where all the roses are grown from cuttings and then sold in pots.

The bottom of 8000 steps that have to be climbed to get to the top of Mount Emei.

CHESTNUT ROSE, *ROSA ROXBURGHII* This is very distinctive because of the spines on its buds, hips that look rather like small, spiny chestnuts hanging from the branches and its thin, peeling bark. It has a great many tiny leaflets, up to 19 on each leaf. Summer flowering. Common in Sichuan and Yunnan on roadsides and between paddy fields. In cultivation it grows to about 250 cm (8 ft) high. Quite well scented, and with a long flowering season.

FAILURE This is the rose that we thought was going to be the wild China Rose but which turned out to be a Multiflora hybrid. However, I think it is very interesting. It looks exactly like *Rosa multiflora* var. *platyphylla* as illustrated by Redouté, known in cultivation as Seven Sisters, a Rambler up to 350 cm (12 ft) high. It was a great favourite in Victorian times and gained its name because the flowers vary in colour, in theory showing seven different tones from white to deep pink. Very fragrant.

side with tremendous expectations. When we get to it we find that it is an escaped garden variety of *Rosa multiflora*, known in cultivation as Seven Sisters! However, we find another treasure later in the day: *Rosa cymosa*, which Martyn calls the Elderflower Rose because it has about twenty or thirty tiny flowers in a flat bunch. It is a great, drooping plant with very long stems hanging down from the trees.

We are now about to tackle the 8000 steps that lead up Mount Emei. Whether we'll make it or not is highly debatable. After no more than a thousand steps we are in a state of collapse, but at this point we are rescued by rickshaw men who, it seems, run a regular service carrying wrecked sightseers to the heights.

We leave Mount Emei and head for Père David's seminary in Boaxing. Our first stop is at a tea plantation. Beautiful rows of clipped hedges run right round the mountain looking rather like a giant maze. The tea plant is a species of camellia and only grows well at very particular altitudes. However, from the rose point of view, what concerns us about tea is the fragrance. The fresh leaves don't have a strong scent. It is only when they are dried, and especially when water is added, that they release the tea aroma. Yet this 'tea scent' has given its name to a whole class of roses: the Tea-scented Roses, parents of the Hybrid Teas of modern rose culture.

Do the so-called Tea Roses really smell of tea? This is the question. Some people say they do, others that they were called Tea Roses because they smelled of tea after the plants had been shipped to Europe from Canton on tea clippers. No doubt everything on a tea clipper eventually smelt strongly of tea. Another reason that is given for the name is that the plants were all bought from a nursery in Canton called Fa Tee. Martyn has yet another solution to this tea-scented rose controversy: he wonders whether the tea that was imported was scented, perhaps with orange blossom or jasmine or even rose petals. The plot thickens.

After driving through a dramatic gorge we get to within five miles of Boaxing only to find an enormous rock in the middle of the road. Teams of

Hips of the Chestnut Rose, *Rosa roxburghii*.

THE CHESTNUT ROSE, *ROSA ROXBURGHII* This can be found in many different shades of colour in the wild from very pale pink to a deep reddish pink.

A CHINA ROSE Found in the first temple on the climb up Mount Emei. Now unknown in the West, but a rather primitive China hybrid that may have existed up here for a thousand years. One of the characteristics is that the red petals show white streaks, a character common to many of the early Chinas introduced in the West.

The Redouté drawing of *Rosa multiflora* var. *platyphylla* from *Les Roses* (Vol. II, page 69). It looks very similar to our Failure (opposite).

A view of the gardens of the first temple on Mount Emei, with the China Rose climbing through the shrubs.

This drawing from the Reeves' Collection in the Lindley Library looks very similar to the remarkable rose we found on the Emperor's Tea Mountain (below).

TEA MOUNTAIN ROSE As we started to climb the Emperor's Tea Mountain we came across this rose on the side of the track. It looked like a Rugosa hybrid, but *rugosa* is a seaside plant and here we are over 1600 km (1000 miles) from the ocean. The locals when questioned confirmed its identity as Mai Kwa. Back in Britain we compared our photographs to the Reeves' drawings to find that a very similar rose had been drawn in Canton in around 1825!

The growth habit of the rose that so resembles the Reeves' drawing (above).

The road to Boaxing. A most beautiful China Rose growing in front of a typical, mountain farmer's house. In the background the Jeepo and the ever-inquisitive locals who gathered to find out what on earth was going on. A semi-double pink China, it looks very similar to Old Blush but is perhaps a little darker.

workers are blasting a new road through a gorge. The road builders erect a tripod over the rock and, using a pulley system, lift it very, very gradually and put it on the back of a truck for removal. Only man power is used. At last we are able to get past. We go down the road another 300 yards and BOOM – another blast! This time a few hundred tonnes block the road. No choice. We must think again.

* * * *

We have just had a super lunch at a roadside café. The main feature was Ma Po's bean curd, cubes of tofu cooked in a spicy sauce then sprinkled with chilli powder while still sizzling hot. Very spicy, very delicious. Said to have been called after a local cook Ma Po because the red surface of the bean curd looked like her pock-marked skin!

Roses are grown very differently in China from the way they are grown in the West where people have collections of ten, twenty, thirty, 100 or 200 different roses. In China you travel 200 miles to a village and find only one kind of cultivated rose in its gardens. You go another 200 miles and find another rose, different from the previous one. I think that when a good rose is developed its cuttings are passed from hand to hand.

DAY NINE

Off to the Emperor's Tea Mountain. One of our tasks today is to search for a yellow rose. Our guide Vegetable thinks the symbolism of the colour yellow could have affected the popularity of yellow roses. Yellow, he says, is now the colour of playboys or pimps, though before the Cultural Revolution it was the imperial colour. If you refer to a girl as being a 'yellow girl' you are almost certainly referring to a prostitute. The Communist's red, on the other hand, is now the good luck colour and pink signifies sweet dreams.

After climbing a good way up the mountain we find a big, white rose with twenty or thirty small flowers in each flowerhead. It reminds Martyn of Wedding Day. The inflorescence, stems and flower buds are very glandular and softly hairy. It is beautifully scented with a rather unusual, musky scent. Martyn says perhaps we've discovered the original musk rose. Well, we can but hope. Later, on looking it up, we find there is only one rose with really

Using water buffalo is the only real way to plough deep, wet, heavy clay.

ROSA RUBUS Discovered in western and central China by Henry in 1888. We found it growing on a hillside in western Sichuan. It is remarkable for having downy hairs on leaves, buds and stems. It is called *rubus* because the foliage looks exactly like that of the blackberry *Rubus fruticosus*. Summer flowering. Little grown in gardens but it makes a very nice plant, a tall shrub up to about 450 cm (15 ft) high with a good red foliage when young. Strongly scented of musk.

A view of *ROSA RUBUS* tumbling out of the luscious vegetation on the lower slopes of the Emperor's Tea Mountain, with *Iris japonica*.

THE ELDERFLOWER ROSE, *ROSA CYMOSA* It is just about to come into full flower. We should have been here two weeks later. Wonderfully scented, like violets.

Looking down over the tea plantation as we climb the Sky Steps up the Emperor's Tea Mountain.

THE ELDERFLOWER ROSE, *ROSA CYMOSA* Found in a hedge in Sichuan. Elegant, long branches hang down from low trees and swing gently in the breeze. Masses of tiny white flowers are bunched together, just like the flowers of an elderberry except for the creamy yellow appearance caused by bright yellow stamens. Summer flowering. Grows up to 750 cm (25 ft) high. Rather tender, probably best grown in a greenhouse or conservatory in frosty climates.

hairy, glandular coatings on the flower buds, stems and even the leaf backs: *Rosa rubus*, the Blackberry Rose, so-called because its hairy foliage resembles blackberry leaves!

Having found examples of pink and red garden roses in China, it left only the yellow garden rose unaccounted for. We had failed to find any on the trip so far, but here, on the last leg of our journey, we are told of a remote monastery where there is a single yellow rose. However, when we finally get there, the rose master (a priestess) tells us that the poor, naughty, yellow thing had died; so, a second failure.

Answers

The evidence certainly shows that China and Tea Roses have been bred in the Chinese interior, and it seems quite possible that the original 'stud Chinas' were bred not in Canton but somewhere in the hinterland. We found roses very close to Hume's Blush and others that were related to Parson's Pink, Parks' Yellow and Slater's Crimson. It also seems very likely that botanists and plant collectors of the past could have discovered other garden roses if they had been able to journey inland and not been restricted to within a six-mile radius of Canton. This is not only true of the past. It is still the case that there are some very interesting roses to be found in the gardens of deepest China, even today.

A still, misty evening. Looking back towards the Sky Steps from the top of the Emperor's Tea Mountain.

THE WILD CHINA ROSE, *ROSA CHINENSIS* VAR. *SPONTANEA* This rose had been seen by two botanists, Wilson and Henry, in the last 100 years, but had then been lost again. This photograph was taken by Mikinori Ogisu, the Japanese botanist who rediscovered it in May 1983 growing in the wild in Leibo, south-west Sichuan at about 1700 m (5500 ft). A once-flowering Climber, it has flowers that open pale and darken to red as they age. This is the wild type of the China Rose that has so changed rose breeding, the remote ancestor of the Hybrid Tea and Floribunda roses. This photograph saves our bacon: it is the rose we thought we had found in the gorge but which turned out to be Seven Sisters.

We had come miles to this temple to see a rare yellow rose. On our arrival the priestess and her acolyte told us it had died.

ROSA RUBIGINOSA, EGLANTINE, SWEETBRIAR Sweet Briars are a group of several species of Dog Rose usually found on dry or chalky soils; they were popular garden plants in medieval times because of their sweetly aromatic leaves, which smell of apples, especially after rain. Summer flowering. Height to 320 cm (10½ ft). Well scented. Photographed in the gardens at Hatfield House, Hertfordshire.

ROSA CANINA The Dog Rose forms a large, stiff shrub and is very pretty for the few weeks when it is in full flower. The flowers are usually pale pink, the leaves and hips smooth. Found wild in hedges and rough pastures throughout Europe and much of western Asia. Once flowering, in early summer. To about 200 cm (7 ft) high, a little wider. Scented.

CHAPTER FIVE

Wild Roses

The wild roses and their cultivars are arranged by group: Dog Roses, Scotch Roses, Yellow Briars, American Roses, Rugosas, Moyesii, Chinese Roses, Giant Climbers.

Dog Roses are the commonest wild roses in Britain and northern Europe. They can be recognized by their stiff, twiggy bushes and usually pale pink, but sometimes deep pink or white, flowers in small groups. The styles in the middle of the flower are short and do not stick up in a group as those of the musk roses do. Eglantine is a form of Dog Rose with aromatic leaves.

They were the first roses to be grown in northern Europe, in both single and double forms, before Gallicas and Damasks were brought back from the Middle East by the Crusaders in the fourteenth century. In the early seventeenth century yellow roses were introduced from Turkey and the first American roses were grown in English gardens. By 1656, John Tradescant the Younger, whose father had been gardener to the Earl of Salisbury at Hatfield House, Hertfordshire, was growing all these roses in his garden at Lambeth in London. His collection amounted to thirty-two different kinds, including Francofurtana and Muscovita which his father had collected in 1618 while accompanying an embassy from James I to Moscow.

The double-flowered Dog Rose is still found in gardens, usually under the name Abbotswood. Dog Roses are also commonly used in Europe as stocks and so often appear as suckers in abandoned or poorly kept gardens.

RAUBRITTER A very lovely, low, spreading shrub. Its sprawling habit and incurving petals are characteristic. Raised by Kordes in Germany, launched 1936. (Daisy Hill × Solarium.) Quite long flowering around midsummer. Liable to mildew. Stems to 200 cm (7 ft). Well scented.

DUPONTII A large shrub or low climber. Its shapely flowers are up to 7.5 cm (3 in) across, with an upright tuft of styles in the centre. Known in France since the early nineteenth century. Of unknown origin but probably *Rosa arvensis* or possibly *Rosa moschata* crossed with *Rosa gallica*. Once flowering, in midsummer. Height up to 250 cm (8 ft), more if supported. Well scented.

ROSA FEDTSCHENKOANA A grey-leaved rose with flowers about 5 cm (2 in) across. From the mountains of Central Asia. Discovered by the great Russian botanist, Alexei Fedtschenko, and his wife, Olga, around 1871. Introduced in Britain 1900. The plant suckers. Flowers are produced over a long period from midsummer. Height of stems to 200 cm (7 ft). Well scented.

MEG MERRILIES A shrub with aromatic foliage like the wild species. One of Lord Penzance's Sweet Briar hybrids, introduced 1894. Summer flowering. Height to 300 cm (10 ft). Well scented.

ROSA GLAUCA formerly *ROSA RUBRIFOLIA* A large shrub with arching branches and lovely grey or purplish, delicate ornamental foliage and deep purple young twigs. Small flowers are followed by numerous bright red hips. Found wild in the mountains of Europe from the Pyrenees to Albania. Summer flowering. Seems unaffected by disease. Height to 400 cm (13 ft). Some scent. Photographed at Hatfield House, Hertfordshire.

DAISY HILL A large shrub. Raised by Smith in Northern Ireland *c.*1900. A seedling of the old hybrid, Macrantha, a sprawling plant thought to be a hybrid between *Rosa gallica* and *Rosa canina* or *Rosa alba*. Once flowering, in midsummer, but sets a good crop of hips. To 150 cm (5 ft) high × 350 cm (11 ft) wide. Well scented.

ANDERSONII A large bush, a good version of a single Dog Rose, with larger flowers. First recorded in a Hillier catalogue in Britain 1912. Possibly a Gallica hybrid – it is reminiscent of a small Complicata (page 35). Once flowering in midsummer. To 200 × 200 cm (7 × 7 ft). Scented.

SCOTCH BRIAR, BURNET ROSE, *ROSA PIMPINELLIFOLIA*, formerly *ROSA SPINOSISSIMA* Usually a short suckering shrub in the wild. Stems are characteristically bristly and covered with numerous slender, spines. Found in Europe from Iceland eastwards to Siberia, Turkey and Central Asia, growing on partially stabilized sand dunes and in sandy or chalky soil in hills and mountains. Flowers in late spring are followed by rather round black hips. Height to 100 cm (3 ft).

MRS COLVILLE (HIPS) The hips are interesting as they show the influence of *Rosa pendulina*, the Alpine rose, being elongated and reddish.

MRS COLVILLE A low, much-branched shrub with rich purplish-crimson flowers with a paler eye, large reddish hips and broad stipules. A *Rosa pendulina × pimpinellifolia* hybrid. Height to 100 cm (3 ft). Scented.

DOORENBOS SELECTION An upright-growing variety with bright crimson single flowers raised in The Hague, photographed in California.

The wild Scotch or Burnet Rose is common throughout Europe. Early cultivars were all selections of the wild type with pink, white, double or bicoloured flowers. Later hybrids between this and other wild roses were raised, or found wild and brought into gardens. Finally, in the 1930s, Kordes produced the lovely large shrubs which share the prefix 'Frühlings' (spring) by crossing the Burnet Rose with Hybrid Teas. All do well on sandy soils and in cold gardens where most roses grow poorly.

STANWELL PERPETUAL A very pretty perpetual flowering rose that forms a rather upright shrub. Parentage uncertain; it was found in a garden at Stanwell, Middlesex and introduced by Lee of Hammersmith in 1838. Graham Thomas suggests that *Rosa pimpinellifolia* was one parent, an Autumn Damask probably the other. Flowers in midsummer but always has a few flowers into autumn and in wet seasons when more modern roses are destroyed by blackspot. Height to 150 cm (5 ft). Sweetly scented.

DOUBLE WHITE An easy-to-grow old variety of Scotch Briar that makes a thicket of shoots and has masses of pretty, incurved flowers. Summer flowering. Disease resistant. Height to 200 cm (7 ft). Sharp, fresh scent.

WILLIAM III A very dwarf Scotch Briar with greyish leaves and purplish flowers that are paler on the back of the petals. The hips are black. Suckers to produce a thicket of stems. Summer flowering. Height to 50 cm (1½ ft). Scented.

ALBERT EDWARDS An exceptionally free-flowering shrub with arching stems. Introduced by Hillier in Britain 1961. A hybrid between the large-flowered form of *Rosa pimpinellifolia altaica* from the mountains of Siberia and *Rosa xanthina* forma *hugonis*, from China. Spring flowering. Height to 300 cm (10 ft). Light scent.

ROSA PERSICA, HULTHEMIA PERSICA A semi-desert plant that suckers widely and sends up low sprawling shoots. Flowers are bright yellow with a large red eye, the leaves have only one greyish leaflet. It should do well in dry, hot regions. Summer flowering. Height to 60 cm (2 ft). Scented. Photographed near Urumuchi in north-western China.

ROSA CANTABRIGIENSIS A chance hybrid with bristly young shoots and reddish hips. Appeared in Cambridge Botanic Garden in *c.* 1930. The parents were probably *Rosa xanthina* forma *hugonis* and *Rosa sericea*. Spring flowering. Height to 200 cm (7 ft). Scented.

PERSIAN YELLOW The double form of *Rosa foetida*, a good garden plant in warm climates. Introduced from Iran 1837. Summer flowering. Height to 150 cm (5 ft). Photographed near Sutter's Creek in the California Gold Country, where it had naturalized.

ROSA HARDII An early *Rosa persica* hybrid. Requires more heat and warmth than most roses. Raised in the Luxembourg Gardens, Paris by its director, Alexandre Hardy, in *c.* 1786; *Rosa clinophylla* was said to be the seed parent. Summer flowering. Susceptible to mildew. Height to 180 cm (6 ft). Some scent.

THE YELLOW ROSE OF TEXAS, HARISON'S YELLOW, *ROSA × HARISONII* This rose is said to have been carried westwards across America with the pioneers and planted wherever they stopped. Raised by George Folliott Harison, or possibly his father Richard; both were New York lawyers and keen gardeners in the early 19th century. (*Rosa foetida* × *Rosa pimpinellifolia*.) Flowers in midsummer. Height to 200 cm (7 ft).

AUSTRIAN BRIAR, *ROSA FOETIDA* Introduced in England in the late 16th century. Its origin is a mystery. It probably arose as an ancient hybrid between the very glandular *Rosa kokanica* from Central Asia and the wild Turkish *Rosa hemisphaerica*, which has greyish leaves. Thrives best in a sunny position. Summer flowering. Liable to blackspot in dank gardens. Height to 250 cm (8 ft). The flowers are said to be unpleasantly scented, of bed bugs.

The bright yellow, small-flowered roses are all found wild in the dry parts of Asia, from Turkey eastwards to northern China and Mongolia. They usually grow on rocky hillsides or in hedges, in much the same places as Dog Roses grow in England or *Rosa californica* in the Sierra Nevada foothills. The double and red forms are of great antiquity, long grown by the Turks in the case of *Rosa foetida,* or the Chinese in the case of *Rosa xanthina.*

TIGRIS A low, sprawling shrub. Requires as hot and sunny a place as possible to do well. Tigris is one of only three hybrids (the others are Euphrates and Nigel Hawthorne) which have been introduced since 1968 when Alec Cocker and Jack Harkness in Britain obtained seeds of *Rosa persica* and started a breeding programme to try to raise roses with a red eye. Flowers continuously. Height to 45 cm (1½ ft).

FATHER HUGO'S ROSE, *ROSA XANTHINA*, FORMA *HUGONIS* A shrub with pale yellow, rather cup-shaped flowers. It is the common wild yellow rose in north-western China, named after Father Hugh Scallan, a missionary, who sent seed to Kew in around 1900. Flowers in early summer. Height to 250 cm (8 ft). Scented.

CANARY BIRD, *ROSA XANTHINA* A large shrub with arching stems and neat, small leaves; a particularly fine form of *Rosa xanthina.* Lindley's original description of the species was taken from a Chinese drawing of a double yellow rose. Spring flowering. Height of stems to 250 cm (8 ft). Scented.

AUSTRIAN COPPER, *ROSA FOETIDA* BICOLOR The flowers are yellow in bud and on the reverse; and intense red when open. Grown in Arab countries at least since the 12th century. Summer flowering. Prone to blackspot. Height to 250 cm (8 ft).

THE SULPHUR ROSE, *ROSA HEMISPHAERICA, ROSA RAPINII* A low shrub with curved or hooked prickles and orange or yellow hips. This wild form from central Turkey is very similar to *Rosa foetida.* Summer flowering. Height to 180 cm (6 ft).

BASYE'S THORNLESS A complex hybrid. Raised by Basye in USA 1977. (Basye's Amphidiploid × *Rosa carolina* seedling × Hugh Dickson.) It is tetraploid and fertile, so is able to be crossed with modern garden roses. Basye's Purple is now in commerce. (*Rosa rugosa* × *Rosa foliolosa*.) Height to 200 cm (7 ft). Some scent.

SACRAMENTO ROSE, *ROSA STELLATA* var. *MYRIFICA* Forms large thickets. Needs a dry, hot place to grow and flower well. Found in the Sacramento and White Mountains in New Mexico. Flowers from midsummer to autumn. Height to 200 cm (7 ft) in wild, shorter in gardens.

ROSA BELLA A relative of *Rosa moyesii* from north-western China. Flowers are about 5 cm (2 in) across, hips about 2 cm (¾ in) long. Raised at the Arnold Arboretum, Massachusetts from seed collected by Purdom in *c.* 1914. Summer flowering. Height to 250 cm (8 ft). Good scent.

ROSA ARKANSANA A native American, ranging from Wisconsin and Minnesota to Colorado and Kansas, growing on dry hills and prairies. Flowers throughout summer. Height to 60 cm (2 ft). Scented.

ROSA VIRGINIANA syn. *ROSA LUCIDA* A leafy bush with flowers 6 cm (2½ in) across. Common in north-eastern North America, from Newfoundland south to Pennsylvania and east to Ontario and Arkansas. Midsummer flowering. Height to 200 cm (7 ft).

ROSA CALIFORNICA Forms spreading thickets of stems with flowers up to 5 cm (2 in) across. The common wild rose in California on the west side of the Sierra Nevada, it grows in rather damp places below 1800 m (6000 ft). Flowers throughout summer and autumn. Height to 200 cm (7 ft). Scented.

BASYE'S AMPHIDIPLOID Raised by Basye in USA 1955. (*Rosa abyssinica* × *Rosa rugosa*.) *Rosa abyssinica* is a member of the *synstylae*, so this rose is similar in background to a Damask. By doubling of the chromosomes, Basye's Amphidiploid becomes fertile, and able to cross with tetraploid garden roses. Height to 200 cm (7 ft). Scented.

ROSA MINUTIFOLIA An interesting, dwarf rose with leaflets that are up to 6 mm ($\frac{1}{4}$ in) long with very hairy undersides and flowers 2.5 cm (1 in) across. From the dry mountains of Baja, California and now very rare in the wild. Flowers are produced from autumn to spring, followed by very spiny fruit. Height to 60 cm (2 ft).

ROSA CALIFORNICA PLENA A tall shrub. A cultivated form of *Rosa californica*, with bright, deep pink, semi-double flowers with a pale centre, in masses along the branches. The stipules are broad and the bracts leafy. Summer flowering. Height to 250 cm (8 ft). Well scented.

SCABROSA A round shrub with fresh green leaves and single flowers up to 14 cm ($5\frac{1}{2}$ in) across. Hips are large and red. Introduced by Harkness in Britain 1960. A form or hybrid of *Rosa rugosa* of unknown origin. Flowers throughout summer and autumn. Height to 200 cm (7 ft). Well scented.

ROSERAIE DE L'HAŸ A wonderful form of *Rosa rugosa*, or possibly a hybrid, with huge flowers, thorny stems and bright green, narrow leaflets. Raised by Gravereaux at the Roseraie de l'Haÿ, Paris 1901. Flowers well into autumn. Height to 200 cm (7 ft). Strong, heavy scent.

MRS ANTHONY WATERER A Rugosa hybrid. Raised by Waterer in Britain 1898. (*Rosa rugosa* seedling × Général Jacqueminot.) Flowers over a long period; best in midsummer. Height to 150 cm (5 ft). Very fragrant.

ROSA RUGOSA A native of the coasts of Japan, eastern Siberia, northern China and Korea where it grows mainly on sand dunes near the sea, forming low, suckering patches. Also found naturalized on the coasts of Europe. Flowers throughout summer and autumn. Both species and its hybrids are exceptionally disease resistant. Height to 180 cm (6 ft). Well scented. Photographed at West Wittering, Sussex.

ROSA RUGOSA PLENA Double forms of *Rosa rugosa* are rather inaccurately placed under this name.

RUSKIN A large shrub which can be trained as a climber, or pegged down like a Hybrid Perpetual. A Rugosa hybrid. Raised by Van Fleet in USA 1928; the other parent was the Hybrid Perpetual, Victor Hugo. Flowers mainly in midsummer with a few later. Height to 120 cm (4 ft). Very well scented.

F.J. GROOTENDORST A tall, rather lanky bush. Unusual because of the frilly edges to the petals. Flowers are small, but carried several in a tight head. (*Rosa rugosa* Rubra × Mme Norbert Levavasseur.) Flowers throughout summer and autumn. Height to 200 cm (7 ft). Some scent.

CIBLES A Rugosa hybrid raised by Kaufmann 1893.

A view of the garden at Hidcote Manor, Gloucestershire, showing the rose F.J. GROOTENDORST.

DELICATA One of the least vigorous of the Rugosa hybrids, as its name suggests. Raised by Cooling 1898. Repeat flowering. Height usually to 150 cm (5 ft). Good scent.

MAX GRAF Forms a dense ground cover of trailing shoots, with clusters of large pink flowers. Raised by Bowditch in USA 1919. (*Rosa rugosa* × *Rosa wichuraiana*.) A seedling from this rose, which proved to be a fertile tetraploid, became the basis of the Kordesii Roses. Summer flowering with the occasional flower in autumn. Height to 75 cm (2½ ft). Scented.

NEW CENTURY A Rugosa hybrid with smoother leaves. Raised by Van Fleet in USA. (*Rosa rugosa* Alba × Clotilde Soupert.) Flowers continuously. Height to 150 cm (5 ft). Very well scented.

THÉRÈSE BUGNET A very hardy, bushy shrub. Raised by Bugnet in Canada 1950. A complex Rugosa hybrid. Flowers continuously. Height to 180 cm (6 ft). Well scented.

BLANC DOUBLE DE COUBERT A dense, bushy plant. Raised by Cochet-Cochet in France 1892. Summer flowering. Height to 120 cm (4 ft). Wonderfully scented.

The collection of old *Rosa rugosa* varieties in a cool border along a north-facing wall at Mottisfont Abbey, Hampshire.

PINK GROOTENDORST A tall, lanky bush. A sport of F.J. Grootendorst, with flowers of a prettier colour. Robust and healthy. Height to 200 cm (10 ft) or more. Fragrant.

PAULII, *ROSA RUGOSA REPENS* There are two hybrids under this name, one white and one pink, both thorny shrubs with long, trailing stems, suitable for ground cover. Raised by Paul in Britain before 1903. The pink form appears to be a sport of the white. (*Rosa rugosa × Rosa arvensis.*) Height to 30 cm (1 ft). Mostly midsummer flowering. Well scented.

PINK SURPRISE A bushy shrub with flowers about 7.5 cm (3 in) across. Raised by Lens in Belgium, introduced by Austin in Britain in 1987. (*Rosa rugosa × Rosa bracteata*). Flowers from summer into autumn. Height to 150 cm (5 ft).

NYVELDT'S WHITE A large shrub with pure white, sweetly scented flowers from pale pink buds, and coarse, green leaves. Raised by Nyveldt 1955. ((*Rosa rugosa* × *Rosa majalis*) × *Rosa nitida*.) Height to 200 cm (6 ft). Flowers continuously from midsummer into autumn. Fragrant.

FRAU DAGMAR HARTOPP, FRU DAGMAR HASTRUP A bushy shrub, one of the most beautiful of all single roses. Very large, clear rose-pink flowers are followed by bright red hips. Raised by Hastrup in Denmark 1914. Flowers from midsummer to autumn. Height to 150 cm (5 ft), smaller than most Rugosas. Scented.

SARAH VAN FLEET A free-flowering Rugosa hybrid. Raised by Van Fleet in USA, launched 1926. (*Rosa rugosa* × My Maryland.) Flowers continuously. Some rust. Height to 120 cm (4 ft). Fragrant.

LADY CURZON A large shrub, sometimes grown as a climber. A lovely, single rose with a pale centre. Raised by Turner in Britain 1901. (*Rosa rugosa* × *Rosa macrantha*.) Once flowering, in midsummer. Height to 300 cm (9 ft). Scented.

SCHNEEZWERG, SNOW DWARF A good, hardy rose for a hedge. Semi-double flowers are followed by red hips. Raised by Lambert in Germany 1912. (*Rosa rugosa* × *Rosa bracteata*.) Flowers throughout summer and autumn. Height to 150 cm (5 ft). Fragrant.

NOVA ZEMBLA A rather upright shrub. Introduced by Mees in Britain 1937. A sport of Conrad Ferdinand Meyer. Flowers as well or better in autumn as in summer. Height to 300 cm (10 ft). Well scented.

AGNES An exceptional, very double, pale yellow rose with glandular leaves, like *Rosa foetida*, and arching stems. Raised by Saunders in Canada 1922. (*Rosa rugosa* × *Rosa foetida* Persiana.) Repeat flowering. Height to 150 cm (5 ft). Fragrant.

SOUVENIR DE CHRISTOPHE COCHET A pink, double-flowered Rugosa hybrid. Raised by Cochet-Cochet in France 1894. Height to 200 cm (7 ft). Well scented.

MARTIN FROBISHER A rounded shrub with the appearance of an Old Rose, although it is reputedly a Schneezwerg seedling. Raised by Svedja in Canada 1968. Leaves more like *Rosa pimpinellifolia* than *Rosa rugosa*. A good succession of flowers after the initial flush. Height to 150 cm (5 ft). Good scent.

The roses on the following four pages, *Rosa moyesii* and related species, are all natives of China. They form large, open shrubs with pink or red flowers and, usually, large, beautiful hips. They are easily grown in climates with wet summers and not very cold winters. *Rosa macrophylla*, the most tender of the group, is considered zone 7 in North America.

ARTHUR HILLIER Numerous deep pink flowers are followed by a good crop of large, bright red hips. Raised at Hillier's nurseries in Britain 1938. (*Rosa moyesii* × *Rosa macrophylla*.) Summer flowering. Height to 250 cm (8 ft). Some scent. Photographed in the Heather Garden at Windsor Great Park, Berkshire.

WINTONIENSIS. A *Rosa moyesii* seedling, with scented foliage, very glandular hips. Raised by Hillier in Britain, launched 1928. (A *Rosa moyesii* seedling × *Rosa setipoda*.) Summer flowering. Height to 360 cm (12 ft). Some scent.

HIGHDOWNENSIS A large shrub with crimson flowers, reddish stems and small leaves with bluish undersides. Hips are prolific. Raised in Sir Frederick Stern's garden in Sussex, before 1925. A *Rosa moyesii* seedling. Summer flowering. Height to 300 cm (10 ft).

ROSA FORRESTIANA Similar to *Rosa multibracteata* in its leafy bracts, but the bunch of hips is almost stemless. A native of north-western Yunnan in China. Collected by Forrest in 1918. Usually flowers late summer. Height to 200 cm (7 ft). Some scent.

ROSA MACROPHYLLA A large shrub, with rich pink flowers and oval leaflets. Hips are variable, but sometimes very large, particularly in Schilling 2079, a form from Nepal. This species is found wild in forest clearings from Pakistan eastwards along the Himalayas to Bhutan and western Yunnan. Summer flowering. Height to 300 cm (10 ft). Some scent.

EDDIE'S JEWEL A Moyesii hybrid. Raised by Eddie in Canada 1962. (Donald Prior × *Rosa moyesii*.) Repeat flowers well. Height to 250 cm (8 ft). Some scent.

ROSA MOYESII A very large shrub when established. A distinctive rose with bright red flowers in the cultivated form and numerous small, rounded leaflets. Flowers are often pink in the wild. Originally collected in western China, near Kanding, by Pratt and named after the Reverend J. Moyes, a missionary in China. Summer flowering. Height to 600 cm (20 ft).

GERANIUM A clone of *Rosa moyesii*, chosen for its compact growth and good hips. Raised from wild seed at Wisley in Britain 1938. Summer flowering. Height to 250 cm (8 ft).

ROSA MOYESII The flask-shaped hips make a lovely autumn show.

THREEPENNY-BIT ROSE, *ROSA ELEGANTULA, ROSA FARRERI* PERSETOSA An elegant, spreading bush with tiny leaves and flowers. Collected by Farrer in Gansu, north-west China in 1915. This form was selected by Bowles in Britain. Summer flowering. To 200 × 200 cm (7 × 7 ft).

CORYANA A compact bush with dense leaves and bright reddish-pink flowers. Raised by Hurst at Cambridge 1926. (*Rosa roxburghii* × *Rosa macrophylla*.) Midsummer flowering. Height to 200 cm (7 ft). Little scent.

COOPER'S BURMESE, COOPER'S BURMA ROSE Almost certainly a hybrid between *Rosa laevigata* and *Rosa gigantea*. Unlike *Rosa laevigata* the receptacle is smooth, not bristly, but the petals curl and go pinkish as they age like *Rosa gigantea*. Hardier and freer flowering then *Rosa laevigata*. Repeat flowering. Height to 450 cm (15 ft). Scented.

RAMONA, RED CHEROKEE A lovely climber for a warm wall. Rather tender, but excellent in the Mediterranean or other warm climate. Originated as a sport from the paler-flowered Anemonoides. Found by Dietrich Turner in California in 1913. Flowers produced for a long period from early summer. Height to 300 cm (10 ft). Faint scent.

FORTUNIANA An ancient Chinese garden hybrid between *Rosa banksiae* and *Rosa laevigata*. A rampant climber with scented double flowers about 7.5 cm (3 in) across. Introduced in Europe by Fortune in *c.* 1845. Does not do well in cold climates, but popular in California where it was often used as an understock. Summer flowering. To 1200 cm (40 ft).

CHEROKEE ROSE, *ROSA LAEVIGATA* A rampant climber which will climb into trees or cover a pergola. Hardy only on a warm wall in frosty areas. A native of China where it is widespread in warmer areas, but it has also gone wild in the USA's southern states. Spring flowering. Height to 600 cm (20 ft). Some scent.

A drawing of the double form of *Rosa roxburghii* commissioned by Reeves in China *c*. 1814.

ROSA ROXBURGHII var. *ROXBURGHII* A small shrub. This double, ancient Chinese garden rose, sent back to Europe in 1824, was the original form of *Rosa roxburghii*. Flowers over a long period in midsummer. Height to 150 cm (5 ft). Well scented. The single form of *Rosa roxburghii* is illustrated on pages 54 and 55.

ROSA MULTIBRACTEATA A Chinese rose forming a dense bush with elegant, small leaves and broad, crowded bracts and elongated hips in loose bunches. Collected by Wilson in the Min Valley in 1908. Flowers appear in late summer. Height to 180 cm (6ft). An attractive plant with a long flowering period.

ROSA WILLMOTTIAE Like a pink version of Canary Bird with small rounded leaflets and elongated hips; forms an arching bush. Named after Ellen Willmott, a great Edwardian gardener and author of *The Genus Rosa* (1914). A native of China, in dry valleys in western Sichuan, particularly in the Min Valley. Flowers in early or midsummer. Width to 200 cm (7 ft). Slightly scented.

ROSA SETIPODA. An attractive rose with pale, white-centred flowers with distinct, sticky, bristly stalks and very long tapering sepals. The *Rosa moyesii*-like hips are very fine. Collected in China by Wilson in 1901. Found in western Hubei (Hupeh) and neighbouring Sichuan. Summer flowering. Height to 250 cm (8 ft). Some scent.

ROSA FILIPES KIFTSGATE A climber with small flowers produced in huge heads. Native of China in north-west Sichuan and Gansu. Flowers profusely in late summer. Height to 1200 cm (40 ft). Well scented. This fine form of the species was photographed at Kiftsgate Court near Hidcote, Gloucestershire. Since being planted in 1938, it has attained huge size growing into a beech tree.

THE BAMBOO ROSE, *ROSA MULTIFLORA* WATSONIANA A mutation with very narrow leaflets and weak stems. Produces few flowers. Summer flowering. Height to 60 cm (2 ft).

ROSA BRUNONII LA MORTOLA A particularly fine clone of *Rosa brunonii*, or possibly a hybrid, with large, narrow, bluish, pubescent leaflets and large flowers. It originated in the gardens at La Mortola on the Italian Riviera, but its provenance is uncertain. Summer flowering. Height to 900 cm (30 ft).

ROSA SEMPERVIRENS This is the Mediterranean equivalent of all these Chinese climbers. It has evergreen leaves and only 5–6 flowers, with glandular stalks, in a head. Found from North Africa and Spain to Greece and Turkey. Flowers from early to midsummer. Height to 600 cm (20 ft). Some scent.

ROSA LONGICUSPIS var. *SINOWILSONI* A hardier and more rampant variety than normal *Rosa longiscuspis*, with larger leaves and horribly thorny stems. Petals are silky on the back. From Mount Emei in Sichuan. Summer flowering. Height to 200 cm (7 ft) or more. Scented.

ROSA SOULIEANA On railings in Eccleston Square, London.

ROSA BRUNONII A very strong climber. Native of the Himalayas from Kashmir and Afghanistan eastwards to western China, growing in warm, wet valleys at up to 2400 m (8000 ft). Summer flowering. Height to 900 cm (30 ft) or more. Well scented.

ROSA SOULIEANA A climber with long, slender branches. Flowers are yellow in bud and white on opening. Leaves are bluish with rounded leaflets. Native of western Sichuan where it grows on rocky hillsides. Flowers in late summer. Height to 530 cm (18 ft). Scented.

WEDDING DAY A seedling of *Rosa longicuspis* var. *sinowilsoni*. Raised in Sir Frederick Stern's garden in Sussex. Summer flowering. Height to 700 cm (23 ft). Well scented. Photographed in the garden of Sir David and Lady Beattie, Wellington, New Zealand.

CHAPTER SIX

Old Roses

Roses developed between 1800 and 1920 are arranged by group: Moss Roses, Portlands, Noisettes, Bourbons, Hybrid Perpetuals, Chinas, Tea Roses and Early Hybrid Teas.

GLOIRE DES MOUSSEUX, MME ALBONI A rather upright Damask Moss. Raised by Laffay in France, launched 1852. Occasionally flowers in autumn. Height to 130 cm (4 ft). Well scented.

Moss Roses are sports of other groups, mainly Damask and Centifolia, and have been known from around 1650. They are recognized by the numerous small glands on the flower buds and upper stems which create the damp mossy effect. The glands are scented and add to the fragrance of the flowers.

WHITE BATH, SHAILER'S WHITE MOSS, ROSA CENTIFOLIA MUSCOSA ALBA A sport from the Common Moss, recorded in 1788. A reversion to the pink has been noted. Summer flowering. Height to 130 cm (4 ft). Well scented.

CHAPEAU DE NAPOLÉON

EMPRESS JOSEPHINE

GÉNÉRAL KLÉBER An upright Damask Moss named after the French general who commanded Napoleon's army in Egypt. Raised by Robert in France, launched 1856. Summer flowering. Height to 160 cm (5½ ft). Well scented. Photographed in the Christchurch Botanic Gardens, New Zealand.

CHAPEAU DE NAPOLÉON, CRESTED MOSS, *ROSA CENTIFOLIA* CRISTATA A sport of *Rosa centifolia* which occurred on the wall of a convent in Fribourg, Switzerland around 1820. Not a Moss, but a sport with mossy outgrowth on the sepals. Summer flowering. Height to 150 cm (5 ft). Very good scent.

EMPRESS JOSEPHINE, IMPÉRATRICE JOSÉPHINE A Gallica hybrid, probably with *Rosa majalis*. Known since 1820. Summer flowering. Height to 160 cm (5½ ft). Slight scent.

WILLIAM LOBB, OLD VELVET MOSS A tall Damask Moss with a quarter China. Its purplish flowers fade to greyish-mauve. Raised by Laffay in France, launched 1855. Summer flowering. Height to 300 cm (10 ft). Well scented. Photographed at Hidcote Manor, Gloucestershire.

MME DELAROCHE-LAMBERT, AUTUMN DAMASK A Damask Moss with purplish-pink flowers, usually darker than shown here, and very broad leaflets. Raised by Robert in France, launched 1851. Repeat flowering. Height to 150 cm (5 ft). Well scented, with sticky moss.

MOUSSUE BLANCHE NOUVELLE A Centifolia Moss. Summer flowering. Height to 160 cm (5½ ft). Photographed at Malmaison, France.

BARON DE WASSENAER A spreading Damask Moss. Raised by Verdier in France, launched 1854. Summer flowering over a long period. Height to 150 cm (5 ft). Well scented.

ALFRED DE DALMAS, MOUSSELINE A rather short, not very mossy, Damask Moss with rounded leaflets. Raised by Laffay in France, launched 1855. Repeat flowers on and off. Height to 120 cm (4 ft). Well scented.

La Quatre Saisons Continué A Portland. Raised by Lelieur in France, launched 1811. Repeat flowering. Height to 150 cm (5 ft). Well scented. Photographed at Malmaison, Paris.

Although many of the Portland roses were probably grown at Malmaison in France, they get their name from the English Duchess of Portland. She sent a plant to the château and the gardener there, Andre Dupont, called the first rose of the group after her. The origin of Portland roses is debatable but they were very probably bred from a China × Damask cross. They repeat flower, although less reliably than the modern Hybrid Teas, and grow to around 120 cm (4 ft). The flowers, which retain a strong Damask scent, are on short stems so that, when open, they tend to be closely surrounded by the leaves.

Rose de Puteaux A Damask mentioned by Philip Miller in *The Gardener's Dictionary* in 1698. Good scent.

Marie Robert A Portland. Raised by Moreau-Robert in France, launched 1850. Repeat flowering. Height to 120 cm (4 ft). Photographed at the Roseraie de l'Haÿ, Paris.

Comte de Chambord A Portland-China cross perhaps. Large leaves. Raised by Moreau-Robert in France, launched 1860. Repeat flowering, often well into autumn. Disease resistant. Height to 150 cm (5 ft). Good scent.

JAPONICA, MOUSSEUX DU JAPON A very mossy (even on the leaves) Moss. Leaves are purplish when young. An old variety, perhaps raised in Japan. Once flowering. Height to 100 cm (3½ ft). Sweetly scented.

MME LOUIS LÉVÊQUE A Moss-Damask, one of the largest-flowered Mosses. Raised by Lévêque in France, launched 1873. Repeat flowering. Height to 150 cm (5 ft). Good, sweet scent.

STRIPED MOSS, OEILLET PANACHÉE A small, bushy Damask Moss. Possibly raised by Dupont, launched by Verdier in 1888. Striped Moss Roses appeared several times before 1800 and we cannot be certain when this one arose; it is likely that it is Dupont's which is still cultivated. Summer flowering. Height to 130 cm (4 ft). Well scented.

ROSE DU ROI, LEE'S CRIMSON PERPETUAL A Portland, important as parent of some Hybrid Perpetuals. Raised by Lelieur in France, launched 1815. Repeat flowers well. Height to 100 cm (3½ ft). Well scented. Photographed at Malmaison, Paris.

JAMES VEITCH Not very mossy, possibly a Portland. Flowers are purplish, fading to grey. Raised by Verdier in France, launched 1864. Repeat flowering. Height to 100 cm (3½ ft). Very good scent. Photographed at Mottisfont Abbey, Hampshire.

GOETHE One of the few single Mosses. It has numerous red spines on the stem and small, single or semi-double flowers. Raised by Lambert in Germany, launched 1911. Summer flowering. Height to 200 cm (7 ft) or more.

L'HÉRITIERANA A Boursault rose. A hybrid between *Rosa chinensis* and probably *Rosa blanda*, or perhaps *Rosa pendulina* which is often quoted but less likely. Photographed at the Roseraie de l'Haÿ, Paris.

IMPORTANT ROSE BREEDERS II

Philippe-Victor Verdier, nephew of Antoine A. Jacques (page 84), was born in 1803. He collaborated with his uncle in breeding *Rosa sempervirens* ramblers such as Félicité et Perpétue, and raised peonies, irises and gladioli. He also bred many good Hybrid Perpetuals – first once-flowering varieties such as Général Athalin and, later, repeat-flowering ones – and raised Moss, China, Tea and Noisette Roses. He died in 1878. His son Louis-Eugène-Jules concentrated on rose breeding and was a prolific breeder of Hybrid Perpetuals. He died in 1902.

Noisette Roses have their origin in a cross between *Rosa moschata* and Parson's Pink China, made by Champneys in South Carolina in 1802 and called Champneys' Pink Cluster. Seed from this was raised by Philippe Noisette in Charleston and cuttings were sent to France, where it was called Blush Noisette and crossed with yellow Tea Roses to produce the typical yellow Noisettes, such as Desprez à Fleurs Jaunes.

CHAMPNEYS' PINK CLUSTER A Noisette. Raised by Champneys in USA, launched 1811. (*Rosa moschata* × Parson's Pink China.) This was the original cross which gave rise to the Noisette Roses. Summer flowering. Height to 300 cm (10 ft). Very good scent.

BLUSH NOISETTE A Noisette with small flowers, in clusters, that turn pale pink from a red-flushed bud. Raised by Noisette, launched in France 1817. Continuous flowering. Good disease resistance. Height from 180 cm (6 ft) to 450 cm (15 ft). Good, clove-like scent.

MME ALFRED CARRIÈRE A Noisette. Raised by Schwartz in France, launched 1879. Repeat flowers well. Height to 600 cm (20 ft) or more. Good scent. Photographed in Eccleston Square, London.

AIMÉE VIBERT, BOUQUET DE LA MARIÉE A Noisette-*Rosa sempervirens* Rambler. Raised by Vibert in France, launched 1828. Repeat flowers well, into autumn. Height to 450 cm (15 ft). Slight scent.

FÉLICITÉ ET PERPÉTUE A *Rosa sempervirens* Rambler with evergreen leaves. Very good in cold, windy gardens. Close to the Noisettes, though with *Rosa sempervirens* rather than *Rosa moschata* as a parent. Raised by Jacques in France, launched 1827. (*Rosa sempervirens* × *Rosa chinensis*.) Summer flowering. Liable to mildew. Height to 650 cm (22 ft). Delicate, primrose-like scent.

IMPORTANT ROSE BREEDERS III

Antoine A. Jacques was head gardener to the Duc d'Orléans at Château de Neuilly from 1824 to 1832, and later to the duke's son, who became king Louis-Philippe. In 1819 he received from a M. Breon of the Île de Bourbon (now Réunion) seeds that gave rise to the original Bourbon Rose. It first flowered in 1821 and was illustrated by Redouté.

Using *Rosa sempervirens*, an evergreen, early-flowering rose from the Mediterranean, Jacques raised Adélaïde d'Orléans (1826), named after the duke's sister, who was a pupil of Redouté. Other Ramblers that he bred, and which have survived and are still popular, are Félicité et Perpétue (1827), Flora (1830) and Princess Marie (1829), named after Louis-Philippe's wife, Marie Amélie.

DESPREZ À FLEURS JAUNES, JAUNE DESPREZ A Tea-Noisette. Raised by Desprez in France, launched 1830. (Blush Noisette × Parks' Yellow.) Repeat flowering. Height to 450 cm (15 ft). Very good scent.

Large-flowered Noisette Roses on a wall at Mottisfont Abbey, Hampshire.

JEANNE D'ARC A Rambler. Raised by Verdier in France, launched 1848. (*Rosa arvensis* × a Noisette). Summer flowering. Height to 270 cm (9 ft). Good scent. Photographed in Fred Boutine's garden, California.

FELLEMBERG, LA BELLE MARSEILLAISE A China hybrid probably with *Rosa multiflora*. Known since 1835. Very perpetual. Height to 210 cm (7 ft). Little scent, of sweet peas. We found similar roses growing in old monastery gardens in China.

BALTIMORE BELLE A Rambler. Very hardy. Raised by Feast in USA, launched 1843. (*Rosa setigera* × a Gallica, possibly.) Summer flowering but late. Very resistant to disease. Height to 360 cm (12 ft). Well scented.

LAMARQUE A Tea-Noisette. The buds are pale yellowish. Needs a warm climate. Raised by Maréchal in France, launched 1830. (Blush Noisette × Parks' Yellow Tea-scented China.) Repeat flowering. Height to 360 cm (12 ft). Good scent. Photographed in the Cypress Hill Cemetery, California.

FLORA A Rambler. Raised by Jacques in France, launched 1830. (*Rosa sempervirens* × a China.) Summer flowering. Height to 360 cm (12 ft). Delicate, primrose scent.

The first Bourbon Rose was a natural hybrid between the China Rose Old Blush and the Autumn Damask, found in a hedge on the Île de Bourbon (now Réunion) by a French botanist, A.M. Perichon, and propagated by him. M. Breon, a government botanist, sent seeds to the future Louis-Philippe of France and two plants were raised by his gardener, Antoine A. Jacques. Bourbons are repeat flowering but usually retain the good Damask scent. A great many really fine Old Roses are found in this group.

CÉLINE A Bourbon. Launched by Laffay 1825. Flowers mainly in midsummer with a few later flowers. Height to 240 cm (8 ft). Photographed in the Roseraie de l'Haÿ, Paris.

BOURBON ROSE, ROSIER BOURBON, ROSE JACQUES, *ROSA BOURBONIANA* The original Bourbon. Raised by Jacques in France, launched 1819. (Autumn Damask × Pink China.) Flowers mid-summer. To 150 cm (5 ft). Good scent.

BOULE DE NEIGE A Bourbon. Flowers reflex in good weather to form a ball. Raised by Lacharme in France, launched 1867. Repeat flowering. Height to 300 cm (10 ft). Very good scent.

DUCHESSE D'AUERSTÄDT A climbing Noisette. Raised by Bernaix in France, launched 1888. A sport of a Rêve d'Or seedling. Repeat flowers well. Height to 300 cm (10 ft). Good scent.

QUEEN OF BOURBONS, BOURBON QUEEN, REINE DES ÎLES BOURBON A Bourbon. Raised by Mauget in France, launched 1834. Repeat flowers a little. Height to 210 cm (7 ft). Slight scent.

WILLIAM ALLEN RICHARDSON A Noisette. Raised by Ducher in France, launched 1878. A sport of Rêve d'Or. Repeat flowering. Height to 360 cm (12 ft). Slight tea scent. Photographed in the Roseraie de l'Haÿ, Paris.

CLAIRE JACQUIER A Noisette. Flowers fade as they age. Raised by Bernaix in France, launched 1888. Flowers in midsummer, some later flowers. Height to 1000 cm (33 ft). Very good scent. Photographed in the Garden of the Rose, St Albans, Hertfordshire.

Mme Isaac Pereire

Mme Grégoire Staechelin

Mme Caroline Testout

Zéphirine Drouhin

Mme Isaac Pereire A Bourbon with deep pink flowers which become magenta. Raised by Garçon in France, launched 1881. Flowers continuously. Height to 180 cm (6 ft). Very good scent.

Zéphirine Drouhin A Bourbon with very few thorns. Raised by Bizot in France, launched 1868. Repeat flowers well. Liable to mildew, especially on a wall. Height to 240 cm (8 ft). Good scent.

Mme Grégoire Staechelin A large-flowered Climber. Raised by Dot in Spain, launched 1927. (Frau Karl Druschki × Château de Clos Vougeot.) Repeat flowering. Good disease resistance. Height to 250 cm (8 ft) or more. Very good scent.

Mme Caroline Testout A Hybrid Tea. Raised by Pernet-Ducher in France, launched 1890. The climbing form appeared 1901. (Mme de Tartas × Lady Mary Fitzwilliam.) Repeat flowering. Height to 250 cm (8 ft) or more as a climber. Little scent.

HONORINE DE BRABANT A Bourbon with large leaves. Unknown origin. Repeat flowers well in autumn. Height to 180 cm (6 ft). Very good, rich scent. Photographed at Malmaison, Paris.

VARIEGATA DI BOLOGNA A Bourbon. Background colour of the flowers is white or palest pink. Raised by Bonfiglioli in Italy, launched 1903. Summer flowering; produces a few late flowers. Liable to mildew, blackspot on dry soils. Height to 250 cm (8 ft). Very good scent.

LA REINE VICTORIA A Bourbon with wonderfully incurved flowers. Raised by Schwartz in France, launched 1872. Mme Pierre Oger is a pale sport of this. Repeat flowers well. Liable to blackspot. Height to 180 cm (6 ft). Very well scented.

COUPE D'HEBE A Bourbon-China hybrid with cupped and quartered flowers. Raised by Laffay in France, launched 1840. Once flowering. Height to 240 cm (8 ft) or may be trained as a climber. Well scented.

IMPORTANT ROSE BREEDERS IV

Jean Laffay was born in Paris in 1794 and began as gardener to a nurseryman, Ternaux. Although his earliest roses were introduced in 1815, his main period of activity was from 1837 to 1855 in Bellevue-Meudon. His early introductions were mostly Chinas and Teas such as Bengale d'Automne (1825) and Mme Desprez (1835), his later ones mostly Hybrid Perpetuals, Bourbons and Mosses of which Great Western (1838) and Gloire des Mousseux (1852) are still widely grown.

MME PIERRE OGER A Bourbon. Raised by Oger and introduced by Verdier in France 1878. A sport of La Reine Victoria. Repeat flowers well. Liable to blackspot. Height to 180 cm (6 ft) or more. Very good scent.

PHILÉMON COCHET A Bourbon, not to be confused with the white double Rugosa hybrid, Souvenir de Philémon Cochet. Raised by Cochet-Cochet in France, launched 1895. A Mme Isaac Pereire seedling. Height to 300 cm (10 ft) as a climber. Good scent.

MME LAURIOL DE BARNY A Bourbon. Raised by Trouillard in France, launched 1868. Flowers mainly in midsummer with a few later flowers. Height to 200 cm (7 ft), higher if trained as a climber. Good, fruity scent.

COMTESSE DE ROCQUIGNY A Bourbon with globular, white-tinted rosy-salmon flowers. Raised by Vaurin in France, launched 1874. Height to 150 cm (5 ft). Good scent.

ZIGEUNERKNABE, GIPSY BOY A Bourbon-like modern shrub with coarse leaves and crimson flowers that become purplish. Very hardy and tolerant of poor conditions. Raised by Lambert in Germany, launched 1909. A Russeliana seeding. Summer flowering. Height to 180 cm (6 ft) or more. Little scent.

ZIGEUNERKNABE Photographed at Sellindge, Kent.

LA REINE A strong-growing Hybrid Perpetual. Raised by Laffay in France, launched 1842. Flowers mostly in midsummer but some later flowers. Height to 150 cm (5 ft). Very well scented.

Hybrid Perpetuals were the result of an attempt to combine the large flowers and rich scent of the Gallica Roses with the perpetual flowering of the Chinas. The forerunner of this class was Rose du Roi, a seedling of the Portland rose raised in France in 1815. The true, large-flowered Hybrid Perpetuals, or *Hybrides Remontant* as they were called in France, were first raised by Laffay at Auteuil, starting with Princesse Hélène in 1837. He crossed Hybrid Chinas with Portlands and Bourbons and produced a proportion of repeat-flowering roses; the recessive, repeat-flowering genes were present in both parents.

Hybrid Perpetuals have huge flowers on strong shoots and inherited rather short flower stalks from the Portlands, so that the flowers sit down among the leaves. Most are red, pink or white. No yellows were ever raised. The great years of the Hybrid Perpetuals were between 1858 and 1899 after which, like the Tea Roses, they lost popularity to their descendants, the Hybrid Teas.

GRÜSS AN TEPLITZ A China-Bourbon-Tea raised by Geschwind in Hungary, introduced 1897. ((Sir Joseph Paxton × Fellenberg) × (Papa Gontier × Gloire des Rosomanes).) Repeat flowering. Height to 180 cm (6 ft). Good scent. Photographed in Union Hill Cemetery, California.

DEMBROSKY, DEMBROWSKI A Hybrid Perpetual. Raised by Vibert in France, launched 1849. Repeat flowering. Height to 150 cm (5 ft). Some scent.

Graham Thomas, the Old Rose expert, in his garden near Woking, outside London, with the rose Souvenir de St Anne's.

SOUVENIR DE ST ANNE'S A Bourbon. A sport of Souvenir de la Malmaison discovered in Lady Ardilaun's garden, St Anne's, Dublin, before 1916. Repeat flowers well. Height to 210 cm (7 ft). Very good scent.

BARONNE PRÉVOST A Hybrid Perpetual. Flowers do not open properly in wet weather. Raised by Desprez in France, launched 1842. Repeat flowers well. Susceptible to blackspot. Height to 150 cm (5 ft). Very well scented.

The Old Rose Garden at the Roseraie de l'Haÿ, Paris.

SIDONIE, SYDONIE A Hybrid Perpetual. Raised by Dorisy in France, launched by Vibert 1847. Repeat flowering. Liable to blackspot. Height to 90 cm (3 ft). Scented.

YOLANDE D'ARAGON A Hybrid Perpetual with strong, upright stems. Raised by Vibert in France, launched 1843. Repeat flowering. Height to 150 cm (5 ft). Fantastic scent.

EMPEREUR DU MAROC A Hybrid Perpetual. The flowers become dark blackish-maroon, but are damaged by wet weather. Raised by Guinoisseau in France, launched 1858. A hybrid of Géant des Batailles. Produces a few later flowers. Height to 150 cm (5 ft). Very good, heavy scent.

ENFANT DE FRANCE A Hybrid Perpetual with velvety-textured petals and narrow, dark green leaflets. Raised by Lartay in France, launched 1860. Repeat flowering. Height to 180 cm (6 ft). Very good scent.

BARONESS ROTHSCHILD, BARONNE ADOLPH DE ROTHSCHILD A Hybrid Perpetual with greyish foliage close up around the flower. Raised by Pernet (père) in France, launched 1868. A sport of Souvenir de la Reine d'Angleterre. Repeat flowers well. Height to 120 cm (4 ft). Little scent. Photographed in David Austin's garden at Albrighton, Shropshire.

TRIOMPHE DE L'EXPOSITION A Hybrid Perpetual with flowers that open very flat. Raised by Margottin in France, launched 1855. Repeat flowers well. Height to 150 cm (5 ft). Good scent.

KATHLEEN HARROP A Bourbon. Launched by Dickson in Northern Ireland, 1919. Pale sport of Zéphirine Drouhin. Repeat flowers well. Liable to mildew. Height to 240 cm (8 ft), more on a wall. Very good scent.

SOUVENIR DU DOCTEUR JAMAIN A Hybrid Perpetual. Better in a cool position. Raised by Lacharme in France, launched 1865. (Général Jacqueminot × Charles Lefèbvre.) Repeat flowers well in autumn. Height to 300 cm (10 ft). Very good rich scent.

REINE DES VIOLETTES, QUEEN OF VIOLETS A Hybrid Perpetual with grey-green foliage. Flowers, with incurved petals, are velvety purple fading to soft violet. Raised by Millet-Malet in France, launched 1860. A seedling of Pius IX. Repeat flowering. Height to 150 cm (5 ft). Very good scent.

GENERAL WASHINGTON A Hybrid Perpetual with large, flat flowers. Raised by Granger in France, launched 1861. A sport of Triomphe de l'Exposition. Good flowers in autumn. Height to 150 cm (5 ft). Photographed in the Huntington Rose Garden, Los Angeles.

PAUL NEYRON Very robust Hybrid Perpetual with huge flowers, pink with a lilac flush. Raised by Levet in France, launched 1869. (Victor Verdier × Anna de Diesbach.) Repeat flowers well. Height to 180 cm (6 ft). Little scent.

JULES MARGOTTIN A Hybrid Perpetual. Raised by Margottin in France, launched 1853. A La Reine seedling. Repeat flowering. Height to 120 cm (4 ft). Good, strong scent.

BARON DE BONSTETTEN A Hybrid
Perpetual with upright, strong growth.
Raised by Liabaud in France, launched
1871. (Général Jacqueminot × Géant des
Batailles.) Some flowers in autumn.
Height to 210 cm (7 ft). Very good scent.
Photographed in Fred Boutine's garden,
California.

MAGNA CHARTA A Hybrid Perpetual.
Raised by Paul in Britain, launched 1876.
Repeat flowers well. Height to 120 cm
(4 ft) or more. Good scent.

ROGER LAMBELIN An interesting Hybrid Perpetual with white petal edges. A sport of
Fisher Holmes. Launched by Schwartz in France, 1890. Repeat flowering. Susceptible to
mildew. Height to 120 cm (4 ft). Well scented.

ANDRÉ LEROY D'ANGERS A Hybrid
Perpetual. Its flowers are deeper pink,
often purplish, in cool weather. Raised by
Trouillard in France, launched 1866.
Height to 140 cm (5 ft).

DUKE OF EDINBURGH A Hybrid
Perpetual. Raised by Paul in Britain,
launched 1868. A Général Jacqueminot
seedling. Repeat flowers well in autumn.
Height to 90 cm (3 ft). Very good scent.

EUGÈNE FÜRST A Hybrid Perpetual.
Raised by Soupert et Notting in
Luxemburg, launched 1875. A seedling of
Baron de Bonstetten. Repeat flowering.
Height to 120 cm (4 ft). Good scent.

ULRICH BRUNNER A Hybrid Perpetual with deep pink flowers. Raised by Levet in France, launched 1881. Repeat flowering. Height to 180 cm (6 ft). Good scent. Photographed at Sissinghurst Castle, Kent. Président de Sèze, the paler rose in the background, is described on page 33.

GLOIRE LYONNAISE A Hybrid Perpetual. Raised by Guillot (fils) in France, launched 1885. (Baroness Rothschild × Mme Falcot.) Flowers continuously. Height to 180 cm (6 ft). Good scent.

MME SCIPION COCHET A Hybrid Perpetual with silvery foliage and cerise-pink flowers with crinkled petals. Raised by Cochet in France, launched 1873. Repeat flowering. Height to 120 cm (4 ft). Very good scent.

FRAU KARL DRUSCHKI, SNOW QUEEN, REINE DES NEIGES, WHITE AMERICAN BEAUTY A very robust Hybrid Perpetual with light green leaves. Raised by Lambert in Germany, launched 1901. (Merveille de Lyon × Mme Caroline Testout.) Repeat flowering. Sometimes gets mildew. Height to 180 cm (6 ft). Little scent.

HUGH DICKSON A Hybrid Perpetual. Raised by Dickson in Northern Ireland, launched in 1905. (Lord Bacon × Gruss an Teplitz.) Repeat flowering. Height to 210 cm (7 ft), taller as a climber, or can be pegged down. Very good scent.

MRS JOHN LAING A Hybrid Perpetual. Raised by Bennett in Britain, launched 1887. A François Michelon seedling. Repeat flowering. Height to 120 cm (4 ft). Very good scent. Bennett is said to have received $45,000 for the rights of this rose in the USA.

CAPTAIN HAYWARD A tall-growing Hybrid Perpetual that often sets hips. Raised by Bennett in Britain, introduced posthumously in 1893 by his son Edmund. A Triomphe de l'Exposition seedling. Few late flowers. Height to 250 cm (8 ft) with support. Very good scent. Photographed at Mottisfont Abbey, Hampshire.

IMPORTANT ROSE BREEDERS V

Henry Bennett was a prosperous tenant farmer at Stapleford in the Wylye Valley near Salisbury, Wiltshire, but felt that his farm needed an alternative source of income. Perhaps he foresaw the decline of English agriculture in the late 1870s caused by the opening up of the American prairies. He decided to breed roses, the growing and showing of which was fast becoming a craze. His first attempts in 1868 were unsuccessful, so from 1870 to 1872 he made yearly visits to the major breeders in France. He was surprised to find that they did not practise the systematic breeding he had learnt while raising cattle, but raised hundreds of thousands of seedlings and selected a few of the best. At Stapleford he established up-to-date breeding facilities, with heated glasshouses for earlier flowers and to ripen the rose seed properly.

Bennett's first seedlings were ready for launching in 1879, when he introduced ten 'Pedigree Hybrids of the Tea Rose' emphasizing that they had been raised scientifically from known parents. These first roses were not very enthusiastically received as some were prone to mildew, but Bennett's ideas were soon taken up by other breeders. The Horticultural Society of Lyon invited him to lecture there and decided to call his new hybrids, between Teas and Hybrid Perpetuals, *Hybrides de Thé* or Hybrid Teas. In 1880 Bennett moved from Stapleford to Shepperton, near London, where he died in 1890. Of his later roses Lady Mary Fitzwilliam (1882), a Hybrid Tea, is important as a parent of Mme Caroline Testout; Captain Hayward (1893) and Mrs John Laing (1887), both Hybrid Perpetuals, are still widely grown today.

J.B CLARK A Hybrid Perpetual with very dark flowers. Raised by Dickson in Northern Ireland, launched 1905. (Lord Bacon × Gruss an Teplitz.) Repeat flowering. Height to 450 cm (15 ft) on a pillar. Photographed at the Roseraie de l'Haÿ, Paris. Very good scent.

CHAMPION OF THE WORLD, MRS DE GRAW A Hybrid Perpetual with spreading shoots. Raised by Woodhouse in Britain, launched 1894. (Hermosa × Magna Charta.) The late flowers are often better than the early ones. Height to 150 cm (5 ft), arching. Some scent.

MME ERNEST CALVAT A Bourbon Rose. Strong growing and bushy for a Bourbon. A sport of Mme Isaac Pereire. Launched by Schwartz in France, 1888. Repeat flowers very well. Height to 180 cm (6 ft). Very good scent.

BARON GIROD DE L'AIN A Hybrid Perpetual. Raised by Reverchon in France, launched 1897. A sport of Eugene Furst. Repeat flowering. Height to 120 cm (4 ft). Some scent.

SPENCER A Hybrid Perpetual with petals that are almost white on the back. Often fails to open in wet weather. A sport of Merveille de Lyon. Launched by Paul in Britain, 1892. Repeat flowering. Height to 120 cm (4 ft). Very good scent.

GLOIRE DE CHÉDANE-GUINOISSEAU A Hybrid Perpetual. Raised by Chédane-Pajotin in France, launched 1907. (Gloire de Ducher × unknown.) Repeats with a few flowers. Height to 120 cm (4 ft). Good scent.

JEANNY SOUPERT A Polyantha. Raised by Soupert et Notting in Luxemburg, launched 1912. (Mme Norbert Levavasseur × Petite Léonie.) Repeat flowers continuously. Height to 90 cm (3 ft). Light scent.

Polyantha Roses were formed by crossing a China Rose with a dwarf, repeat-flowering form of *Rosa multiflora*. The first hybrids were once flowering but repeat flowering appeared in the second generation. Pâquerette and Mignonette, introduced by Guillot (fils) in 1875 and 1881, were pretty, dwarf roses with stiff heads of small, double, short-petalled flowers, like dwarf Ramblers. Numerous roses of this type were introduced in the later nineteenth century. It was only when Tea Roses were introduced into the parentage that more elegant, dwarf roses appeared. Mlle Cécile Brünner and Perle d'Or (page 101) both have loose sprays of miniature, Hybrid-Tea-shaped flowers and are still familiar roses; Clotilde Soupert is another of the same type, alas only good in warm, dry weather. Polyanthas, which reached their pinnacle of success in 1909, never achieved the popularity of Teas or Hybrid Perpetuals, but have continued as a minor group until today, although completely overshadowed by their successors, the Floribundas.

BABY FAURAX A Polyantha with purplish-pink, very double, small flowers. Raised by Lille in France, launched 1924. Repeat flowers continuously. Height to 30 cm (1 ft). Little scent.

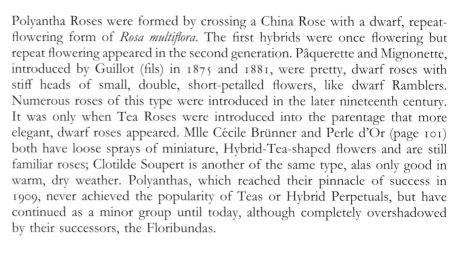

LA MARNE An almost thornless Polyantha with very dark green, shiny leaves. Raised by Barbier in France, launched 1915. (Mme Norbert Levavasseur × Comtesse du Cayla.) Repeat flowering. Resistant to mildew; very healthy foliage. Height to 125 cm (4 ft). Little scent. Photographed in the Cypress Hill Cemetery, California.

ARRILLAGA A Hybrid Perpetual with very large flowers. Raised by Schoener in USA, launched 1929. ((*Rosa centifolia* × Mrs John Laing) × Frau Karl Druschki.) Flowers mostly in midsummer. Height to 180 cm (6 ft). Slight scent.

NYPELS PERFECTION (foreground) A Polyantha with flowers that usually fade from pink to white. Raised by Leenders in The Netherlands, launched 1930. Repeat flowering. Height to 60 cm (2 ft). Little scent. Photographed in David Austin's garden at Albrighton, Shropshire.

FERDINAND PICHARD A Hybrid Perpetual with pink, crimson-striped flowers. Raised by Tanne in France, launched 1921. Flowers mainly in midsummer with a few later flowers. Height to 250 cm (8 ft). Good scent.

GEORG ARENDS, FORTUNÉ BESSON A Hybrid Perpetual. Raised by Hinner in Germany, launched 1910. (Frau Karl Druschki × La France.) Flowers continuously. Height to 150 cm (5 ft) arching. Very good scent.

SYMPHONY A Hybrid Perpetual. Raised by Weigand in Germany, launched 1935. (Frau Karl Druschki × Souvenir de Claudius Pernet.) Repeat flowering, especially good in autumn. Height to 180 cm (6 ft). Some scent.

A view of trained roses at the Roseraie de l'Haÿ, Paris.

EVEREST A Hybrid Perpetual with very large, creamy-white flowers. Raised by Easlea in Britain, launched 1927. (Candeur Lyonnaise × ? Mrs Wakefield Christie-Miller.) Repeat flowering. Height to 120 cm (4 ft). Good scent.

LE VÉSUVE, LEMESLE A very thorny China that grows as a twiggy, branching shrub. Raised by Laffay in France, launched 1825. Repeat flowers well. Very healthy. Height to 90 cm (3 ft), eventually 150 cm (5 ft). Good scent. This large plant was photographed at Mottisfont Abbey, Hampshire.

EUGÈNE DE BEAUHARNAIS A Bourbon-China hybrid, named after the Empress Josephine's brother. Raised by Hardy in France, launched 1838. Repeat flowering. Height to 90 cm (3 ft). Some scent.

China Roses developed from old Chinese garden roses introduced to Europe at the end of the eighteenth and beginning of the nineteenth centuries. They are usually small shrubs with red, pink or white flowers, and were originally especially valued for their continuous flowering in warm climates. When crossed with the original Tea Rose, Parks' Yellow Tea-scented China, they gave rise to Teas. They were also crossed with other groups to introduce their repeat-flowering character to European roses. One of the original introductions, Old Blush, remains an excellent garden rose and some early hybrids such as Hermosa (1834) and Mutabilis, which has been known since 1896, are still widely grown today.

LADY ANN KIDWELL A Poly-pom. A beautiful rose, like a large, purplish-pink Cécile Brünner. Raised by Krebs in USA, launched 1948. Found by Fred Boutine at Marsh Nursery, Pasadena. Repeat flowering. Height to 150 cm (5 ft). Good scent.

CRAMOISI SUPÉRIEUR, AGRIPPINA, LADY BRISBANE A China. Raised by Coquereau in France, launched 1832. Repeat flowers well. Height to 90 cm (3 ft), 180 cm (6 ft) as a climber. Good scent. Photographed in Georgetown Cemetery, California Gold Country.

CÉCILE BRÜNNER, MLLE CÉCILE BRÜNNER, SWEETHEART ROSE, MIGNON, MALTESE ROSE A Poly-pom. Raised by Pernet-Ducher in France, launched 1881. A Mme de Tartas seedling. Repeat flowering. Height to 90 cm (3 ft). Little scent.

CLIMBING CÉCILE BRÜNNER A vigorous climbing sport that is good growing up into trees. Introduced by Hosp in USA 1904. Summer flowering. Height to 600 cm (20 ft). Scented.

PERLE D'OR A Poly-pom, like a pale yellow version of Cécile Brünner. Raised by Rambaux in France, launched 1883. (Mme Falcot × a Polyantha.) Flowers continuously. Height to 120 cm (4 ft). Good scent.

YVONNE RABIER A Polyantha hybrid with very glossy leaves. Raised by Turbat in France, launched 1910. (*Rosa wichuraiana* × a Polyantha.) Repeat flowering. Very healthy. Height to 90 cm (3 ft). Good scent.

PERLE D'OR Photographed in the garden of Miriam Wilkins in California. Miriam is the founder of the Heritage Rose Group.

MATEO'S SILK BUTTERFLIES A very graceful and free-flowering China × hybrid musk cross. Raised by Lettunich in USA, launched 1993. (Mutabilis × ? Francis E. Lester.) Repeat flowers continuously. Height to 150 cm (5 ft). Slight scent. Photographed in the garden of the breeder Kleine Lettunich in Aptos, California. This is the original bush of this variety.

MATEO'S SILK BUTTERFLIES In close-up.

MUTABILIS, the Noisette MARY WASHINGTON and their hybrid in Fred Boutine's garden, California.

MUTABILIS, TIPO IDEALE A China with flowers that open yellow then turn pink and finally crimson. Known since 1896 but of unknown origin. An Old Rose, also found in China. Repeat flowering. Good disease resistance. Height to 150 cm (5 ft), to 750 cm (25 ft) as shown here on Kiftsgate Court, Gloucestershire.

SANGUINEA

MISS LOWE

SINGLE PINK A China. Trevor Griffiths shows a single, pink China similar to this called L'Admiration. Introduced by Robert in France 1856. Possibly a reversion of Old Blush. Repeat flowering. Height to 130 cm (4 ft). Scent of sweet peas.

SLATER'S CRIMSON CHINA, SEMPERFLORENS, BENGALE SANGUINAIRE, LE BENGALE À BOUQUETS (OF REDOUTÉ) A dwarf China with very slender stalks. An old Chinese garden rose introduced to Europe 1792. Repeat flowering. Height to 90 cm (3 ft). Little scent.

SANGUINEA, BENGAL CRIMSON, ROSA INDICA A China. Introduced from China in 1804. Repeat flowering. Height to 300 cm (10 ft) on a wall. Little scent. This old variety, photographed in the Chelsea Physic Garden, London, appears larger and taller than the dwarf Miss Lowe.

MISS LOWE, SANGUINEA A China. There is doubt as to whether Sanguinea and Miss Lowe are really distinct, though most authorities acknowledge that two forms do exist. Repeat flowering. Height usually to about 60 cm (2 ft). Little scent.

BENGALE D'AUTOMNE, ROSIER DES INDES A China. Raised by Laffay in France, launched 1825. Repeat flowering. Height to 120 cm (4 ft). Photographed at Malmaison, Paris.

INDICA PURPUREA (possibly the same as Bengale Pourpre, raised by Vibert in France, launched 1827). A very dwarf China. Its purplish-crimson flowers are slightly more double than those of Miss Lowe. Repeat flowering. Height to 50 cm (1½ ft) at most.

BLAIRII No 2 In full bloom at Mottisfont Abbey, Hampshire.

BLAIRII No.2. A China hybrid. Raised by Blair in Britain, launched 1845. (A China Rose × Tuscany.) Flowers mostly in summer with a few later flowers. Susceptible to mildew. Height to 300 cm (10 ft). Can be trained as a climber. Good scent.

VIRIDIFLORA, GREEN ROSE A China. Known since 1843. A sport of Old Blush in which the sepals have proliferated at the expense of the petals. Flowers continuously. Height to 120 cm (4 ft).

SOPHIE'S PERPETUAL A China hybrid. The contrast of pale centre and deep red edge may be very striking. Found and named by Humphrey Brooke, a great connoisseur of Old Roses, launched 1960. Repeat flowers well. Height up to 240 cm (8 ft). Very good scent.

BLAIRII No.1 A China-Bourbon hybrid. Raised by Blair in Britain, launched before 1844. Flowers mostly in summer but a few autumn flowers. Height to 200 cm (7 ft). Good scent.

IRENE WATTS A very free-flowering China. Raised by Guillot in France, launched 1896. Repeat flowers continuously. Height to 50 cm ($1\frac{1}{2}$ ft). Good tea scent.

COMTESSE DU CAYLA A China. Leaves are purplish when young, flowers reddening as they age. Raised by Guillot in France, launched 1902. Repeat flowers well. Height to 90 cm (3 ft). Good tea scent.

THE DRAGON'S EYE A China hybrid. Raised by Heirloom Old Garden Roses in USA, launched 1991. Repeat flowering. Height to 75 cm (2½ ft). Good musk-like scent.

GLOIRE DES ROSOMANES, RAGGED ROBIN, RED ROBIN A China. Raised by Vibert in France, launched 1825. Much used as an understock in California. Repeat flowers continuously. Height to 180 cm (6 ft). A little scent.

HERMOSA, ARMOSA A China. Raised by Marchesseau in France, launched 1840. Repeat flowers very well. Good disease resistance. Height to 100 cm (3½ ft). There is also a climbing form. Good scent.

IMPORTANT ROSE BREEDERS VI

Jean-Pierre Vibert was born in 1777 in Paris and began collecting roses in 1810. He fought under Napoleon in the Peninsular War but retired after sustaining many wounds to run a hardware store near St Germain des Prés, Paris. André Dupont, a well-known breeder and collector patronized by the Empress Josephine, had his rose garden nearby and encouraged in young Vibert an interest in roses. In 1812 Vibert sold his hardware business and moved to Chennevières-sur-Marne on the outskirts of Paris where he began to grow roses himself. In 1815 he bought the stock and business of M. Descemet in St Denis which had been sacked by the allied armies after the defeat at Waterloo. Although the roses were moved to his nursery in August most of them survived. In 1827 he left Chennevières-sur-Marne because of infestations of cockchafer grubs and moved to St Denis where he grew roses until his first retirement in 1835, when he moved his seedlings and choicest plants to Longjumeau. But the roses were again plagued by cockchafers so he moved south from Paris to Angers where he continued breeding roses until he finally retired in 1851. He sold the business to his gardener, M. Robert. Shortly before his death in 1866 Vibert told his grandson, 'I have loved only Napoleon and roses ... after all the evils from which I have suffered there remain to me only two objects of profound hatred, the English, who overthrew my idol, and the white worms that destroyed my roses.'

CATHERINE MERMET A Tea with lilac-pink flowers. Susceptible to wet weather. Much used as a greenhouse rose for cut flowers. Raised by Guillot (fils) in France, launched 1869. Repeat flowering. Height to 120 cm (4 ft). Quite good scent.

Tea Roses are like delicate Hybrid Teas and are the result of crosses between forms of the wild Tea Rose, *Rosa gigantea*, and forms of the China Rose, *Rosa chinensis*. Their original parents were two Chinese garden roses imported to Europe in the early years of the nineteenth century: Hume's Blush Tea-scented China and Parks' Yellow Tea-scented China. They were soon crossed with dwarf China Roses, Bourbons and Noisettes and formed a new, perpetual-flowering class with graceful growth and delicate scent. The years 1882 to 1910 were the great years of the Tea Rose, after which they quickly lost popularity to the more robust Hybrid Teas. Although yellow, pink and pale orange colours predominate, there were also whites and dark reds.

MAMAN COCHET A Tea. Long-lived in California Gold Country cemeteries. Raised by Cochet in France, launched 1893. (Marie Van Houtte × Mme Lombard.) Flowers continuously. Height to 200 cm (7 ft) in a mild climate. Good scent.

FORTUNE'S FIVE-COLOURED ROSE, SMITH'S PARISH A Tea. Introduced from China by Fortune, launched 1844. Recently rediscovered in Smith's Parish, Bermuda. Repeat flowering. Height to 120 cm (4 ft). Photographed in the Huntington Rose Garden, Los Angeles.

MME DE TARTAS A Tea with globular flowers. Important as the seed parent of Mme Caroline Testout. Raised by Bernède in France, launched 1859. Repeat flowering. Height to 90 cm (3 ft).

BON SILÈNE A free-flowering and vigorous Tea. Raised by Hardy in France, launched 1835. Repeat flowering. Very good scent. Photographed at the Vintage Gardens Nursery, California.

RIVAL DE PAESTUM A rather tender Tea China hybrid. Its leaves are purplish when young. Raised by Paul in Britain, launched 1848. Repeat flowers well, better in autumn. Height to 130 cm (4 ft). Good scent.

SAFRANO, AIMÉ PLANTIER A Tea with semi-double flowers that are best in bud. Known as the best cut rose in France until 1900, sent from the Mediterranean to Paris in vast quantities. Raised by Beauregard in France, launched 1839. (Possibly Parks' Yellow × Mme Desprez.) Repeat flowers well. Height to 200 cm (7 ft) in a warm climate. Good scent.

MARIE VAN HOUTTE A Tea with nodding flowers. Raised by Ducher in France, launched 1871. (Mme de Tartas × Mme Falcot.) Flowers continuously. Height to 200 cm (7 ft) on a warm wall. Good scent.

SOMBREUIL A Tea, usually a climber. Very hardy for a Tea. Raised by Robert in France, launched 1850. (Gigantesque × a Hybrid Tea.) Repeat flowers well. Height to 400 cm (13 ft) as a climber on a wall. Good scent.

LEY'S PERPETUAL, LAÏS A Tea. Raised by Damaizin in France, launched 1867. Repeat flowering. Height to 350 cm (11 ft) as a climber. Very good scent.

DEVONIENSIS, MAGNOLIA ROSE A Tea. Hardy for a Tea Rose. Raised by Foster in Britain, launched 1841 (climbing sport, 1858). Repeat flowers well. Height to 300 cm (10 ft) as a climber (shown here). Very good scent.

MONSIEUR TILLIER A Tea with blood-red flowers with purple markings. Hardy for a Tea Rose. Raised by Bernaix in France, launched 1891. Repeat flowering. Height to 100 cm (3½ ft). Little scent.

BARONNE HENRIETTE DE SNOY A Tea. Raised by Bernaix in France, launched 1897. (Gloire de Dijon × Mme Lambard.) Flowers continuously. Prone to mildew in wet weather. Height to 120 cm (4 ft). Little scent.

ARCHIDUC JOSEPH A Tea with flowers that vary in colour according to temperature. Raised by Nabonnand in France, launched 1892. A Mme Lambard seedling. Repeat flowering. Height to 120 cm (4 ft). Little scent.

MLLE LA COMTESSE DE LEUSSE A Tea. Raised by Nabonnand in France, launched 1878. Repeat flowering. Height to 120 cm (4 ft). Slight scent.

BURBANK A Tea. Raised by Burbank in USA, launched 1900. (Hermosa × Bon Silène.) Continuous flowering. Very disease resistant. Little scent.

ÉTOILE DE LYON A Tea. Needs a warm climate to open well. Raised by Guillot (fils) in France, launched 1881. A Mme Charles seedling. Continuous flowering. Height to 80 cm (2½ ft). Good tea scent.

IMPORTANT ROSE BREEDERS VII

Gilbert Nabonnand of Golfe Juan, France, specialized in raising Chinas and Teas, of which he introduced no less than seventy-eight between 1872 and 1903. He was born in 1829 at Guezolles in the Loire and worked as an agricultural labourer until the age of sixteen, when he was apprenticed to various nurserymen including Guillot (père). His first rose nursery was near Avignon, but in 1864 he moved to Golfe Juan on the Mediterranean coast. Of his most famous Tea Roses, General Schablikine (1878) and Archiduc Joseph (1892) are still widely grown, also the Hybrid Tea, Lady Waterlow (1903).

MLLE FRANZISKA KRÜGER, GRAND-
DUC HÉRITIER DE LUXEMBOURG A
Tea. Heat tolerant. Raised by Nabonnand
in France, launched 1879. (Catherine
Mermet × General Schablikine.) Repeat
flowering. Liable to mildew. Height to
100 cm (3½ ft). Good scent.

FRANCIS DUBREUIL A Tea with very
dark red, velvety petals. Raised by
Dubreuil in France, launched 1894.
Repeat flowers well. Height to 60 cm
(2 ft). Good scent.

GENERAL
SCHABLIKINE

RÊVE D'OR

GENERAL SCHABLIKINE A Tea that has
purple shoots when young and curved
flower stalks. Hardy for a Tea Rose.
Raised by Nabonnand in France,
launched 1878. Almost never without a
flower. Height to 150 cm (5 ft), higher
when trained. Slight scent.

RÊVE D'OR, GOLDEN DREAM,
GOLDEN CHAIN, CONDESA DA FOZ A
Noisette. Raised by Ducher in France,
launched 1869. A Mme Schultz seedling.
Repeat flowers well in autumn. Height to
350 cm (11 ft) or more. Tea scent.

WILLIAM R. SMITH, CHARLES DINGEE, JEANETTE HELLER A Tea. Raised by Bagg in USA, launched 1908. (Maman Cochet × Mme Hoste.) Repeat flowers well. Height to 60 cm (2 ft). Good scent.

ROSETTE DELIZY A Tea with large, full flowers. Raised by Nabonnand in France, launched 1922. (Général Galliéni × Comtesse Bardi.) Repeat flowers well. Height to 180 cm (6 ft) on a wall. Good fruity scent.

PERLE DES JARDINS A Tea. Raised by Levet in France, launched 1874. A Mme Falcot seedling. Continuous flowering in warm climates. Height to 100 cm (3½ ft). Good scent.

MME ANTOINE MARI One of the hardier Teas. Raised by Mari, launched 1901. Repeat flowers well. Height to 75 cm (2½ ft), more on a wall. Some scent.

DR GRILL A very free-flowering Tea with deep pink or yellowish flowers depending on temperature. Raised by Bonnaire in France, launched 1886. (Ophirie × Souvenir de Victor Hugo.) Repeat flowers well. Height to 100 cm (3½ ft). Good scent.

MOLLY SHARMAN-CRAWFORD A Tea which becomes pure, slightly greenish-white in cooler weather. Raised by Dickson in Northern Ireland, launched 1908. Repeat flowers well. Suffers a little from mildew. Height to 100 cm ($3\frac{1}{2}$ ft). Little scent. Photographed in the Georgetown Cemetery in the California Gold Country.

MRS CAMPBELL HALL A Tea with tough, dark foliage. Raised by Dickson in Northern Ireland, launched 1915. Repeat flowering. Height to 30 cm (1 ft). Good scent.

MRS B.R. CANT A Tea. Its flowers are usually deep red on the edges in cold weather. Raised by Cant in Britain, launched 1901. Repeat flowers well, very good in autumn. Height to 125 cm (4 ft). Slight scent.

WHITE MAMAN COCHET A Tea. Raised by Cook in USA, launched 1890. A sport of Maman Cochet. Repeat flowering. Height to 120 cm (4 ft). Good scent. Photographed at the Vintage Gardens Nursery, California.

ADAM RACKLES A Hybrid Tea. Raised by Rommel in Germany 1905. A sport of Mme Caroline Testout. Repeat flowering. To 240 cm (8 ft). Slight scent.

The first Hybrid Teas were formed by crossing two existing groups of roses: the robust and rather coarse Hybrid Perpetuals and the delicate Teas. The earliest roses of this parentage were not immediately hailed as a new race. Victor Verdier, a large, bright pink rose raised by François Lacharme in Lyon in 1859 from Jules Margottin (a Hybrid Perpetual) × Safrano (a Tea), is still classed as a Hybrid Perpetual. La France, said to be a seedling of Mme Falcot, an orange-yellow Tea, is now generally considered the first Hybrid Tea. However, it was a stray seedling and some authorities have considered a more likely parentage to be Mme Victor Verdier (a red Hybrid Perpetual) × Mme Bravy (a pale blush Tea). Hybrid Teas were first recognized as a class in 1880 as a result of the pioneering work of Henry Bennett (page 96), who applied breeding principles he had learnt with cattle to roses. The early Hybrid Teas were direct crosses between Hybrid Perpetuals and Teas, but from about 1898 began to be raised from crosses within the group.

LADY WATERLOW A climbing Hybrid Tea Noisette hybrid. Raised by Nabonnand in France, launched 1903. (La France de '89 × Mme Marie Lavalley.) Repeat flowering, good in autumn. Very resistant to mildew and rust; susceptible to blackspot. Height to 350 cm (12 ft). Photographed on a wall at Mottisfont Abbey, Hampshire.

MME CAROLINE TESTOUT A Hybrid Tea. Raised by Pernet-Ducher in France, launched 1890. (Mme de Tartas × Lady Mary Fitzwilliam.) Repeat flowering. Gets a little mildew. Height to 120 cm (4 ft), 600 cm (20 ft) as a climber. Good scent.

LADY MARY FITZWILLIAM A Hybrid Tea with rather globular flowers. A very important parent of Hybrid Teas. Raised by Bennett in Britain, launched 1882. (Devoniensis × Victor Verdier.) Repeat flowering. Height to 60 cm (2 ft). Slight scent.

CAPTAIN CHRISTY A Hybrid Tea. Its young leaves are often likened to those of Mahonia. Raised by Lacharme in France, launched 1873. (Victor Verdier × Safrano.) Repeat flowers well. Height to 120 cm (4 ft). Tea scented. Photographed at the Roseraie de l'Haÿ, Paris.

SOUVENIR DE GILBERT NABONNAND A Tea. Raised by Nabonnand in France, launched 1920. Repeat flowers well. Height to 30 cm (1 ft). Slight scent.

IMPORTANT ROSE BREEDERS VIII

Jean-Baptiste Guillot (père) founded a nursery outside Lyon in 1829, and introduced his first rose, a Hybrid Perpetual called Lamartine, in 1842. His son Jean-Baptiste started work in the nursery at the age of fourteen. Very soon he made the significant discovery that seedling briars (of Eglantines or Dog Roses) made better stocks than cuttings. In 1852 he set up on his own and his father went into partnership with another breeder, Joseph Schwartz, with whom he had already been collaborating. Guillot (père) introduced over eighty new roses, mainly Hybrid Perpetuals and Bourbons, and, in around 1845, Mme Bravy, the lovely pale Tea Rose that had been raised by another Guillot from the nearby village of Pont-de-Chéruy.

The first introduction by Guillot (fils) was a winner: the Tea, Mme Falcot, in 1858. In 1866 he produced an even more famous rose, La France, later considered the first Hybrid Tea, and in 1875 the first dwarf repeat-flowering Polyantha, Ma Pâquerette. Guillot's present head, Jean-Pierre, is the fifth generation and is also breeding for new types of roses. He is about to introduce repeat-flowering Climbers based on the large Chinese species like *Rosa filipes* and is experimenting with Climbers derived from *Rosa cymosa*, *Rosa laevigata* and *Rosa bracteata* to raise 'brothers' for Mermaid.

LA FRANCE One of the earliest Hybrid Teas, though this class was not recognized until the 1880s. Raised by Guillot (fils) in France, launched 1867. Repeat flowers well. Height to 130 cm (4 ft), or 300 cm (10 ft) as a climber. Very good scent.

GRÜSS AN AACHEN A Floribunda or Hybrid Tea. Raised by Geduldig in Germany, launched 1909. (Frau Karl Druschki × Franz Deegen.) Repeat flowers well. Height to 100 cm (3½ ft). Very good scent. There is also a climbing sport. Photographed at Hidcote Manor, Gloucestershire.

SOUVENIR DE MME BOULLET A climbing Hybrid Tea. Raised by Pernet-Duchet in France, launched 1921. Repeat flowering. Height to 240 cm (8 ft).

SOUVENIR DE GEORGES PERNET A climbing Hybrid Tea. Raised by Pernet-Duchet in France, launched 1927. Repeat flowering. Height to 300 cm (10 ft). Good scent.

IMPORTANT ROSE BREEDERS IX

The Pernet-Ducher name arose from the marriage of two great families of rose breeders in 1881. Joseph Pernet was the son of Claude Pernet, who had started a rose nursery in Lyon in 1845. After working for his father for some years he went to gain more experience with another Lyon nurseryman, Claude Ducher, who had begun breeding roses in 1835. Ducher raised many fine roses, some of which are still grown, notably the Noisettes Rêve d'Or (1869) and Bouquet d'Or (1872) and the Tea Marie van Houtte (1871). Claude Ducher died in 1874 and the business was taken over by his widow. Joseph had become foreman in the Ducher nursery by 1880, at the age of twenty-two, and when he married Ducher's daughter, Marie, a year later he took on both the Ducher name and the business. Cécile Brünner was introduced in that same year and in 1890 the still-famous Hybrid Tea Mme Caroline Testout was launched.

For some years it had been the goal of breeders to raise a yellow-flowered Hybrid Perpetual. By persevering with what little pollen was produced by Persian Yellow, Joseph raised an unsatisfactory seedling in 1891 from Antoine Ducher, a Hybrid Perpetual. This seedling was planted out in the nursery and in 1893 a yellow chance seedling was found nearby. It was introduced in 1900 as Soleil d'Or. Using a *Rosa foetida* seedling, he obtained Rayon d'Or in 1910. The first yellow Hybrid Tea, it is now recognized as the first of the Pernetianas and an important ancestor of Peace. Joseph's two sons were to have taken over the business but both were killed in the First World War. Their roses, Souvenir de Claudius Pernet and Souvenir de Georges Pernet, are still grown. Joseph arranged for Jean Gaujard to take over in 1924.

CUPID A climbing Hybrid Tea. Raised by Cant in Britain, launched 1915. Summer flowering, with good hips in autumn. Height to 450 cm (15 ft), or more. Good scent.

JOANNA HILL A Hybrid Tea, said to be the seed parent of Peace. Raised by Hill in USA, launched 1928. An Ophelia seedling. Repeat flowering. Height to 120 cm (4 ft). Good scent.

LULU A Hybrid Tea. Raised by Easlea in Britain, launched 1919. Repeat flowering. Liable to mildew. Height to 120 cm (4 ft).

SOLEIL D'OR A *Rosa foetida* hybrid. An interesting, historic rose for a hot, dry climate. Raised by Pernet-Duchet in France, launched in 1900. (A seedling from Antoine Ducher × *Rosa foetida persiana*.) Once flowering, with a few later flowers. Height to 120 cm (4 ft). Good scent.

MME BUTTERFLY A Hybrid Tea. Its flowers are deeper coloured than Ophelia. A sport of Ophelia. Launched by Hill in USA, 1918. Flowers continuously. Height to 75 cm (2½ ft). There is also a climbing sport.

PAUL'S LEMON PILLAR A climbing Hybrid Tea. Raised by Paul in Britain, launched 1915. (Frau Karl Druschki × Maréchal Niel.) Summer flowering. Height to 600 cm (20 ft) on a wall. Very good scent.

CHAPTER SEVEN

Found Roses

Some of the roses that have been found in old gardens or graveyards.

ARCHIDUC CHARLES, ARCHDUKE CHARLES A China with pink petals that change to crimson. Illustrated in *Beauties of the Rose* (1850–1853) by Henry Curtis. Raised by Laffay in France, launched 1825. (A Parson's Pink China seedling × *? Rosa sempervirens*.) Flowers continuously. Height to 120 cm (4 ft). Slight scent.

AN UNKNOWN CHINA A low shrub. Flowers vary from pink to red. This is very similar to, and indeed may well be, Archduke Charles, shown above in a contemporary illustration. Found in the Union Hill Cemetery in the California Gold Country.

LITTLE FANNY SHEPHERD So named because it grows by her grave in the Georgetown Cemetery, California. Similar to the rose Lamarque, but pure white flushed with pink at the base. Height to 180 cm (6 ft). Good scent.

GEORGETOWN YELLOW TEA A rounded, free-flowering bush with large, very double flowers. Similar to Étoile de Lyon which was popular in California in the 1920s. Good in hot, dry weather. Repeat flowering. Height to 180 cm (6 ft). Tea scented. Photographed in the Georgetown Cemetery in the California Gold Country in late May.

A ROSE OF UNKNOWN NAME A very strong-growing Hybrid Tea, possibly a climber. Seen in a garden in California, this huge single-flowered rose is probably a hybrid of *Rosa gigantea*. In some ways it is similar to the much smaller Dainty Bess or Schoener's Nutkana, a Nutkana hybrid (page 8). Repeat flowering. Height to 180 cm (6 ft). Slight scent.

Fred Boutine with a bouquet of Found Roses in his garden in Tuolumne, California. Formerly curator at the Huntington Botanic Gardens, Los Angeles, Fred now spends much of his time searching for and identifying Old Roses, especially in the cemeteries of the gold-mining areas of California. The graveyards are especially rich in ancient Teas and Chinas that continue to flourish today, long after the settlements have become ghost towns.

ROSA CANINA An understock flowering in the Brompton Cemetery, London. There are many old Hybrid Teas dating from the 1920s onwards in the graveyard.

RXL UNDERSTOCK A large shrub with long shoots, much used as an understock. Probably *Rosa chinensis* × *Rosa multiflora*. Often found when the original rose has died and the plant has reverted.

RED RUN AROUND A loose shrub, that forms large thickets by suckering, hence its common name. A semi-double red *Rosa gallica* of unknown origin, often naturalized near old cottages in California. Summer flowering. Height to 150 cm (5 ft). Good scent.

FUN JWAN LO, INDICA MAJOR, ODORATA A Tea hybrid, probably × *Rosa multiflora*. Long smooth canes are easily rooted for stocks. Often used as a rootstock in California, so survives when the original rose has died. Repeat flowering. Height to 180 cm (6 ft). Slight scent.

CHAPTER EIGHT

Climbers

Climbers are arranged by colour: white, pink, purple, red, orange and yellow

ICEBERG (CLIMBING) Scrambling up an ash tree in Eccleston Square, London.

ICEBERG (CLIMBING), SCHNEEWITTCHEN A climbing sport of the Floribunda Iceberg of Kordes 1958. Tolerates some shade. Launched by Cants in Britain 1968. (Robin Hood × Virgo.) Summer flowering. Some mildew. Height to 550 cm (18 ft). Slight scent.

A new white Climber developed at Jackson & Perkins in Somis, California, by Keith Zary.

TREASURE TROVE A giant sprawling Rambler. A seedling found by John Treasure in Britain, launched 1977. (Kiftsgate × Hybrid Tea.) Summer flowering. Height to about 800 cm (26 ft). Very good scent.

LONG JOHN SILVER A Climber. Bred to withstand cold winters. (*Rosa setigera* × Sunburst.) Raised by Horvath in USA, launched 1934. Summer flowering. Height to 450 cm (15 ft). Fragrant.

SNOWBIRD CLIMBING A climbing Hybrid Tea. Raised by Weeks in USA, launched 1949. Height to 320 cm (10 ft). Scented.

A general view of Climbers trained up poles and along thick ropes, in the Bagatelle Rose Garden, Paris.

SUMMER SNOW CLIMBING A climbing Floribunda. Raised by Cocteau, launched 1936. Height to 200 cm (7 ft).

WHITE DAWN A free-flowering, healthy Climber. Raised by Langley, launched 1949. (New Dawn × Lily Pons.) Height to 400 cm (13 ft). Sweet scent. Photographed in the Roseto di Cavriglia, Italy.

CITY OF YORK, DIREKTOR BENSCHOP A Rambler, good for shady areas. Raised by Tantau in Germany, launched 1945. (Prof. Gnau × Dorothy Perkins.) Summer flowering. Height to 250 cm (8 ft). Fragrant.

ADÉLAÏDE D'ORLÉANS A *Rosa sempervirens* Rambler. Raised by Jacques in France, launched 1826. Flowers in midsummer. Susceptible to mildew. Height to 450 cm (15 ft). Pleasant primrose-like scent.

PAUL'S PERPETUAL WHITE, PAUL'S SINGLE WHITE PERPETUAL A form of musk rose. Raised by Paul in Britain, launched 1883. Flowers from summer to autumn. Height to 250 cm (8 ft). Sweetly scented.

BETTY SHERRIFF Probably a natural hybrid. Found on the Bhutan Tibet border by Mrs Sherriff. Summer flowering. Height to 600 cm (20 ft). Good scent. Photographed at Cockermouth Castle in the Lake District, England.

AUGUSTE GERVAIS A large-flowered Rambler. Raised by Barbier in France, launched 1918. (*Rosa wichuraiana* × Le Progrès.) Summer flowering. Height to 500 cm (17 ft). Well scented.

ALBERTINE A large-flowered Rambler. Immensely popular for its wonderful show of flowers. Raised by Barbier in France, launched 1921. (*Rosa wichuraiana* × Mrs A.R. Waddell.) Summer flowering. Disease resistant. Height to 600 cm (20 ft). Very well scented. Photographed at the pottery of Stephen Pierce near Cork, Ireland.

DR W. VAN FLEET A large-flowered Rambler. New Dawn is a seedling of this rose. Raised by Van Fleet in USA, launched 1910. ((*Rosa wichuraiana* × Safrano) × Souvenir du Président Carnot.) Summer flowering. Height to 600 cm (20 ft). Well scented.

SIR CEDRIC MORRIS Raised by Sir Cedric Morris and launched by Beales in Britain 1979. A *Rosa glauca* seedling. Summer flowering. Height to a gigantic 900 cm (30 ft). Strongly scented.

VENUSTA PENDULA Photographed in the Garden of the Rose, St Albans, Hertfordshire

VENUSTA PENDULA (DETAIL) An old *Rosa arvensis* Rambler. Rediscovered by Kordes in Germany, reintroduced 1928. Summer flowering. Height to 500 cm (17 ft). Negligible scent.

PAUL'S HIMALAYAN MUSK A rampant Climber. Its origin has been lost, probably the *Rosa himalaica alba magna* of Paul of Cheshunt. Raised by Paul in Britain, launched later 19th century. A *Rosa brunonii* seedling. Summer flowering. To 1000 cm (33 ft). Some scent.

BELLE PORTUGAISE, BELLE OF PORTUGAL Free-flowering Climber. Will withstand shade; needs protection in cold areas. Raised by Cayeux in Portugal, launched 1900. Summer flowering. Height to 450 cm (15 ft). Good scent.

IMPORTANT ROSE BREEDERS X

Dr Walter Van Fleet worked in the US Department of Agriculture Plant Introduction Station at Glenn Dale, Maryland, from 1905 to the 1920s. One of the department's main aims was to raise plants that were hardy enough, and suitable in other ways, for the climate of North America which is, by European standards, very cold in winter and hot and wet in summer.

The rose Dr W. Van Fleet, a good pink Climber, is a Wichuraiana hybrid crossed with a Tea, and that seedling then crossed with a Hybrid Tea. Its repeat-flowering sport, New Dawn, is now much more common. American Pillar, a popular, single-flowered Rambler, is a hybrid of *Rosa setigera*, an American climbing species. Using *Rosa rugosa*, Van Fleet raised several very tough hybrids including Sarah Van Fleet (page 72). A cross with a Hybrid Tea, it was introduced in 1926.

SILVER MOON A large-flowered Rambler, very popular in USA. Raised by Van Fleet in USA, launched 1910. A *Rosa laevigata* hybrid. Repeat flowering. Height to 900 cm (30 ft). Rich scent.

MARY WALLACE A large Rambler. Raised by Van Fleet in USA, launched 1924. (*Rosa wichuraiana* × a pink Hybrid Tea.) Summer flowering. Height to 600 cm (20 ft). Sweetly fragrant. Photographed in David Austin's rose garden at Albrighton, Shropshire.

COMPASSION, BELLE DE LONDRES A climbing Hybrid Tea. A strong, healthy grower it is a superb rose in every way. Raised by Harkness in Britain, launched 1974. (White Cockade × Prima Ballerina.) Good repeat flowering. Disease resistant. Height to 300 cm (10 ft). Very good scent.

TIFFANY CLIMBING A climbing Hybrid Tea. Recommended by Peter Beales as one of the best 1950s roses. Commonly grown in the bush form. Raised by Lindquist and launched by Howard in USA 1954. (Charlotte Armstrong × Girona.) Flowers for a long period. Height to 365 cm (12 ft). Good scent.

A view across Monet's garden at Giverny in France with lovely rose arches and pillars, and some standards nearer the camera.

CLAIR MATIN A climbing Floribunda. Raised by Meilland in France, launched 1960. (Fashion × Independence) × *Rosa multiflora* seedling.) Very free-flowering over a long season. To 300 cm (10 ft) high × 125 cm (4 ft) wide. Photographed in the Bagatelle Rose Garden, Paris.

LÉONTINE GERVAIS A large Rambler. Quite tolerant of shade once flowering. Raised by Barbier in France, launched 1903. (*Rosa wichuraiana* × Souvenir de Catherine Guillot.) Summer flowering. Height to 450 cm (15 ft). Good scent.

A thatched cottage near the old gardens of Mottisfont Abbey, Hampshire, with a superb selection of climbers.

MORGENGRUSS, MORNING GREETING A Kordesii Climber. Raised by Kordes in Germany, launched 1962. Repeat flowers well. Height to 375 cm (12 ft). Fragant.

COLCESTRIA A Modern Climber. Graham Thomas says it should be grown more often. Raised by Cant in England, launched 1916. Repeat flowers a little. Height to 250 cm (8 ft). Very fragant.

SANTA CATALINA A climbing Floribunda. A superb rose that should be grown more often. Raised by McGredy in Northern Ireland, launched 1970. (Paddy McGredy × Heidelberg.) Free flowering until autumn. Height to 275 cm (9 ft). Fragant.

ALIDA LOVETT An almost thornless Rambler. Raised by Van Fleet in USA, launched 1905. (Souvenir du President Carnot × *Rosa wichuraiana*.) Summer flowering. Height to 360 cm (12 ft).

SORAYA A climbing Hybrid Tea. Raised by Meilland in France, launched 1955. ((Peace × Floradora) × Grand'mère Jenny.) Height to 300 cm (10 ft). Fragrant. Photographed in the Bagatelle Rose Garden, Paris.

PAUL TRANSOM More a Hybrid Tea than a Rambler. Raised by Barbier in France, launched 1900. (*Rosa wichuraiana* × L'Idéal.) Flowers over a long period with a good late spurt. Height to 425 cm (14 ft). Good fragrance.

COLETTE A free-flowering Modern Climber that has wonderful, old-fashioned flowers. Raised by Meilland in France, to be launched by Selection Meilland in 1994. Good disease resistance. Repeat flowering. Height to 175 cm (6 ft). Light scent.

PINK CLOUD A Modern Climber. A good pillar rose, extremely popular in France but little known elsewhere. Raised by Boerner in USA, launched 1952. Height to 300 cm (10 ft). Good scent. Photographed at the Roseraie de l'Haÿ, Paris.

CHAPLIN'S PINK CLIMBER, CHAPLIN'S PINK One of the most free-flowering of all the Ramblers. Raised by Chaplin in Britain, launched 1967. (Paul's Scarlet × American Pillar.) Summer flowering. Height to 450 cm (15 ft). Very little scent. Photographed in the Garden of the Rose, St Albans, Hertfordshire.

AMERICA A Modern Climber. Raised by Warriner in USA, launched 1976. (Fragrant Cloud × Tradition.) Repeat flowering. Height to 375 cm (12 ft). Very good fragrance.

BANTRY BAY One of the best climbing Floribundas. Raised by McGredy in Northern Ireland, launched 1967. (New Dawn × Korona.) Repeat flowering. Height to 300 cm (10 ft). Good scent. Photographed on the walls at Hampton Court Palace, England.

GERBE ROSE A good healthy Climber. Quite good in shade. Raised by Fauque in France, launched 1904. (*Rosa wichuraiana* × Baroness Rothschild.) Flowers over a very long period. Height to 375 cm (12 ft). Good scent, especially in the evening.

DAUPHINE A Hybrid Tea. A good healthy climber, now very difficult to find. Raised by Gaujard in France, launched 1959. Height to 300 cm (10 ft). Some scent.

MORNING JEWEL A climbing Floribunda. Raised by Cocker in Scotland, launched 1968. (New Dawn × Red Dandy.) Continues to flower into autumn. Height to 300 cm (10 ft). Fragrant.

BLOSSOMTIME A Modern Climber with lovely deeper colour on the backs of the petals. Should be grown much more. Raised by O'Neal in USA, launched 1951. (New Dawn × a Hybrid Tea.) After the first crop of flowers it continues to repeat well. Height to 450 cm (15 ft). Very fine scent.

LAVINIA, LAWINIA Always listed as a Climber but it grows more like a very large shrub. Raised by Tantau in Germany, launched 1980. Repeat flowers very well. Height to 275 cm (9 ft). Fragrant.

MEISARDAN A low Modern Climber. Raised by Meilland in France, to be launched by Selection Meilland in 1994. Repeat flowering. Good disease resistance. To 175 cm (6 ft). Light scent.

RHONDA A vigorous Modern Climber. Raised by Lissemore in USA, launched 1968. (New Dawn × Spartan.) Repeat flowering. Height to 300 cm (10 ft). Fragrant.

ORIENTAL CLIMBER A climbing Hybrid Tea, quite popular in France and Italy. Raised by Robichon, launched 1946. Height to 250 cm (8 ft). Some scent. Photographed in the Roseto di Cavriglia, Italy.

ORIENTAL CLIMBER A close-up.

PINK MERMAID No one knows the origin of this lovely pink, single Climber. Probably grown from a seedling in California. Mermaid is very possibly one of the parents. Repeat flowering. Height to 1000 cm (33 ft).

EDEN ROSE 88, PIERRE DE RONSARD A superb, low Climber or large shrub rose. Raised by Francis Meilland before he died, launched posthumously in France 1987. Flowers throughout summer. Good disease resistance. Height to 250 cm (8 ft). Some scent.

EDEN ROSE 88 Note the green buds and outer petals. Collected in Eccleston Square, London.

ANTIQUE, ANTIKE 88 A vigorous Modern Climber with bushy foliage. Raised by Kordes in Germany, launched 1989. Flowers continuously. Height to 250 cm (8 ft). Some scent.

IMPORTANT ROSE BREEDERS XI

From 1900 onwards Barbier & Cie of Orleans, France, raised a group of beautiful, large-flowered Ramblers using *Rosa luciae*, a trailing species from Japan, as the source of the climbing habit and for its glossy, dark green, evergreen foliage, and various Tea and Hybrid Tea Roses to provide size and colour in the flowers. These mostly appear together in midsummer, although a few varieties continue to flower into autumn. Barbier's Ramblers include Albéric Barbier raised in 1900, Paul Transom (1901), Alexandre Girault (1909) and, the most famous of all, Albertine (1921). Alexandre Girault covers the great arbour which is the *pièce de résistance* of the garden at the Roseraie de l'Haÿ, Paris.

FANDANGO A low Modern Climber. Raised by Meilland in France, launched 1989. Repeat flowering. Height to 250 cm (8 ft). Some scent. Photographed in the Bagatelle Rose Garden, Paris.

ALEXANDRE GIRAULT A massive Rambler. Raised by Barbier in France, launched 1909. (*Rosa wichuraiana* × Papa Gontier.) Summer flowering. Height to 600 cm (20 ft) at least. Fragrant. Photographed in the Huntington Rose Garden, Los Angeles.

SHOT SILK (CLIMBING) A climbing Hybrid Tea launched by Knight in Australia 1931; the shrub was raised by Dickson, launched 1924. (Hugh Dickson seedling × Sunstar.) Flowers continuously. To 500 cm (17 ft). Good scent.

HANDEL A climbing Floribunda. Raised by McGredy in Northern Ireland, launched 1965. (Columbine × Heidelberg.) Repeats and repeats right through to winter. Height to 350 cm (11 ft). Slight scent.

ALOHA A Hybrid Tea. A superb shrub or low climber. Raised by Boerner in USA, launched 1949. (Mercedes Gallart × New Dawn.) Repeat flowers very well. Good disease resistance. Height to 300 cm (10 ft). Superb scent.

MISS HELYETT, MISS HEYLETT A *Rosa wichuraiana* Rambler, very free flowering. Raised by Fauque in France, launched 1909. Summer flowering. Height to 350 cm (11 ft). Some scent.

MRS F.W. FLIGHT A *Rosa multiflora* Rambler, excellent on pillars. Raised by Cutbush in Britain, launched 1905. (Crimson Rambler × unknown.) Summer flowering. Height to 300 cm (10 ft). Some fragrance. Photographed in the Roseraie de l'Haÿ, Paris.

NEW DAWN A sport of the Rambler Dr W. Van Fleet. One of the all-time best roses. Introduced by Dreer Somerset in USA 1930. Repeat flowering. Height to 600 cm (20 ft). Good disease resistance. Light scent.

NEW DAWN Growing at Cockermouth Castle, England.

BLUE GIRL A climbing Hybrid Tea that has unaccountably dropped out of the catalogues. Raised by Kordes in Germany, launched 1964. Height to 250 cm (8 ft). Good scent.

PARADE A healthy, glossy, climbing Floribunda. Will tolerate some shade. Raised by Boerner in USA, launched 1953. (New Dawn seedling × World's Fair.) Good repeat flowering. Height to 300 cm (10 ft). Some scent.

WINIFRED COULTER A climbing Floribunda. The breeder is not recorded; probably a climbing sport of Winifred Coulter, the shrub. Flowers continuously. Height to 450 cm (15 ft). Slight scent. Photographed on the rose arches in the Huntington Rose Garden, Los Angeles.

CLIMBING AMERICAN BEAUTY A healthy, long-lived, free-flowering Climber. Not a sport of American Beauty the bush rose. Raised by Hoopes Bros & Thomas in USA, launched 1909. Repeat flowering. Height to 375 cm (12 ft). Some scent. Our specimen was photographed in the Cypress Hill Cemetery, California, where it had been growing since before the First World War.

FLAME DANCE, FLAMMENTANZ A large-flowered Modern Climber. Raised by Kordes in Germany, launched 1955. Height to 300 cm (10 ft). Some scent.

SUMMER WINE A delicate, attractive, almost single Modern Climber. Raised by Kordes in Germany, launched 1985. Repeat flowering. Height to 300 cm (10 ft). Good scent.

PINK WONDER (CLIMBING), KALINKA (CLIMBING) A climbing Floribunda. Raised by Meilland in France, launched 1976. Flowers continuously. Height to 275 cm (9 ft). Some scent.

The main path up to Monet's house at Giverny in France is still decorated with rose arbours.

FUGUE A Modern Climber, grown less than it should be. Raised by Meilland in France, launched 1958. (Alain × Guinée.) Flowers throughout summer. Height to 300 cm (10 ft). Lightly scented.

IMPORTANT ROSE BREEDERS XII

James Cocker & Sons of Aberdeen was founded in 1841, soon after James Cocker left his job as gardener at Castle Fraser following a disagreement with his employer, who had told him to pick fruit for the house on the sabbath. Rose breeding began in the 1890s and the company's first important rose was Mrs Cocker, introduced in 1899. The business closed in 1923 soon after the early death of Alexander Cocker, the founder's grandson, but in 1936 it was revived by Alexander's son, Alec Cocker, as a general nursery. By the early 1950s he and his wife, Anne, had decided to specialize in roses. Alec's first new introductions were in 1968: three climbers and seedlings of New Dawn called Morning Jewel, White Cockade and Rosy Mantle. Alec's Red, a fine Hybrid Tea with excellent scent, was introduced in 1970. Silver Jubilee, raised from a seedling of the Kordesii Climber Parkdirektor Riggers, and introduced the year after Alec's death in 1977, was also widely acclaimed. The firm continues under Alec's wife Ann. Recently, Cockers have raised several good dwarf Floribundas.

DR HUEY, SHAFTER A Wichuraiana hybrid, extensively used as an understock in USA but really a good plant in its own right. Raised by Thomas in USA, launched 1920. (Ethel × Gruss an Teplitz.) Summer flowering. Height to 250 cm (8 ft). Slight scent. Photographed in the Grafton Cemetery, California, presumably a reverted understock.

DORTMUND A Kordesii Climber. Raised by Kordes in Germany, launched 1955. Repeat flowering. Height to 250 cm (8 ft). Some scent. Photographed on the house of Dr Ernest Scholtz, California.

SURPASSING BEAUTY, WOOLVERSTONE CHURCH ROSE An old Climber. Rediscovered by Humphrey Brooke in Woolverstone, Suffolk. Introduced by Beales in Britain 1980. Repeat flowering. Height to 250 cm (8 ft). Strong scent.

PARKDIREKTOR RIGGERS A Kordesii Climber. Raised by Kordes in Germany, launched 1957. (Rosa kordesii × Our Princess.) Repeat flowering. Height to 400 cm (13 ft). Slight scent.

Pillar roses in the Roseraie de l'Haÿ, Paris.

GUINÉE

ENA HARKNESS

ALEC'S RED

GUINÉE A climbing Hybrid Tea with wonderful dark flowers and foliage. Raised by Mallerin in France, launched 1938. (Souvenir de Claudius Denoyel × Ami Quinard.) Sometimes repeats a little. Height to 500 cm (17 ft). Intensely fragrant.

ENA HARKNESS A climbing sport of the shrub Hybrid Tea raised by Norman in Britain and launched by Harkness in 1946. This sport was introduced by Murrell in 1954. (Crimson Glory × Southport.) Flowers continuously. Height to 365 cm (12 ft). Good scent.

ALEC'S RED A Hybrid Tea with vigorous upright growth, best used as a climber. Raised by Cocker in Scotland, launched 1973. (Fragrant Cloud × Dame de Coeur.) Continues to flower through summer. Height to 200 cm (7 ft). Very good scent.

DUBLIN BAY A climbing Floribunda. Raised by McGredy in Northern Ireland, launched 1976. (Bantry Bay × Altissimo.) Flowers all summer. Height to 250 cm (8 ft). Some scent.

DANSE DES SYLPHES A climbing Floribunda. Raised by Mallerin in France, launched 1959. (Danse du Feu × (Peace × Independence).) Good repeat flowering. Height to 300 cm (10 ft). Little scent.

ALLEN CHANDLER A vigorous modern Hybrid Tea climber. Has nice big orange hips. Raised by Chandler in England, launched 1923. (Hugh Dickson × seedling.) Some repeat flowering. Height to 500 cm (17 ft). Slight scent.

AMERICAN PILLAR A vigorous *Rosa setigera* Rambler. Does well in sun or shade. Raised by Van Fleet in USA, launched 1902. Only once flowering but makes a superb show. Summer flowering. Susceptible to mildew. Height to 500 cm (17 ft). Scent slight. Photographed in the Auckland Botanic Gardens, New Zealand (see also page 144).

DANSE DU FEU, SPECTACULAR A very free-flowering Floribunda climber that grows well on a north wall. Raised by Mallerin in France, launched 1953. (Paul's Scarlet Climber × *Rosa multiflora* seedling.) Good repeat flowering. Height to 360 cm (12 ft). Little scent. Photographed in the Bagatelle Rose Garden, Paris.

DYNAMITE A red climbing seedling of Symphathie in the Jackson & Perkins rose fields which we hope will soon be introduced. Repeat flowering. Height to about 300 cm (10 ft). Slight scent.

ALTISSIMO A large Floribunda shrub that is best grown as a climber. Raised by Delbard-Chabert in France, launched 1967. (Tenor × unknown.) Flowers continuously. Height to 350 cm (11 ft). Slight scent. Photographed in the garden of Sharon Van Enoo, Los Angeles, with the rose Ballerina.

PAUL'S SCARLET CLIMBER A very hardy Modern Climber. Raised by Paul in Britain, launched 1915. Height to 600 cm (20 ft). Repeats and repeats. Little scent. Photographed at the Roseto di Cavriglia, Italy.

PORTHOS A Floribunda that can be used as a low climber. Raised by Laperrière in France, launched 1971. Height to 200 cm (7 ft). Little scent. Photographed on the walls in the Bagatelle Garden, Paris.

DIABLOTIN, LITTLE DEVIL CLIMBING A wonderful Floribunda that is only grown in France. Raised by Delbard in France, launched 1970. Height to 300 cm (10 ft). Some scent.

GALWAY BAY A climbing Floribunda. Raised by McGredy in Northern Ireland, launched 1966. (Heidelberg × Queen Elizabeth.) Repeat flowering. Height to 300 cm (10 ft). Little scent.

MEG A climbing Hybrid Tea with almost single blooms. Raised by Gosset in Britain, launched 1954. (Paul's Lemon Pillar × Mme Butterfly.) Repeat flowering. Height to 400 cm (13 ft). Some scent.

POLKA A delightful new Modern Climber. Raised by Meilland in France, launched 1992. Good disease resistance. Repeat flowers well. Height to 180 cm (6 ft). Light fragrance.

POLKA In the Meilland rose fields in southern France.

TENOR A good, Modern Climber that is very difficult to find. Raised by Delbard in France, launched 1962. Height to 300 cm (10 ft). Some scent. Photographed in the Bagatelle Rose Garden, Paris.

BREATH OF LIFE A Hybrid Tea climber. Raised by Harkness in Britain, launched 1982. (Red Dandy × Alexander.) Repeat flowering. Height to 250 cm (8 ft). Scented.

ARIELLE BOMBASLE A Modern Climber. Raised by Meilland in France, introduced 1991. Repeats. Disease resistant. To 190 cm (6½ ft). Light scent.

JOSEPH'S COAT A Floribunda that is probably best grown as a low climber. Flowers open yellow and change to red. Raised by Armstrong in USA, launched 1964. (Buccaneer × Circus.) Repeat flowers right into winter. Height to 250 cm (8 ft). Little scent.

LAWRENCE JOHNSTON

MAIGOLD

GOLDEN SHOWERS

GOLDEN SHOWERS A Floribunda climber. Raised by Lammerts in USA, launched 1956. (Charlotte Armstrong × Captain Thomas.) One of the best repeating climbers. Good disease resistance. Height to 375 cm (12 ft). Fragrant.

MAIGOLD The earliest of the large-flowered Climbers to come into bloom. Raised by Kordes in Germany, launched 1953. (Poulsen's Pink × Frühlingstag.) Spring flowering. Disease resistant. Height to 360 cm (12 ft). Good scent.

LAWRENCE JOHNSTON Climber grown by Major Lawrence Johnston at Hidcote Manor, Gloucestershire. Rediscovered by Graham Thomas in 1948. Raised by Pernet-Ducher in France, launched 1923. (Mme Eugène Verdier × *Rosa foetida* Persiana.) Repeat flowering. Height to 900 cm (30 ft). Fragrant.

LAWRENCE JOHNSTON To 900 cm (30 ft) or even more. Photographed on a wall at Powis Castle, Shropshire.

PHYLLIS BIDE A rather large-flowered Rambler. Raised by Bide in Britain, launched 1923. Said to be (Perle d'Or × Gloire de Dijon). Keeps on flowering into autumn. Height to 400 cm (13 ft). Good scent.

A new yellow Climber being tested by Jackson & Perkins, California, in their rose fields.

GOLDEN SHOWERS Around the tennis court at Eccleston Square, London.

HIGH NOON A Hybrid Tea climber. Raised by Lammerts in USA, launched 1946. Flowers continuously until winter. Height to 450 cm (15 ft). Fragrant. Photographed in the garden of Miriam Wilkins, California.

EASLEA'S GOLDEN RAMBLER A Floribunda climber. Raised by Easlea in Britain, launched 1932. Summer flowering. Height to 450 cm (15 ft). Good scent.

MERMAID A vigorous, single Climber with wonderful rich green foliage that is almost evergreen. Raised by Paul in Britain, launched 1918. (*Rosa bracteata* × a Tea Rose.) Continues to flower after the first flush. Good disease resistance. Height to 900 cm (30 ft). Scented.

OPHELIA (CLIMBING) A climbing sport of the shrub Hybrid Tea. Raised by Paul in Britain; the shrub was launched 1912, the climber 1920. Repeat flowering. Height to 600 cm (20 ft). Very fragrant. Photographed at Sellindge, Kent.

PRIMAVÈRE, PRIMROSE A Wichuraiana hybrid, yellow in bud then paler. Raised by Barbier in France, launched 1929. Height to 250 cm. (8 ft). Light scent.

IMPORTANT ROSE BREEDERS XIII

Paul & Son of Cheshunt, Hertfordshire, was founded by Adam Paul in 1806. By 1872, his grandson George Paul was the owner and introduced an early Hybrid Tea: Cheshunt Hybrid. Important roses which were introduced by the company and are still available are Paul's Single White, a *Rosa moschata* hybrid introduced in 1883, Paul's Lemon Pillar, a hybrid of Maréchal Niel and Frau Karl Druschki, launched in 1915, and Goldfinch, a Rambler (1907).

William, Adam's son, started life at the Cheshunt nursery and it was from here that he wrote the first edition of his famous book *The Rose Garden*, published in 1848. Later, in 1860, he left to start his own nursery at Waltham Cross. Beauty of Waltham, a pink Hybrid Perpetual (1862), Ophelia (1912), Paul's Scarlet Climber (1915) and Mermaid (1917) were all introduced from there.

ALCHEMIST Photographed growing through a holly in Eccleston Square, London.

ROSA BANKSIAE LUTEA Photographed at the Chelsea Physic Garden, London.

ALCHEMIST This Modern Climber has flowers that look more like an Old Rose. Raised by Kordes in Germany, launched 1956. (Golden Glow × *Rosa eglanteria*.) Summer flowering. Good disease resistance. Height to 600 cm (20 ft). Scented.

ROSA BANKSIAE LUTEA The double yellow Lady Banks' Rose. This tender double Banksian rose is still to be found in the depths of China (page 50). Introduced to Britain from China by John Parks 1824. Summer flowering. Height to 600 cm (20 ft). Fragrant.

ROYAL GOLD A Hybrid Tea climber. Slightly tender. Raised by Morey in USA, launched 1957. (Goldilocks × Lydia.) Continuous flowering. Height to 250 cm (8 ft). Lovely fragrance.

CAPTAIN THOMAS A climbing Hybrid Tea. One of the parents of Golden Showers. Raised by Thomas in USA, launched 1935. This rose seems never to have come to Europe. Repeat flowering. Height to 300 cm (10 ft). Some scent.

PARURE D'OR A large-flowered Climber. Raised by Delbard-Chabert in France, launched 1970. Height to 250 cm (8 ft). Some scent. Photographed in the Bagatelle Rose Garden, Paris.

GLOIRE DE DIJON Photographed on the wall at Mottisfont Abbey, Hampshire.

DREAMING SPIRES A Hybrid Tea climber. Raised by Mattock in Britain, launched 1977. (Buccaneer × Arthur Bell.) Repeat flowering. Height to 400 cm (13 ft). Some scent.

MARÉCHAL NIEL

GLOIRE DE DIJON

LADY HILLINGDON

MARÉCHAL NIEL A slightly tender Tea-Noisette, very popular in Victorian conservatories. Raised by Pradel in France, launched 1864. A seedling from Cloth of Gold. Repeat flowering. Height to 450 cm (15 ft). Very fragrant.

GLOIRE DE DIJON One of the all-time favourite Climbers. Raised by Jacotot in France, launched 1853. (A Tea Rose × Souvenir de la Malmaison.) Some flowers in autumn. Height to 400 cm (13 ft). Excellent scent.

LADY HILLINGDON (CLIMBING) A climbing Tea, but not really tender except in very cold areas. Raised by Lowe & Shawyer in Britain, launched 1910. (Papa Gontier × Mme Hoste.) Repeat flowering. Height to 400 cm (13 ft). Fine scent.

CHAPTER NINE

Ramblers

Wichuraiana Ramblers are first, followed by the Multifloras.

ALBÉRIC BARBIER A large-flowered Rambler. Raised by Barbier in France, launched 1900. (*Rosa wichuraiana* × Shirley Hibbard.) After the main flowering it continues to flower spasmodically to autumn. Height to 500 cm (17 ft). Good scent.

AMERICAN PILLAR

EXCELSA

SANDER'S WHITE A small-flowered, rampant Rambler, an excellent plant. Raised by Sander in Britain, launched 1912. Summer flowering. Height to 400 cm (13 ft). Some scent.

AMERICAN PILLAR A vigorous *Rosa setigera* Rambler. Very hardy. Does well in sun or shade. Raised by Van Fleet in USA, launched 1902. Once flowering (see also page 134).

EXCELSA, RED DOROTHY PERKINS A small-flowered Rambler. Raised by Walsh in USA, launched 1909. Summer flowering. Prone to mildew. Height to 600 cm (20 ft).

DEBUTANTE A vigorous, small-flowered Rambler. Raised by Walsh in USA, launched 1902. (*Rosa wichuraiana* × Baroness Rothschild.) Summer flowering. Height to 400 cm (13 ft). Scent of primroses.

NEWPORT FAIRY A *Rosa multiflora* and *Rosa wichuraiana* hybrid only available in USA. Raised by Gardner in USA, launched 1908. Summer flowering. Height to 400 cm (13 ft). Some scent. Photographed at Rose Acres, California.

RASPBERRY RIPPLE A large-flowered Rambler. Raised by Wyant in USA. A *Rosa sempervirens* hybrid. Height to 450 cm (15 ft). Photographed climbing an old olive tree, Oneto Ranch, California. Some scent.

MAY QUEEN A medium-sized Rambler. The flowers tinge mauve in maturity. Tolerant of cold sites. Raised by Manda in USA, launched 1898. (*Rosa wichuraiana* × Champion of the World.) Summer flowering. Height to 500 cm (17 ft). Good scent. Photographed on David Austin's shed, Albrighton, Shropshire.

FRANÇOIS GUILLOT A large-flowered Rambler, should be much better known. Raised by Barbier in France, launched 1907. Summer flowering. Height to 300 cm (10 ft). Slightly scented. Photographed in the Bagatelle Rose Garden, Paris.

EVANGELINE A late-flowering single Rambler, but a double-flowering Rambler sometimes goes by this name. Raised by Walsh in USA, launched 1906. (*Rosa wichuraiana* × Crimson Rambler.) Summer flowering. Height to 500 cm (17 ft). Sweetly scented.

FRANÇOIS JURANVILLE A large-flowered Rambler with lovely, mixed-up petals. Raised by Barbier in France, launched 1906. (*Rosa luciae* × Mme Laurette Messimy.) Summer flowering. Height to 750 cm (25 ft). Good scent.

MME ALICE GARNIER A large-flowered Rambler, quite good in the shade. Raised by Fauque in France, launched 1906. (*Rosa wichuraiana* × Mme Charles Small.) Summer flowering. Height to 300 cm (10 ft). Some scent.

ETAIN A free-flowering Rambler. Almost evergreen. Raised by Cant in Britain, launched 1953. A Wichuraiana hybrid. Summer flowering. Height to 400 cm (13 ft). Fragrant.

RUSSELLIANA, OLD SPANISH ROSE, RUSSELL'S COTTAGE ROSE, SOUVENIR DE LA BATAILLE DE MARENGO An old Rambler of unknown origin. Probably bred in Spain around 1840. Summer flowering. Height to 600 cm (20 ft). Well scented. Photographed in the California Gold Country.

BLUSH RAMBLER A small-flowered Rambler. Almost thornless. Raised by Cant in Britain, launched 1903. (Crimson Rambler × The Garland.) Summer flowering. Height to 500 cm (17 ft). Good scent. Photographed at Cockermouth Castle in the Lake District, England.

ROSE-MARIE VIAUD A small-flowered Rambler. The flowers fade to a greyish-mauve. Almost thornless. Raised by Igoult in France, launched 1924. (Crimson Rambler × Erinnerung an Brod.) Summer flowering. Height to 400 cm (13 ft). Good apple-like scent.

RAMBLING RECTOR A small-flowered giant shrub or Rambler. Known since 1912. The parentage is probably *Rosa multiflora* × *Rosa moschata*. Summer flowering. Height to 600 cm (20 ft). Scented. Photographed in the Garden of the Rose, St Albans, Hertfordshire.

SEAGULL A small-flowered Rambler. Raised by Pritchard in Britain, launched 1907. (*Rosa multiflora* × Général Jacqueminot.) Summer flowering. Height to 500 cm (17 ft). Well scented. Photographed at the Roseraie de l'Haÿ, Paris.

GOLDFINCH A small-flowered Rambler. Almost thornless. Raised by Paul in Britain, launched 1907. (Hélène × unknown.) Summer flowering. Height to 250 cm (8 ft). Some scent. Photographed at Rose Acres, California.

TOBY TRISTAM A small-flowered
Climber, only found in Europe. A
Kiftsgate hybrid. Summer flowering.
Height to 500 cm (17 ft). Slight scent.

TRIER A shrub or low Climber. Raised
by Lambert in Germany, launched 1904.
A complicated parentage includes *Rosa
multiflora* and the Noisette Rêve d'Or.
Repeat flowering. Height to 250 cm
(8 ft). Heavily scented.

APPLE BLOSSOM A free-flowering Rambler. Raised by Burbank in USA, launched 1932.
(Dawson × *Rosa multiflora*.) Summer flowering. Height to 350 cm (11 ft). Only slightly
scented.

BLEU MAGENTA A late-flowering Rambler with superb, dark
purple flowers that fade to a deep mauvish-grey. Unknown origin,
arrived 1910. Summer flowering. Height to 500 cm (17 ft). Some
fragrance. Photographed at Kiftsgate Court, Gloucestershire.

TAUSENDSCHÖN, THOUSAND BEAUTIES A shrub or Climber.
The flowers show an enchanting variation in colour. Raised by
Schmidt in Germany, launched 1906. (Daniel Lacombe × Weisser
Herumstreicher.) Summer flowering. Height to 300 cm (10 ft).
Some scent. Photographed in the Grafton Cemetery, California.

CHAPTER TEN

Modern Roses

Hybrid Teas and Floribundas are arranged by colour: white, pink, red, orange and yellow. These are followed by two-coloured, painted, striped, grey, green, brown and single roses from both groups.

ICEBERG, SCHNEEWITTCHEN, FÉE DES NEIGES An elegant Floribunda, still the favourite white modern rose after more than 30 years. Raised by Kordes in Germany, launched 1958. (Robin Hood × Virgo.) Some blackspot. Flowers continuously. To 90 cm (3 ft). Some scent.

This chapter includes two major groups: Hybrid Teas and Floribundas. Hybrid Teas are the biggest and most popular group of all time. They were developed by crossing Tea Roses with Hybrid Perpetuals. The result combined the big, robust, many-petalled flowers of the Hybrid Perpetuals with the repeat flowering and tall, elegant buds of the Teas. The earliest Hybrid Tea was probably La France, bred by Guillot (fils) in France in 1867, although the section was not named until some years later. The earliest members of the group are shown in Old Roses. Here we illustrate the later forms, most of which have been bred by crossing one Hybrid Tea with another.

Floribundas are a more modern group. Polyantha Roses were crossed with Hybrid Teas to get more free flowering and perpetual flowering; the character of having multiple flowers on each stem came from *Rosa multiflora*, one of the parents of Polyantha Roses. In the beginning Floribundas had little scent, but later breeding has improved on this early deficiency. One of the first was Kirsten Poulsen, launched in 1924.

ICEBERG Photographed at Sellindge, Kent.

MARGARET MERRIL A wonderfully scented Floribunda. Raised by Harkness in Britain, launched 1977. ((Rudolph Timm × Dedication) × Pascal.) Flowers continuously. It does get a little blackspot. Height to 75 cm (2½ ft). Excellent scent.

MRS HERBERT STEVENS A Hybrid Tea available both as a shrub and a climber. A long-lived plant. Raised by McGredy in Northern Ireland, launched 1910. (Frau Karl Druschki × Niphetos.) Repeat flowering. Height to 75 cm (2½ ft). Excellent scent.

IVORY FASHION A Floribunda with dark green foliage and compact growth. Raised by Boerner in USA, launched 1958. (Sonata × Fashion.) Quite good repeat flowering. Height to 45 cm (1½ ft). Scent good.

SOLITAIRE A distinctive Hybrid Tea. Raised by McGredy in New Zealand, launched 1987. Repeat flowering. Height to 120 cm (4 ft). Very fragrant.

VIRGO, VIRGO LIBERATIONEM A slender, upright Hybrid Tea. Raised by Mallerin in France, launched 1947. (Blanche Mallerin × Neige Parfum.) Flowers continuously. Some mildew. Height to 100 cm (3½ ft). Good scent.

POLAR STAR, POLARSTERN A Hybrid Tea, free flowering with long stems. Raised by Tantau in Germany, launched 1982. Flowers continuously. Height to 100 cm (3½ ft). Slight scent.

ROYDEN A Floribunda often grown in New Zealand. Raised by Cattermold in New Zealand, launched 1989. Flowers continuously. Height to 90 cm (3 ft). Some scent.

TOUCH OF VENUS A rare Hybrid Tea that is extremely difficult to obtain except in Australia. Raised by Armstrong in USA, launched 1971. Repeat flowering. Height to 90 cm (3 ft). Scented.

TYNWALD A Hybrid Tea. Raised by
Mattock in Britain, launched 1979. (Peer
Gynt × Isis.) Repeat flowering. Good
disease resistance. Height to 120 cm (4 ft).
Well scented.

GARDEN PARTY A tall-growing healthy Hybrid Tea. Raised by Swim in USA, launched
1959. (Charlotte Armstrong × Peace.) Flowers continuously. Height to 120 cm (4 ft).
Scented. Photographed in the Tauranga Gardens, New Zealand.

LEVERKUSEN A Kordesii Rose that can
be grown as a climber or a shrub. Very
hardy. Raised by Kordes in Germany,
launched 1954. (*Rosa Kordesii* × Golden
Glow.) Flowers continuously. Height to
200 cm (7 ft) or more. Sweetly scented.

GRAND SIÈCLE An elegant Hybrid Tea, difficult to obtain. Raised by Delbard-Chabert
in France, launched 1977. Repeat flowering. Height to 110 cm ($3\frac{1}{2}$ ft). Some scent.

FRENCH LACE An ivory-white Floribunda, sometimes showing a
pink flush. Rather tender. Raised by Warriner in USA, launched
1981. (Dr A.J. Verhage × Bridal Pink.) Flowers continuously.
Height to 75 cm ($2\frac{1}{2}$ ft). Light, spicy scent.

AMANECER A charming Hybrid Tea now extremely difficult to
buy. Raised by Dot in Spain, launched 1966. Repeat flowering.
Height to 90 cm (3 ft). Some scent.

MICHÈLE MEILLAND An upright Hybrid Tea. Good for cut flowers. Raised by Meilland in France, launched 1945. (Joanna Hill × Peace.) Flowers continuously. Height to 110 cm ($3\frac{1}{2}$ ft). Well scented.

APRICOT NECTAR A bushy Floribunda. Raised by Boerner in USA, launched 1965. (Seedling × Spartan.) Flowers continuously. Height to 75 cm ($2\frac{1}{2}$ ft). Good scent.

WHISKY MAC A popular Hybrid Tea. Raised by Tantau in Germany, launched 1967. Flowers continuously. Susceptible to some mildew and frost damage. Height to 110 cm ($3\frac{1}{2}$ ft). Strong scent.

HELEN HAYES A Brownell's 'sub-zero' Hybrid Tea. Raised by Brownell in USA, launched 1956. Repeat flowering. Height to 90 cm (3 ft). Slight scent.

The Garden of the Rose, St Albans, Hertfordshire.

SIMPLICITY A Floribunda sold in America, often on its own roots, as a landscaping rose. Raised by Warriner in USA, launched 1978. Flowers continuously. Height to 90 cm (3 ft). Some scent. Photographed lining the drive at Rose Acres, California.

PRISTINE A Hybrid Tea. Raised by Warriner in USA, launched 1978. (White Masterpiece × First Prize.) Flowers continuously. May get some blackspot. Height to 120 cm (4 ft). Good scent.

IMPORTANT ROSE BREEDERS XIV

William A. Warriner, usually called Bill, was director of Jackson & Perkins research department – the company's breeding operation – from 1966 until the late 1980s. After service in the US Marines during the Second World War he finished his degree at Michigan State University, then worked for Howard & Smith, a firm of rose breeders and growers, in California. In 1956 he started his own business, but joined Jackson & Perkins in 1963. He became director of research there on the death of Eugene Boerner.

SILVER LINING A Hybrid Tea with superb, high buds. Raised by Dickson in Northern Ireland, launched 1958. (Karl Herbst × Eden Rose.) Flowers continuously. Height to 120 cm (4 ft). Good scent.

HARRINY An excellent Hybrid Tea, little grown. Raised by LeGrice in Britain, launched 1967. Good repeat flowering. Height to 75 cm (2½ ft). Wonderfully scented. Photographed in autumn.

HONORINE DE BALZAC A very large-flowered, strong-growing Hybrid Tea. Raised by Meilland in France, to be introduced by Selection Meilland in 1994. Repeat flowering. Disease resistant. Height to 100 cm (3½ ft). Peach scent.

ENGLISH MISS A Floribunda. Raised by Cants in Britain, launched 1977. (Dearest × Sweet Repose.) Flowers continuously. Good disease resistance. Height to 60 cm (2 ft). Good scent.

PAUL RICARD A new Hybrid Tea, named for its odd scent. Raised by Meilland in France, launched 1991. Repeat flowering. Height to 90 cm (3 ft). Scent of anise or 'Ricard'.

VALENCIA A compact Hybrid Tea. Raised by Kordes in Germany, launched 1989. Repeat flowering. Height to 60 cm (2 ft). Some scent.

COMTESSE VANDAL A vigorous, classic Hybrid Tea. Raised by Leenders and introduced by Jackson & Perkins in USA 1932. ((Ophelia × Mrs Aaron Ward) × Souvenir de Claudius Pernet.) Flowers continuously. Height to 100 cm ($3\frac{1}{2}$ ft). Well scented.

DIAMOND JUBILEE A large, bushy Hybrid Tea. Raised by Boerner and introduced by Jackson & Perkins in USA 1947. (Maréchal Niel × Feu Pernet-Duchet.) Flowers continuously. Height to 120 cm (4 ft). Good scent.

The Garden of the Rose, St Albans, Hertfordshire.

A view of the rose garden at the Christchurch Botanic Gardens, New Zealand.

CITY OF LONDON A healthy Floribunda. Raised by Harkness in Britain, launched 1987. (New Dawn × Radox Bouquet.) Flowers continuously. Height to 110 cm (3½ ft). Wonderfully scented.

JOHN DAVIS A hardy Kordesii Rose popular in Canada. Raised by Svejda in Canada, launched 1986. Height to 60 cm (2 ft). Some scent.

SWEET VIVIEN A Floribunda that changes colour to a pure white. Only seems to be available in USA. Raised by Raffel in USA, launched 1961. Height to 60 cm (2 ft).

RAPTURE A Hybrid Tea. Raised by Traendly & Schenck, launched 1926. A climbing sport was launched by Dixie in 1933. Height to 75 cm (2½ ft). Some scent.

AOTEAROA A Hybrid Tea, sadly only available in New Zealand to date. Raised by McGredy in New Zealand, launched 1989. Repeat flowering. Height to 75 cm (2½ ft). Scented.

SIERRA GLOW A very free-flowering Hybrid Tea. Raised by Lammerts in USA, launched 1942. Height to 110 cm (3½ ft). Photographed in the Sydney Botanic Garden, Australia.

MRS CHARLES J. BELL, MRS C.J. BELL An unusual Hybrid Tea, difficult to find but surely it should be grown much more? A sport of Red Radiance. Raised by Bell in USA, launched 1917. Height to 90 cm (3 ft). Scented.

IMPORTANT ROSE BREEDERS XV

Sam McGredy I was born in 1828 and rose to be head gardener at a large house before starting his own nursery in Portadown, County Armagh, Northern Ireland, in 1880. His son Sam II began raising rose seedlings in about 1895, and in 1905 achieved his first major success with Countess of Gosford. Sam II was a great enthusiast and a few of his seedlings survive, notably Mrs Herbert Stevens, launched in 1910. He died suddenly in 1926 and was succeeded by twenty-nine-year-old Sam III, who continued to expand the firm and grew around a million roses a year. McGredy's Yellow, one of the finest yellow Hybrid Teas raised before the Second World War, was introduced in 1933. Sam III's early death in 1934, and the destruction of much of the breeding stock during the war meant that Sam IV took over a very poor business in 1952. (See page 193 for the rest of the story.)

MRS WAKEFIELD CHRISTIE-MILLER A Hybrid Tea with fine, glossy foliage. Raised by McGredy in Northern Ireland, launched 1907. Repeat flowering. Height to 60 cm (2 ft). Fragrant.

TOURNAMENT OF ROSES A Hybrid Tea. Raised by Warriner and launched by Jackson & Perkins in USA 1988. Height to 100 cm (3½ ft). Scented.

SUTTER'S GOLD A Hybrid Tea. Our specimen is less yellow than is normal. Raised by Swim in USA, launched 1950. (Charlotte Armstrong × Signora.) Flowers continuously. Height to 90 cm (3 ft). Good scent.

JUST JOEY A Hybrid Tea with frilly-edged petals. Raised by Cants in Britain, launched 1972. (Fragrant Cloud × Dr A.J. Verhage.) Flowers continuously. Height to 75 cm (2½ ft). Some scent.

SWEET REPOSE, THE OPTIMIST A vigorous Floribunda. Raised by de Ruiter in The Netherlands, launched 1955. (Golden Rapture × Floribunda seedling.) Height to 90 cm (3 ft). Sweetly scented.

MR E.E. GREENWELL A good, healthy Floribunda that repeats well. Raised by Harkness in Britain, launched 1979. (Jove × City of Leeds.) Repeat flowering. Height to 60 cm (2 ft). Photographed in the Garden of the Rose, St Albans, Hertfordshire.

SEXY REXY A free-flowering Floribunda. Raised by McGredy in New Zealand, introduced by Sealand 1984. (Seaspray × Dreaming.) Wonderful repeat flowering. Good disease resistance. To 90 cm (3 ft). Some scent. Photographed in the Auckland Botanic Gardens, New Zealand.

A view of the rose garden at the Christchurch Botanic Gardens, New Zealand.

IMPROVED CÉCILE BRÜNNER A charming little Floribunda that is grown in the USA and Australia and should be available elsewhere. Raised by Duehrsen, launched 1948. Height to 90 cm (3 ft). Some scent.

SEA PEARL, FLOWER GIRL A free-flowering Floribunda. Raised by Dickson in Northern Ireland, launched 1964. (Kordes' Perfecta × Montezuma.) Flowers continuously. Height to 90 cm (3 ft). Some scent.

QUEEN ELIZABETH A popular Floribunda that is grown all over the world. Raised by Lammerts in USA, launched 1954. (Charlotte Armstrong × Floradora.) Flowers continuously. Height to 180 cm (6 ft) or even more. Some scent. Photographed in the Alhambra gardens, Spain.

SAVOY HOTEL A very free-flowering Hybrid Tea. Raised by Harkness in Britain, launched 1989. (Silver Jubilee × Amber Queen.) Flowers continuously. Good disease resistance. Height to 90 cm (3 ft). Excellent scent. Photographed in Queen Mary's Rose Garden, Regent's Park, London.

REICHSPRÄSIDENT VON HINDENBERG An old Hybrid Tea that has almost disappeared from cultivation. Raised by Lambert in Germany, launched 1933. To 90 cm (3 ft). Some scent.

MADONA A long-stemmed, strong-growing Hybrid Tea. Raised by Meilland in France, launched 1992. Repeat flowering. Good disease resistance. Height to 90 cm (3 ft). Light scent.

NORWICH SALMON A Kordesii Rose classed as a pillar rose but can be grown as a shrub. Raised by Kordes in Germany, launched 1962. Recurrent flowering. Height to 150 cm (5 ft) as a shrub, twice that as a climber. Some scent.

ANISLEY DICKSON, DICKY, MÜNCHNER KINDL A very free-flowering Floribunda. Raised by Dickson in Northern Ireland, launched 1983. (Coventry Cathedral × Memento.) A terrific repeater. Height to 75 cm (2½ ft). Good scent.

LOVELY LADY, DICKSON'S JUBILEE A very free-flowering Hybrid Tea. Raised by Dickson in Northern Ireland, launched 1986. (Silver Jubilee × (Eurorose × Anabell).) Excellent repeater. Height to 75 cm (2½ ft). Very good scent.

PINOCCHIO, ROSENMÄRCHEN A Floribunda much used in breeding. Raised by Kordes in Germany, launched 1940. (Eva × Golden Rapture.) Flowers continuously. Height to 75 cm (2½ft). Some scent.

TALISMAN An unusual, old Hybrid Tea. Raised by Montgomery in USA, launched 1929. (Ophelia × Souvenir de Claudius Pernet.) Flowers continuously. Height to 90 cm (3 ft). Good scent.

ANNA LIVIA A free-flowering Floribunda. Raised by Kordes in Germany, launched 1989. Excellent repeater. Suffers from rain damage. Height to 90 cm (3 ft). Good scent.

THE McCARTNEY ROSE, PAUL McCARTNEY A strong, free-flowering Hybrid Tea. Raised by Meilland in France, launched 1990. Summer flowering. Height to 90 cm (3 ft). Strongly scented.

CENTENAIRE DE LOURDES, MRS JONES A free-flowering Floribunda. Raised by Delbard-Chabert in France, launched 1958. (Frau Karl Druschki × seedling.) Flowers continuously. Height to 90 cm (3 ft). Slight fragrance.

COLUMBUS A large-flowered Floribunda. Raised by Carruth in USA, launched 1990. Flowers continuously. Height to 75 cm ($2\frac{1}{2}$ ft). Scented.

TEXAS CENTENNIAL A Hybrid Tea that grows well as a shrub. Raised by Watkins in USA, launched 1935. A sport of President Herbert Hoover. Repeat flowering. Height to 120 cm (4 ft). Excellent scent.

CURLY PINK A Hybrid Tea that lives up to its name. A rose that should be grown more. Raised by Brownell in USA, launched 1948. (Pink Princess × Crimson Glory.) Flowers continuously. Height to 90 cm (3 ft). Good scent.

WEST COAST, PENTHOUSE A large-bloomed, frilly-petalled Hybrid Tea. Raised by McGredy in New Zealand, launched 1988. Flowers continuously. Height to 75 cm ($2\frac{1}{2}$ ft). Well scented.

MEISOCRAT A strong, bushy Hybrid Tea that closely resembles an English Rose. Raised by Meilland in France, to be launched by Selection Meilland. Repeat flowering. Good disease resistance. Height to 90 cm (3 ft). Excellent scent of apples.

CONGRATULATIONS, SYLVIA A strong, tall Floribunda. Good for cut flowers. Raised by Kordes in Germany, launched 1978. (Carina × seedling.) Flowers continuously. Height to 150 cm (5 ft). Some scent.

AGÉNA A Hybrid Tea with dark, glossy leaves. Raised by Delbard-Chabert in France, launched 1966. (Chic Parisienne × (Michèle Meilland × Mme Joseph Perraud).) Repeat flowering. Height to 90 cm (3 ft). Some scent.

MINNIE WATSON A Hybrid Tea. Raised by Watson in Australia, launched 1965. Repeat flowering. Height to 75 cm (2½ ft). Some scent.

PAUL SHIRVILLE, HEART THROB A Hybrid Tea. Raised by Harkness in Britain, launched 1983. (Compassion × Mischief.) A very good repeater. May get blackspot. Height to 90 cm (3 ft). Great scent. Photographed in Queen Mary's Rose Garden, Regent's Park, London.

PINK PARFAIT A healthy Floribunda. Raised by Swim in USA, launched 1960. (First Love × Pinocchio.) Flowers continuously. Height to 75 cm (2½ ft). Some scent.

BEAUTY QUEEN A Floribunda. Raised by Cants in Britain, launched 1984. (English Miss × seedling.) Flowers continuously. Height to 75 cm (2½ ft). Very good, heavy scent.

QUEEN MOTHER A low-growing Floribunda or Patio Rose. Raised by Kordes in Germany, launched 1991. Flowers continuously. Height to 45 cm (1½ ft). Some scent.

ELIZABETH OF GLAMIS, IRISH BEAUTY A very free-flowering Floribunda. Raised by McGredy in Northern Ireland, launched 1964. (Spartan × Highlight.) Flowers continuously. Height to 75 cm (2½ ft). Very good scent.

RUTH HARKER A Hybrid Tea. Raised by Harkness in Britain, launched 1981. (Fragrant Cloud × Compassion.) Repeat flowering. Height to 75 cm (2½ ft). Terrific scent. Photographed in Queen Mary's Rose Garden, Regent's Park, London.

DOCTOR DICK A Hybrid Tea that should be much more widely available. Raised by Cocker in Scotland, launched 1986. (Fragrant Cloud × Corso.) Repeat flowering. Height to 90 cm (3 ft). Good scent.

SWEETHEART A tall-growing Hybrid Tea. Raised by Cocker in Scotland, launched 1980. (Peer Gynt × (Fragrant Cloud × Gay Gordons).) A good repeater. Height to 90 cm (3 ft). Wonderful scent.

MANOU MEILLAND A clean, healthy Hybrid Tea. Raised by Meilland in France, launched 1979. ((Meigriso × Baronne Edmond de Rothschild) × (Ma Fille × Love Song).) Height to 90 cm (3 ft).

WANDERING MINSTREL, DANIEL GÉLIN A Floribunda. Raised by Harkness in Britain, launched 1986. (Dame of Sark × Silver Jubilee.) Repeat flowering. Height to 60 cm (2 ft).

TIMOTHY EATON A Hybrid Tea, fast becoming impossible to obtain. Raised by McGredy in Northern Ireland, launched 1968. Flowers continuously. Height to 75 cm (2½ ft). Scented.

MULLARD JUBILEE, ELECTRON A Hybrid Tea. Raised by McGredy in Northern Ireland, launched 1970. (Paddy McGredy × Prima Ballerina.) Flowers continuously. To 90 cm (3 ft). Scented.

BLESSINGS A Hybrid Tea. Raised by Gregory in Britain, launched 1967. (Queen Elizabeth × seedling.) Flowers continuously. Gets some mildew. Height to 75 cm (2½ ft). Scented.

IMPORTANT ROSE BREEDERS XVI

Weeks Roses was established in Ontario, California, by O.L. (Ollie) and Verona Weeks in 1938. Ollie had been working for Armstrong Nurseries, also in Ontario, as had Herb Swim, and the two formed a hybridizing partnership in the 1950s; during this period famous roses such as Mister Lincoln were introduced. Swim returned to Armstrong's in the late 1960s where he raised Double Delight, still a very popular bicoloured Hybrid Tea. The Weeks retired in 1985 but Ollie continued his own hybridizing.

A new programme was set up at Weeks Roses by Tom Carruth, who had previously worked with Jack Christensen at Armstrong's and with Bill Warriner at Jackson & Perkins. Tom is continuing with a broad-based breeding programme and has already introduced some Miniatures such as Heart Breaker, cream with a pink edge, and a deep pink Floribunda, Columbus.

CAREFREE WONDER A free-flowering, Modern Shrub Rose, often sold on its own roots for landscaping. Raised by Meilland in France, launched 1990. Flowers continuously. Height to 75 cm (2½ ft). Some scent.

CENTURY TWO A good Hybrid Tea for hot climates. Raised by Armstrong in USA, launched 1971. (Charlotte Armstrong × Duet.) Repeat flowering. Height to 75 cm (2½ ft). Scented.

PRINCESSE MARGARET D'ANGLETERRE, PRINCESS MARGARET OF ENGLAND A Hybrid Tea. Raised by Meilland in France and introduced by Universal Rose Selection 1968. (Queen Elizabeth × (Peace × Michèle Meilland).) Flowers continuously. Height to 90 cm (3 ft). Some scent.

AUGUSTE RENOIR A wonderful, blowzy Hybrid Tea – very appropriately named. Raised by Meilland in France, launched 1992. Repeat flowering. Height to 90 cm (3 ft). Strong, heavy scent.

PINK FAVOURITE A free-flowering Hybrid Tea. Raised by Von Abrams and introduced by Peterson & Dering in USA 1956. (Juno × (Georg Arends × New Dawn).) Flowers continuously. Good disease resistance. Height to 75 cm (2½ ft). No scent. Photographed in Queen Mary's Rose Garden, Regent's Park, London.

KERRYMAN A Floribunda. Raised by McGredy in Northern Ireland, launched 1971. (Mme Léon Cuny × Columbine.) Repeats. Susceptible to blackspot. Height to 90 cm (3 ft). Fragrant.

ABBEYFIELD ROSE A Hybrid Tea. Raised by Cocker in Scotland, launched 1985. (National Trust × Silver Jubilee.) Good repeater. Some blackspot. Height to 90 cm (3 ft). Some scent.

TENERIFE A Hybrid Tea. Raised by Timmermans, launched 1972. (Fragrant Cloud × Piccadilly.) Flowers continuously. Height to 75 cm (2½ ft). Very good scent.

ISABEL DE ORTIZ A tall Hybrid Tea. Raised by Kordes in Germany, launched 1962. (Peace × Kordes Perfecta.) Height to 110 cm (3½ ft). Scented.

WILLIAM BAFFIN A Kordesii Shrub Rose that can also be grown as a climber or allowed to sprawl as a ground cover rose. Raised by Svejda in Canada, launched 1983. A Kordesii seedling. Flowers over a long season. Very hardy and disease resistant. Height to 150 cm (5 ft) or more. Little scent.

Jo Stromei's exotic garden in Sunland, California.

PACEMAKER A Hybrid Tea. Raised by Harkness in Britain, launched 1981. (Red Planet × Wendy Cussons.) Flowers continuously. Height to 90 cm (3 ft). Terrific scent.

HEIDI JAYNE A Hybrid Tea. Raised by Esser, launched 1986. ((Piccadilly × Queen Elizabeth) × (Fragrant Cloud × seedling).) Repeat flowering. Height to 75 cm ($2\frac{1}{2}$ ft). Scented.

PERNILLE POULSEN An early-flowering, healthy Floribunda. Raised by Poulsen in Denmark, launched 1965. (Ma Perkins × Columbine.) Flowers continuously. Height to 90 cm (3 ft). Fragrant.

SHOCKING BLUE A bushy Floribunda. Raised by Kordes in Germany, launched 1974. (Seedling × Silver Star.) Flowers throughout summer. Height to 75 cm ($2\frac{1}{2}$ ft). Good scent.

SEVEN SEAS A Floribunda. Raised by Harkness in Britain, launched 1971. (Lilac Charm × Sterling Silver.) 75 cm ($2\frac{1}{2}$ ft). Some scent.

BLUE MOON, BLUE MONDAY, SISSI, MAINZER FASTNACHT A Hybrid Tea, the best of the so-called 'blue' group. Flowers throughout summer, sunshine brings out the blue tones. Raised by Tantau in Germany, launched 1964. (Sterling Silver seedling × seedling.) Height to 75 cm ($2\frac{1}{2}$ ft). Excellent scent.

IMPORTANT ROSE BREEDERS XVII

Mathias Tantau started a nursery at Uetersen in northern Germany in 1906 and specialized in growing forest trees. By 1918 he had turned to raising roses and introduced his first three Polyanthas in 1919. The breeding programme continued with increasing success. Floradora, a parent of Queen Elizabeth, was produced in 1944 and in 1951 Garnette was introduced by Jackson & Perkins in the United States where it was very successful as a cut flower.

Tantau also raised Cerise Bouquet, a hybrid of *Rosa multibracteata*, in about 1938. He did not introduce it but gave it to his neighbour, Kordes, who is usually credited with its raising. In *The Makers of Heavenly Roses* Jack Harkness records that Tantau was not at all pleased to hear that it had been introduced. However, it is one of the most distinctive and elegant of all Modern Shrub Roses.

Tantau's son, also Mathias, continued the business after his father's death in 1953. Super Star, called Tropicana in America, one of the nursery's most popular roses, appeared in 1960. Blue Moon and Whisky Mac are good roses in unusual colours and Polar Star is an exceptional white.

CHARLES DE GAULLE, KATHERINE MANSFIELD A Hybrid Tea. Raised by Meilland in France, launched 1974. ((Sissi × Prelude) × (Kordes Sondermeldung × Caprice).) To 90 cm (3 ft). Scented.

NEWS Striking, upright Floribunda with clusters of large, deep purple-red flowers. Raised by LeGrice in Britain, launched 1968. (Lilac Charm × Tuscany Superb.) Flowers throughout summer. Height to 75 cm (2½ ft). Some scent.

MAGENTA, KORDES' MAGENTA Very showy plant, somewhere between a Floribunda and a Hybrid Tea. Raised by Kordes in Germany, launched 1954. (Seedling × Lavender Pinocchio.) Flowers throughout summer. Height to 120 cm (4 ft). Good scent.

LAVENDER PINOCCHIO A large-flowered brownish-lavender Floribunda with a bushy habit. Much used in breeding because of its unusual colours. Raised by Boerner in USA, launched 1948. (Pinocchio × Grey Pearl.) Flowers throughout summer. Height to 60 cm (2 ft). Some scent.

PASADENA TOURNAMENT, RED CÉCILE BRÜNNER A seedling of Cécile Brünner. Raised by Krebs in Germany, launched 1942. To 120 cm (4 ft). Some scent.

ESCAPADE A Floribunda with large clusters of semi-double flowers on an upright plant. Raised by Harkness in Britain, launched 1967. (Pink Parfait × Baby Faurax.) Flowers throughout summer. Height to 90 cm (3 ft). Good scent.

PURPLE SPLENDOUR A Floribunda with good, healthy foliage and upright growth. Raised by LeGrice in Britain, launched 1976. (News × Overture.) Height to 90 cm (3 ft). Some scent.

INTRIGUE Bushy Floribunda. There are two roses of this name. This is the one hybridized by Warriner in USA, launched 1984. (White Masterpiece × Heirloom.) Flowers throughout summer. Height to 75 cm (2½ ft). Excellent scent.

RIPPLES A Floribunda with unusual wavy petals. Raised by LeGrice in Britain, launched 1971. ((Tantau's Surprise × Marjorie LeGrice) × (seedling × Africa Star).) Flowers throughout summer. Height to 60 cm (2 ft). Some scent.

INGRID BERGMAN A Hybrid Tea with wonderful deep red flowers. Raised by Poulsen in Denmark, launched 1984. (Precious Platinum × seedling.) Flowers throughout summer. Height to 60 cm (2 ft). Slightly fragrant. Photographed in Queen Mary's Rose Garden, Regent's Park, London.

THE TIMES ROSE A bushy Floribunda with clusters of deep crimson flowers. Raised by Kordes in Germany, launched 1985. (Tornado × Redgold.) Flowers throughout summer. Good disease resistance. Height to 60 cm (2 ft). Some scent.

IMPORTANT ROSE BREEDERS XVIII

The firm of Kordes Sohne is famous both for the hardiness of its outdoor roses and for the greenhouse roses it produces for the cut-flower trade. It was founded in 1887, at Elmshorn in Schleswig-Holstein, by Wilhelm Kordes. He sent his son, also called Wilhelm, to England in 1912 to learn the nursery trade with a fellow German, Max Krause. At the outbreak of the First World War in 1914 both were interned as aliens on the Isle of Man. This period of enforced idleness enabled Kordes to study all available literature on rose breeding and genetics, and, when he returned after the war to the family nursery, which had moved to Sparrieshoop, he specialized in breeding roses. His brother, Hermann, ran the business.

Dr A. Thomas, the Australian rosarian, considers Wilhelm Kordes the Younger to be 'one of the greatest rose men who has ever lived'. By using species roses combined with Hybrid Teas, he introduced some of the hardiest and best of all shrub roses: Frühlingsgold (1937) and Frühlingsmorgen (1941) are two hybrids that have *Rosa pimpinellifolia* in their breeding, as has the orange-yellow Climber, Maigold (1953). Using a seedling of the Sweet Briar, he raised Fritz Nobis, a tall shrub, and introduced extra toughness into yellow-flowered Floribundas.

Another breakthrough came by chance. Wilhelm noticed an occasional hip or two on Max Graf, a hybrid between *Rosa wichuraiana* and *Rosa rugosa* and, in 1941, succeeded in raising a seedling. It proved to be a new fertile tetraploid species which was named *Rosa kordesii* after its raiser. Crossed with Hybrid Tea Roses it formed the basis of a new group of hardy roses, the Kordesii Roses. In 1964 Wilhelm's son, Reimer Kordes, took over the business.

MARLENA A low, very free-flowering Floribunda. Raised by Kordes in Germany, launched 1964. (Gertrud Westphal × Lilli Marlène.) Flowers continuously. Height to 60 cm (2 ft). Photographed in the Garden of the Rose, St Albans, Hertfordshire.

PAPA MEILLAND A Hybrid Tea with large, prize-winning, crimson flowers on bushy plant. Raised by Meilland in France, launched 1963. (Chrysler Imperial × Charles Mallerin.) Repeat flowering. Susceptible to mildew and blackspot. Height to 90 cm (3 ft). Excellent scent.

LILLI MARLÈNE A free-flowering Floribunda. Raised by Kordes in Germany, launched 1959. ((Our Princess × Rudolph Timm) × Ama.) Flowers continuously. Susceptible to mildew. Height to 75 cm (2½ ft). Slight scent.

DUSKY MAIDEN A Floribunda with flowers in clusters on upright plant. Raised by LeGrice in Britain, launched 1947. ((Daily Mail Scented Rose × Étoile de Hollande) × Else Poulsen.) Flowers throughout summer. Height to 60 cm (2 ft). Excellent scent.

ERNEST H. MORSE An upright bushy Hybrid Tea. Raised by Kordes in Germany, launched 1964. Flowers throughout summer. Good disease resistance. Height to 90 cm (3 ft). Excellent scent.

OLIVE A bushy Floribunda. Raised by Harkness in Britain, launched 1982. (Seedling × Dublin Bay.) Flowers throughout summer. Height to 90 cm (3 ft). Some scent.

RUBY WEDDING A bushy Hybrid Tea. Raised by Gregory in England, launched 1979. (Mayflower × unknown.) Flowers throughout summer. Some blackspot. Height to 60 cm (2 ft). Some scent.

CENTURION A healthy Floribunda. Raised by Mattock in Britain, launched 1975. Height to 75 cm (2½ ft). Some scent.

VALENTINA CORTESE A Floribunda. Raised by Gazzaniga in Italy, launched 1976. Repeat flowering. Height to 90 cm (3 ft). Some scent.

CHRISTIAN DIOR A Hybrid Tea. Raised by Meilland in France, launched 1959. ((Independence × Happiness) × (Peace × Happiness).) Flowers continuously. Height to 90 cm (3 ft). No scent.

BROWN VELVET, COLORBREAK A Floribunda with red flowers that turn brownish in cool weather. Raised by McGredy in New Zealand, launched 1982. (Mary Sumner × Kapai.) Flowers continuously. Height to 90 cm (3 ft). Some scent.

ROB ROY A Floribunda. Raised by Cocker in Scotland, launched 1970. (Evelyn Fison × Wendy Cussons.) Flowers over a long season. Height to 90 cm (3 ft). Some scent.

OLYMPIAD A Hybrid Tea named for the Los Angeles Olympic Games. Raised by McGredy in New Zealand, launched 1984. (Red Planet × Pharaoh.) Flowers continuously. Good disease resistance. Height to 90 cm (3 ft). Some scent.

PRECIOUS PLATINUM, RED STAR, OPA PÖTSCHKE A healthy, bushy Hybrid Tea. Raised by Dickson in Northern Ireland, launched 1974. (Red Planet × Franklin Englemann.) Flowers continuously. Height to 100 cm (3½ ft). Light scent.

FRENSHAM A Floribunda that is often found in old gardens. Raised by Norman in Britain, launched by Harkness 1946. (Seedling × Crimson Glory.) Flowers continuously. Slightly susceptible to blackspot. Height to 120 cm (4 ft).

The old border at Rousham, Oxfordshire.

EVELYN FISON, IRISH WONDER A free-flowering Floribunda. Raised by McGredy in Northern Ireland, launched 1962. (Moulin Rouge × Korona.) Flowers continuously. Height to 75 cm ($2\frac{1}{2}$ ft). Some scent. Photographed at Hampton Court Palace, England.

PLAYGIRL A free-flowering Floribunda. Difficult to get in Europe. Raised by Moore in USA, launched 1986. Repeat flowering. Height to 75 cm (2½ ft). Some scent.

PERMANENT WAVE A loose, frilly-petalled Floribunda. Introduced by Leenders in Holland 1932. Height to 75 cm (2½ ft). Some scent.

ÉTOILE DE HOLLANDE A Hybrid Tea, now most common as a climber but also an excellent shrub. Raised by Verschuren in The Netherlands, launched 1919. (General MacArthur × Hadley.) Height to 90 cm (3 ft). Good scent. Photographed in the Brompton Cemetery, London.

RED DEVIL, COEUR D'AMOUR A typically high-centred Hybrid Tea. Foliage crimson when young. Raised by Dickson in Northern Ireland, launched 1970. (Silver Lining × Prima Ballerina.) Flowers continuously. Good disease resistance. Height to 100 cm (3½ ft). Very good scent.

TOPEKA A vigorous Floribunda. Raised by Wisbech Plant Co. in Britain 1978. (Vera Dalton × seedling.) Repeat flowering. Height to 75 cm (2½ ft). Photographed in the walled garden at Hampton Court Palace, England.

Jo Stromei's garden in Sunland, California.

KORONA A Floribunda. Raised by Kordes in Germany, launched 1955. (Obergärtner Wiebicke × Independence.) Height to 90 cm (3 ft). Light scent. Photographed in a churchyard in Warwickshire.

FOUNTAIN, FONTAINE, RED PRINCE A healthy Floribunda. Raised by Tantau in Germany, launched 1970. Height to 90 cm (3 ft). Some scent.

SPRING HILL'S FREEDOM A tall Hybrid Tea or Shrub Rose. As yet difficult to obtain but hopefully it will become available soon. Raised by Twomey in USA, launched 1989. Height up to 220 cm (7 ft). Some scent. Photographed growing as a big shrub in the Huntington Rose Garden, Los Angeles.

TRUMPETER A compact Floribunda with excellent foliage. Raised by McGredy in New Zealand, launched 1977. (Satchmo × seedling.) Flowers continuously. Height to 60 cm (2 ft).

SATCHMO A free-flowering Floribunda. Raised by McGredy in Northern Ireland, launched 1970. (Evelyn Fison × Diamant.) Flowers continuously. Height to 75 cm (2½ ft). Slight scent.

DISCO DANCER A vigorous, bushy, free-flowering Floribunda. Raised by Dickson in Northern Ireland, launched 1984. (Coventry Cathedral × Memento.) Flowers continuously. Height to 75 cm (2½ ft). Little scent. Photographed in the Auckland Botanic Gardens, New Zealand.

IMPORTANT ROSE BREEDERS XIX

Alexander Dickson was born in Scotland in 1801 but moved to Northern Ireland as a young man. He started his own business in 1836 and the family have been nurserymen in Newtownards, County Down, ever since. George Dickson, son of the founder, began serious rose breeding in 1879, inspired by Henry Bennett's introductions in 1878 (see page 96). Dickson's early roses were Hybrid Perpetuals or Tea Roses, then the most popular groups, but one of their most famous was a Hybrid Tea, Mrs W.J. Grant, a seedling of La France × Lady Mary Fitzwilliam and a very important parent of many Hybrid Teas. Other noteworthy roses were single Hybrid Teas: Irish Elegance in 1905 and, in 1912, the very large-flowered, red George Dickson. More recent varieties include Grandpa Dickson (1966) and Precious Platinum (1974).

In 1977 the rose-breeding was separated from the retail side and continued by Patrick Dickson and his son, Colin, who have raised such popular roses as Beautiful Britain and Peaudouce (both 1983), and Tequila Sunrise (1989).

SCARLET QUEEN ELIZABETH A tall, healthy Floribunda. Raised by Dickson in Northern Ireland, launched 1963. ((Korona × seedling) × Queen Elizabeth.) Flowers continuously. Height to 100 cm (3½ ft). Slight scent.

FRAGRANT CLOUD, NUAGE PARFUMÉ, DUFTWOLKE A Hybrid Tea which has won prizes for its scent. Raised by Tantau in Germany, launched 1968. (Seedling × Prima Ballerina.) Flowers continuously. Can get some blackspot. Height to 90 cm (3 ft). Excellent fragrance.

GERANIUM RED A Hybrid Tea with attractive Old Rose flowers. Raised by Boerner in USA, launched 1947. Height to 75 cm (2½ ft). Wonderful scent.

ALEXANDER A strong, healthy Hybrid Tea. Raised by Harkness in Britain, launched 1972. (Super Star × (Ann Elizabeth × Allgold).) Flowers continuously. Good disease resistance. Height to 200 cm (7 ft). Slight scent. Photographed at Hampton Court Palace, England.

HAROLD MACMILLAN A vigorous Floribunda. Raised by Harkness in Britain, launched 1989. (Avocet × Remember Me.) Flowers throughout summer. Height to 90 cm (3 ft). Slight scent.

LADY TAYLOR A low-growing Hybrid Tea or Patio Rose. Raised by Smith, launched 1983. Height to 60 cm (2 ft). Well scented.

CITY OF LEEDS A Floribunda. Raised by McGredy in Northern Ireland, launched 1966. (Evelyn Fison × (Spartan × Red Favourite).) Flowers continuously. Height to 75 cm (2½ ft). Some scent.

BEAUTIFUL BRITAIN A Floribunda. Raised by Dickson in Northern Ireland, launched 1983. (Red Planet × Eurorose.) Flowers continuously. Height to 75 cm (2½ ft). Some scent.

SUE RYDER A free-flowering Floribunda. Raised by Harkness in Britain, launched 1980. (Southampton × seedling.) Very good repeat flowering. Height to 90 cm (3 ft). Slight scent. Photographed in Queen Mary's Rose Garden, Regent's Park, London.

DAME OF SARK A free-flowering Floribunda. Raised by Harkness in Britain, launched 1976. Flowers continuously. To 75 cm (2½ ft). Scented.

IMPORTANT ROSE BREEDERS XX

R. Harkness & Co of Hitchin, Hertfordshire, were rose growers, but not breeders, until 1962 when Jack Harkness, a cousin of the previous owner, took on the business and began raising new crosses on a large scale. Two of the company's most famous early roses, Ena Harkness and Frensham, both introduced in 1946, were raised by an amateur, Albert Norman, a diamond setter in Hatton Garden, London, and later president of the National Rose Society. Jack Harkness's own first introductions, in 1967, were named after Arthurian characters: Merlin, Sir Lancelot and King Arthur. Using an informed choice of parents, and by breeding for health and vigour, he has raised such excellent roses as Mountbatten, Compassion and Greensleeves and, by using *Rosa persica*, has raised roses with red eyes. Euphrates and Tigris are examples.

ROSEMARY HARKNESS A long-stemmed Hybrid Tea. Raised by Harkness in Britain, launched 1985. Repeat flowering. Height to 90 cm (3 ft). Wonderful scent, reminiscent of passion fruit.

L'ORÉAL TROPHY A shrubby Hybrid Tea. Raised by Harkness in Britain, launched 1981. A sport of Alexander. Flowers continuously. Height to 110 cm (3½ ft). Some scent.

MARINA, RINAKOR A Floribunda. Raised by Harkness in Britain, launched 1985. Flowers continuously. Height to 90 cm (3 ft). Sweet scent rather like passion fruit.

HARKNESS MARIGOLD A Floribunda. Photographed in September; in spring the flowers would be more yellow. Raised by Harkness in Britain, launched 1986. (Judy Garland × Anne Harkness.) Repeat flowering. Height to 90 cm (3 ft).

FELLOWSHIP An outstanding healthy and free-flowering Floribunda. Raised by Harkness in Britain, launched 1992. Repeat flowering. Height to 90 cm (3 ft). Scented.

COURTOISIE A free-flowering Floribunda. Raised by Delbard in France, launched 1984. Repeat flowering. Height to 75 cm ($2\frac{1}{2}$ ft). Slight scent.

SUNSET SONG A Hybrid Tea with fine high-budded flowers. Raised by Cocker in Scotland, launched 1981. ((Sabine × Circus) × Sunblest.) Flowers continuously. Height to 90 cm (3 ft). Some scent.

SOUTHAMPTON, A Floribunda. Raised by Harkness in Britain, launched 1972. ((Ann Elizabeth × Allgold) × Yellow Cushion.) Good repeat flowering. Disease resistant. To 90 cm (3 ft). Good scent.

TROIKA, ROYAL DANE A Hybrid Tea. Raised by Poulsen in Denmark, launched 1971. Flowers continuously. Height to 90 cm (3 ft). Fragrant.

FRAGRANT DELIGHT A Floribunda. Raised by Tysterman in USA, launched by Wisbech Plant Co. in Britain 1978. (Chanelle × Whisky Mac.) Flowers continuously. To 90 cm (3 ft). Good scent.

MEMENTO An open-flowered Floribunda. Raised by Dickson in Northern Ireland, launched 1978. (Bangor × Korbell.) Flowers continuously. Height to 75 cm (2½ ft). Some scent.

TZIGANE A Hybrid Tea with a strong yellow reverse to the scarlet petals. Raised by Meilland in France, launched 1951. (Peace × J.B. Meilland.) Repeat flowering. Gets some mildew. Height to 60 cm (2 ft). Fragrant.

PAINTED MOON A Hybrid Tea. Raised by Dickson in Northern Ireland, launched 1989. Flowers continuously. Height to 90 cm (3 ft). Scented.

SILVER JUBILEE A free-flowering Hybrid Tea with very healthy foliage. Raised by Cocker in Scotland, launched 1978. Flowers continuously. Good disease resistance. Height to 100 cm (3½ ft). Some scent.

DAME WENDY A very free-flowering Floribunda. Raised by Cants in Britain, launched 1990. (English Miss × Memento.) Flowers continuously. Height to 60 cm (2 ft). Some scent.

PRISCILLA BURTON A heavily veined, interesting Floribunda. Raised by McGredy in New Zealand, launched 1978. Flowers continuously. Some blackspot. Height to 75 cm (2½ ft). Slight scent.

MOLLY MCGREDY A free-flowering Floribunda. Raised by McGredy in Northern Ireland, launched 1969. (Paddy McGredy × (Mme Léon Cuny × Columbine).) Repeats. To 90 cm (3 ft).

LADY RACHEL

ALPINE SUNSET

LADY RACHEL A Floribunda. Raised by Cants in Britain, launched 1990. (English Miss × Margaret Merril.) Repeat flowering. Good disease resistance. Height to 75 cm (2½ ft). Scented.

ALPINE SUNSET A Hybrid Tea. Raised by Cants in Britain, launched 1974. (Dr A.J. Verhage × Grandpa Dickson.) Flowers continuously. Height to 75 cm (2½ ft). Very good scent.

IMPORTANT ROSE BREEDERS XXI

Cants of Colchester have been nurserymen for over 220 years: George Cant is recorded as being a gardener in the town in 1728 and taking on an apprentice in 1759. The family began to grow roses on a large scale in 1858, by which time the proprietor was Benjamin R. Cant. His wife is commemorated by the famous Tea Rose, Mrs B.R. Cant, introduced in 1901. Benjamin Cant trained his nephew, Frank, who then started his own nursery nearby in competition. There was considerable confusion and acrimony between the two firms until 1967, when they amalgamated to form Cants of Colchester. The firm is now run by the Pawsey family, descendants of Benjamin. Recent introductions include Just Joey and Alpine Sunset.

EYECATCHER A Floribunda. Raised by Cants in Britain, launched 1976. (Arthur Bell × Pernille Poulsen.) Flowers continuously. Height to 75 cm (2½ ft). Good scent.

A view of Monet's garden in Giverny, France.

Royal Romance, Liselle An upright Hybrid Tea. Raised by de Ruiter in 1980. (Whisky Mac × Esther Ofarim.) Flowers continuously. Height to 75 cm (2½ ft). Some scent.

Avocet A Floribunda with dark, glossy foliage. Raised by Harkness in Britain, launched 1984. (Dame of Sark × seedling.) Flowers continuously. Height to 75 cm (2½ ft). Some scent.

Copper Pot A tall Floribunda. Raised by Dickson in Northern Ireland, launched 1968. (Seedling × Spek's Yellow.) Good repeater. Height to 90 cm (3 ft). Slight scent.

Geraldine A Floribunda with light green foliage and orange flowers. Raised by Pearce and introduced by Limes in Britain 1983. Flowers continuously. Height to 75 cm (2½ ft). Slight scent.

PINK CLUSTER A very free-flowering old Floribunda now very difficult to get. Surely this rose should be more available? Raised by Morse in USA, launched 1938. Height to 60 cm (2 ft). Some scent. Photographed in the garden of Sharon Van Enoo, Los Angeles.

ARCADIAN, NEW YEAR An upright Floribunda with dark, glossy foliage. Raised by McGredy in New Zealand, launched 1982. (Mary Sumner × seedling.) Good repeater. Good disease resistance. Height to 75 cm (2½ ft). Some scent.

LOLITA An upright Hybrid Tea. Raised by Kordes in Germany, launched 1973. (Colour Wonder × seedling.) Flowers continuously. Height to 110 cm (3½ ft). Some scent.

CORONATION GOLD A healthy Floribunda. Raised by Cocker in Scotland, launched 1978. ((Sabine × Circus) × (Anne Cocker × Arthur Bell).) Repeats well. Height to 75 cm (2½ ft). Good scent.

TYPHOON A fine healthy Hybrid Tea. Raised by Kordes in Germany, launched 1972. (Dr A.J. Verhage × Colour Wonder.) Flowers continuously. Height to 75 cm (2½ ft). Good fragrance.

CHICAGO PEACE A good strong, healthy Hybrid Tea. Launched by Johnston in USA 1962. A sport of Peace. Good repeater. Good disease resistance. Height to 120 cm (4 ft). Scented. Photographed in the Brompton Cemetery, London.

JOYCE NORTHFIELD A vigorous Hybrid Tea. Raised by Northfield in Britain, launched 1977. (Fred Gibson × Vienna Charm.) Flowers continuously. Height to 90 cm (3 ft). Some scent.

NORWICH CASTLE A Floribunda that opens like a Hybrid Tea. Raised by Beales in Britain, launched 1979. ((Whisky Mac × Arthur Bell) × seedling.) Flowers continuously. Height to 75 cm (2½ ft).

WESTERLAND A tall-growing Floribunda. Raised by Kordes in Germany, launched 1969. (Friedrich Wörlein × Circus.) Good repeater. Height to 180 cm (6 ft). Very fragrant.

THE LADY An exhibition type of Hybrid Tea. Raised by Fryer in Britain, launched 1985. (Pink Parfait × Redgold.) Good repeater. Disease resistant. Height to 75 cm (2½ ft). Scented.

Rose Acres, the garden of Bill and Muriel Humenick, Diamond Springs, California. Photographed at dawn.

JUST JOEY A superb, free-flowering Hybrid Tea with frilly-edged petals. Raised by Cants in Britain, launched 1972. (Fragrant Cloud × Dr A.J. Verhage.) Flowers continuously. Height to 75 cm (2½ ft). Good scent.

ANN ABERCONWAY An upright Floribunda. Raised by Mattock in Britain, launched 1976. (Arthur Bell × seedling.) Flowers continuously. Height to 75 cm (2½ ft). Some scent.

BERNADETTE CHIRAC A tall, shrubby Floribunda. Raised by Delbard in France, launched 1979. Repeat flowering. Height to 140 cm (5 ft). Some scent.

SAMARITAN, FRAGRANT SURPRISE Very full-petalled Hybrid Tea; flowers have an 'Old Rose' appearance. Raised by Harkness in Britain, launched 1991. (Dr A.J. Verhage × Silver Jubilee.) A great repeater. Height to 90 cm (3 ft). Good scent.

Gold Bunny, Gold Badge A free-flowering Floribunda. Raised by Paolino in France, launched 1978. (Poppy Flash × (Charleston × Allgold).) Flowers continuously. To 75 cm (2½ ft).

Chinatown A vigorous, free-flowering Floribunda that can be grown as a shrub. Raised by Poulsen in Denmark, launched 1963. (Columbine × Cläre Grammerstorf.) Good repeater. Height to 120 cm (4 ft). Fragrant. Photographed in Queen Mary's Rose Garden, Regent's Park, London.

IMPORTANT ROSE BREEDERS XXII

Poulsen Nursery was started in 1878 by Dorus Poulsen in Copenhagen. He first grew asparagus and strawberries and later became a seed merchant and breeder. The nursery's first roses were raised in 1907 by Dorus' son, Dines, and included Rödhätte, a cross between a Polyantha and a Hybrid Tea, which was the first of a new group which came to be called Poulsen Roses. They were the forerunners of the Floribundas. Using the same groups as parents, Dorus' brother Svend, who had taken over the breeding in 1914, introduced Kirsten Poulsen (page 199) and Else Poulsen (page 256) in 1924. These were triploids and virtually sterile, so they were slow to lead to a race of new roses. Most of Poulsen's early roses were of this Floribunda type and, in 1938, the first yellow rose in this group appeared.

Svend died in 1974 and was succeeded by his son, Niels Dines, one of whose early introductions was Chinatown (1963), a fine yellow Floribunda with a good scent. In 1976 Niels' daughter, Pernille, and her husband, Mogens N. Osesen, took over the firm. Their Ingrid Bergman is now the most popular red Hybrid Tea and they have introduced a series of Ground Cover Roses such as Kent.

Grandpa Dickson, Irish Gold A free-flowering and popular Hybrid Tea. Raised by Dickson in Northern Ireland, introduced by Jackson & Perkins in USA 1966. ((Perfecta × Governador Brada da Cruz) × Piccadilly.) Flowers continuously. Disease resistant. To 75 cm (2½ ft).

New Day A popular Hybrid Tea in the USA. Raised by Kordes in Germany and introduced by Jackson & Perkins in USA 1977. (Arlene Francis × Roselandia.) Repeat flowering. Height to 75 cm (2½ ft). Good scent.

Pot o'Gold A very free-flowering Hybrid Tea. The flowers are deeper yellow in autumn. Raised by Dickson in Northern Ireland, launched 1980. (Eurorose × Whisky Mac.) Flowers continuously. Height to 90 cm (3 ft). Well scented.

AMATSU-OTOME A very large-flowered Hybrid Tea. Raised by Teranishi in Japan, launched 1960. (Chrysler Imperial × Doreen.) Flowers continuously. Height to 90 cm (3 ft). Slight scent. Photographed at the Vintage Gardens Nursery, California.

DUTCH GOLD A fresh yellow Hybrid Tea. Raised by Wisbech Plant Co. in Britain, launched 1978. (Peer Gynt × Whisky Mac.) Flowers continuously. Height to 120 cm (4 ft). Fragrant.

PEER GYNT A vigorous, bushy Hybrid Tea. Raised by Kordes in Germany, launched 1968. (Colour Wonder × Golden Giant.) Flowers continuously. Height to 90 cm (3 ft). Strong scent.

KING'S RANSOM A Hybrid Tea. Raised by Morey and introduced by Jackson & Perkins in USA 1961. (Golden Masterpiece × Lydia.) Flowers continuously. Height to 120 cm (4 ft). Good scent.

PEAUDOUCE, ELINA A classic, healthy Hybrid Tea. Raised by Dickson in Northern Ireland, launched 1985. (Nana Mouskouri × Lolita.) Flowers continuously. Height to 90 cm (3 ft). Some scent.

SIMBA, GOLDSMITH, HELMUT SCHMIDT A vigorous Hybrid Tea. The flowers tend to 'ball' in autumn. Raised by Kordes in Germany, launched 1981. (Mabella × seedling.) Flowers continuousiy. Height to 75 cm (2½ ft). Some scent.

Gold Medal A strong healthy Floribunda. Raised by Christensen and introduced by Armstrong in USA 1982. (Yellow Pages × (Granada × Garden Party).) Repeat flowering. Height to 75 cm (2½ ft).

SUNSPRITE, KORRESIA, FRIESIA A strong, bushy Floribunda. Raised by Kordes in Germany, launched 1977. (Friedrich Wörlein × Spanish Sun.) Flowers continuously. Height to 75 cm (2½ ft). Good fresh scent.

IMPORTANT ROSE BREEDERS XXIII

Meilland Richardier was founded by Antoine Meilland who, born near Lyon in 1884, was from early boyhood determined to become a rose grower. At sixteen he was apprenticed to Francis Dubreuil, a taïlor who had turned to rose breeding. Dubreuil raised, among others, the miniature China Rose Perle d'Or. Antoine married Dubreuil's daughter in 1909 and a son, Francis, was born in 1912. As a young man Francis was much helped by Charles Mallerin, a heating engineer and an inspired and successful breeder of roses, who produced Virgo (page 149) and Guinée (page 133).

As a result of the royalties produced from the dramatic sales of Peace when it was introduced in the United States in 1945, Francis Meilland was able to sell the main share of the growing business to Francisque Richardier and concentrate on breeding. He bought land near Cap d'Antibes where his wife's family, the Paolinos, had a nursery. Many of the roses he introduced after the Second World War are still grown. We have many of them in this book.

Francis recognized the importance of greenhouse roses and raised Baccara (1954), for a long time a favourite as a cut flower. He died in 1958, at the early age of 46, having fought to get plant patents for new cultivars recognized throughout Europe, and having built up a large international business: Universal Rose Selection. His work is continued by his wife, Louisette, and son, Alain. Louisette is now in charge of the breeding side of the business. Jacques Mouchotte, their chief breeder, is producing, amongst other types, a new range of Landscape Roses (page 220).

ANTHONY MEILLAND A good non-fading yellow Floribunda. Raised by Meilland in France, launched 1990. Repeat flowering. Height to 75 cm (2½ ft). Some scent.

MARCO POLO A dense, erect Hybrid Tea. Raised by Meilland in France, launched 1992. Repeat flowering. Height to 90 cm (3 ft). Distinctive peppery scent.

LIMELIGHT, GOLDEN MEDALLION A Hybrid Tea, popular in the southern hemisphere. Raised by Kordes in Germany, launched 1985. Repeats. Height to 75 cm (2½ ft). Some scent.

YELLOW PAGES A strong, upright Hybrid Tea. Raised by McGredy in Northern Ireland, launched 1971. (Arthur Bell × Peer Gynt.) Flowers continuously. Height to 90 cm (3 ft). Some scent.

Roses undergoing their first trials in the Meilland rose fields in Provence, southern France.

PEACE A detail of the flowers.

PEACE, MME A. MEILLAND, GLORIA DEI, GIOIA The most popular Hybrid Tea of all time with strong, healthy growth. The flowers vary from pink to yellow to red depending on soil, weather and season. Flowers continuously. Height to 120 cm (4 ft) or more. Some scent. The pollination which produced Peace, Francis Meilland's most famous rose, was made in 1935. Its parentage is uncertain but the usual story is that Joanna Hill, a yellow Hybrid Tea, was pollinated with pollen from a seedling (Charles P. Kilham × Margaret McGredy). It has also been suggested that on one side the parentage included George Dickson and Souvenir de Claudius Pernet. The Second World War held up distribution and the rose was only introduced in France in 1943, as Mme A. Meilland in memory of Francis' mother. Meilland had arranged for Conrad-Pyle to be their agents in the United States and in 1939 and 1940 budwood of the rose was sent to America. It was introduced there in 1945 on the day the Armistice was signed. It immediately became a wild success, both for its name and for its superior vigour and size.

AMBER QUEEN A free-flowering, healthy Floribunda. Raised by Harkness in Britain, launched 1984. (Southampton × Typhoon.) Flowers continuously. Height to 60 cm (2 ft). Good scent.

GLENFIDDICH A large-flowered Floribunda. Raised by Cocker in Scotland, launched 1976. (Arthur Bell × (Sabine × Circus).) Flowers continuously. Height to 90 cm (3 ft). Some scent.

HARVEST FAYRE A late-flowering Floribunda that flowers even better into autumn. Raised by Dickson in Northern Ireland, launched 1990. Flowers continuously. To 90 cm (3 ft). Some scent.

MOUNTBATTEN A tall-growing, very healthy Floribunda. Raised by Harkness in Britain, launched 1982. ((Anne Cocker × Arthur Bell) × Southampton.) Flowers continuously. Good disease resistance. Height to 120 cm (4 ft). Good scent.

CONQUEROR'S GOLD A rich-coloured Floribunda that can fade to a red-orange. Raised by Harkness in Britain, launched 1986. Repeat flowering. Height to 60 cm (2 ft). Some scent.

PRINCESS MICHAEL OF KENT A compact, bushy Floribunda. Raised by Harkness in Britain, launched 1981. (Manx Queen × Alexander.) Disease resistant. Flowers continuously. To 60 cm (2 ft).

FREEDOM A Hybrid Tea. Raised by Dickson in Northern Ireland, launched 1984. ((Eurorose × Typhoon) × Bright Smile.) Disease resistant. Repeat flowering. To 75 cm (2½ ft). Light scent.

PRINCESS ALICE, ZONTA ROSE A Floribunda. Raised by Harkness in Britain, launched 1985. (Judy Garland × Anne Harkness.) Repeat flowering. Height to 90 cm (3 ft). Slight scent.

TEQUILA SUNRISE A strong, rich-coloured Floribunda now much used in breeding. Raised by Dickson in Northern Ireland, launched 1988. ((Eurorose × Typhoon) × Bright Smile.) Flowers continuously. Height to 75 cm (2½ ft). Some scent.

ANNE HARKNESS A strong-growing Floribunda. Raised by Harkness in Britain, launched 1979. Flowers continuously; at its best in late summer. Prune hard for best late flowering. Height to 100 cm (3½ ft). Slight scent.

A view across the lake in Queen Mary's Rose Garden, Regent's Park, London.

HANNAH GORDON, (RASPBERRY ICE) A Floribunda with white petals strongly marked and edged in cerise pink. The name Raspberry Ice has been given to this rose but also to the rose Tabris. Raised by Kordes in Germany, launched 1983. (Seedling × Bordure Rose.) Flowers continuously. Height to 90 cm (3 ft). Some scent.

TABRIS, (RASPBERRY ICE) A white Floribunda with pink picotee edges. The name Raspberry Ice has been given to this rose but also to the rose Hannah Gordon. Raised by Kordes in Germany, launched 1986. Flowers continuously. Height to 75 cm (2½ ft). Some scent.

THE COXSWAIN A large, full-flowered Hybrid Tea, creamy-white with red outer petals. Raised by Cocker in Scotland, launched 1985. ((Super Star × Ballet) × Silver Jubilee.) Flowers continuously. Height to 75 cm (2½ ft). Wonderful scent.

PARADISE A Hybrid Tea with flowers that are a blend of bluish-white and strong pink. Raised by Weeks and introduced by Conrad-Pyle in USA 1978. (Swarthmore × seedling.) Flowers continuously. Height to 120 cm (4 ft). Good scent.

STRAWBERRY ICE A very free-flowering, creamy-white Floribunda with cerise-pink edges to the petals. Raised by Bees in Britain, launched by Delbard in France 1975. Flowers continuously. Disease resistant. Height to 60 cm (2 ft). Photographed in the Auckland Botanic Gardens, New Zealand.

HIROSHIMA'S CHILDREN A creamy-yellow Floribunda with pink edges to the petals. Raised by Harkness in Britain, launched 1985. Repeat flowering. Height to 75 cm ($2\frac{1}{2}$ ft). Scent slight.

SUMMER FASHION, ARC DE TRIOMPHE A white Floribunda touched with pink on the petal edges. Raised by Warriner in USA, launched 1986. (Precilla × Bridal Pink.) Height to 75 cm ($2\frac{1}{2}$ ft). Good scent.

SHEILA'S PERFUME A Yellow Floribunda strongly marked and veined with red. Raised by Sheridan in Britain, launched 1985. Flowers continuously. Height to 75 cm ($2\frac{1}{2}$ ft). Wonderful scent.

DOUBLE DELIGHT A creamy-white Hybrid Tea with red-painted edges to the petals. Raised by Swim & Ellis and introduced by Armstrong in USA 1977. (Granada × Garden Party.) Flowers continuously. Susceptible to mildew. Height to 90 cm (3 ft). Delicious scent.

CATHEDRAL, COVENTRY CATHEDRAL A Floribunda with scarlet-edged orange petals. Raised by McGredy in Northern Ireland, launched 1973. ((Little Darling × Goldilocks) × Irish Mist.) Flowers continuously. Some blackspot. Height to 75 cm ($2\frac{1}{2}$ ft).

VICTORIANA A Floribunda. Some petals are brilliant white. Raised by LeGrice in Britain, launched 1977. Repeat flowering. Height to 60 cm (2 ft). Some scent.

Sam McGredy in his greehouse with his last-ever batch of seedlings; he plans to stop work at 70, when he has seen this batch developed to maturity.

MATANGI A healthy, upright Floribunda. The flowers are strongly painted vermilion with a pale pinkish reverse. Raised by McGredy in New Zealand, launched 1974. (Seedling × Picasso.) Flowers continuously. Height to 90 cm (3 ft).

REGENSBERG, BUFFALO BILL, YOUNG MISTRESS A compact, bushy, well-scented Floribunda with pale pink double flowers painted deep cerise-pink. Raised by McGredy in New Zealand, launched 1979. (Geoff Boycott × Old Master.) Flowers continuously. Height to 60 cm (2 ft).

EYEPAINT, TAPIS PERSAN A scarlet Floribunda with a white eye and whitish reverse. Raised by McGredy in New Zealand, launched 1975. (Seedling × Picasso.) Flowers continuously. Disease resistant. Height to 75 cm (2$\frac{1}{2}$ ft).

MAESTRO A painted Hybrid Tea. Raised by McGredy in New Zealand, launched 1981. (Picasso seedling × seedling.) Flowers continuously. To 75 cm (2½ ft).

PICASSO The first of the painted Floribundas. Raised by McGredy in Northern Ireland, launched 1971. Flowers continuously. Height to 60 cm (2 ft).

CHAMPAGNE COCKTAIL A creamy-yellow Floribunda veined with deep pink. Raised by Horner in Britain, launched 1985. (Old Master × Southampton.) Flowers continuously. Height to 75 cm (2½ ft). Well scented.

IMPORTANT ROSE BREEDERS (XXIV)

Sam McGredy IV took over his family's firm in 1952; the nursery had suffered from the Second World War and lack of forceful direction. He sought advice from other breeders, notably Eugene Boerner of Jackson & Perkins, in the USA and made a completely fresh start. His first seedlings were introduced in 1958 and one of the most successful, Elizabeth of Glamis (page 161) was launched six years later in 1964. A breeder of vision, in 1972 he moved his whole operation to New Zealand, to a climate that more or less eliminated the need for greenhouses. There he has specialized in producing a new race of Hand-Painted Roses and Striped Roses. He introduced the Ground Cover Rose Snowcarpet in 1980 and Olympiad (page 170), a Hybrid Tea, in time for the Los Angeles Olympic Games of 1984.

Sam has decided to retire when he has seen through the current batch of seedlings and, as far as I know, the breeding lines and experiments will come to an end. Let us hope he can find some way of making sure his very important work is perpetuated.

LAUGHTER LINES A healthy Floribunda. The pink flowers are painted with red, and bright yellow stamens add to the effect. Raised by Dickson in Northern Ireland, launched 1987. Repeat flowering. Height to 75 cm (2½ ft). Slight scent.

INNER WHEEL A white Floribunda strongly veined in carmine-pink. Raised by Fryer in Britain, launched 1984. (Pink Parfait × Picasso.) Flowers continuously. Disease resistant. Height to 75 cm (2½ ft). Some scent.

CALICO A yellow Hybrid Tea with strong red veining on the petals. Raised by Weeks in USA, launched 1976. Repeat flowering. Height to 75 cm (2½ ft). Lightly scented.

CARELESS LOVE A Hybrid Tea. Launched by Conklin 1955. The striped sport of Red Radiance. Height to 120 cm (4 ft). Good scent. Photograph by Kim Rupert.

PEPPERMINT TWIST A new striped Floribunda raised by Christensen and introduced by Jackson & Perkins in USA 1992. Repeat flowering. Height to 75 cm (2½ ft). Some scent.

CANDY STRIPE A striped Hybrid Tea. Raised by McCummings, launched 1963. Repeats. Height to 60 cm (2 ft).

PURPLE TIGER An exciting purple-and-white striped Floribunda. Raised by Christensen and introduced by Jackson & Perkins in USA 1991. Repeat flowering. Height to 60 cm (2 ft). Good scent.

FIESTA A Hybrid Tea like a simple-flowered version of Harry Wheatcroft. Raised by Hausen in USA, launched 1940. Height to 60 cm (2 ft).

ORANGE SPLASH An exciting new Floribunda. Raised by Christensen and introduced by Jackson & Perkins in USA 1991. Repeat flowering. Height to 60 cm (2 ft). Slight scent.

CHRISTOPHER COLUMBUS A low-growing, strongly striped Floribunda. Raised by Poulsen in Denmark, introduced by Mattocks in Britain 1992. Repeats. Height to 45 cm (1½ ft).

FESTIVAL FANFARE A very free-flowering sport of the Floribunda Fred Loads. Introduced by Ogilvie in 1988. Repeat flowering. Very tall growing, up to 200 cm (7 ft). Can be grown as a large shrub or low climber. Slight scent. Photographed in the garden of Sharon Van Enoo, Los Angeles.

Some of Sam McGredy's seedlings. Sam believes that he can breed some exciting new Hybrid Tea striped roses.

GREENSLEEVES A Floribunda. Raised by Harkness in Britain, launched 1980. ((Rudolph Timm × Arthur Bell) × seedling.) Repeat flowers. Height to 75 cm (2½ ft). Little scent.

JOCELYN A mahogany-brown Floribunda that ages to purple-brown. Raised by LeGrice in Britain, launched 1970. Flowers continuously. Height to 75 cm (2½ ft).

JULIA'S ROSE A parchment-brown Hybrid Tea raised by Tysterman and introduced by Wisbech Plant Co. in Britain 1976. (Blue Moon × Dr A.J. Verhage.) Flowers continuously. Height to 75 cm (2½ ft). Some scent.

MINT JULEP This wonderful, unusual Hybrid Tea is virtually impossible to buy! Raised by Christensen in USA, launched 1983. Repeat flowering. Height to 75 cm (2½ ft).

IMPORTANT ROSE BREEDERS XXV

Edward LeGrice was born in Norfolk in 1902 and apprenticed to Henry Morse & Sons, Norwich, at the age of sixteen. He started his own nursery in 1920 and in 1937 introduced Dainty Maid (page 236), still a popular Floribunda and parent of many of David Austin's English Roses. Dusky Maiden, a dark red single, appeared in 1947 and Allgold, one of his most popular roses, in 1956. More recent introductions from the nursery have included purples, browns and greys as well as the lovely Mermaid hybrid, Pearl Drift (1980).

STERLING SILVER A silver-lilac Hybrid Tea. Better grown under glass in cool climates. Raised by Fisher in USA, launched 1957. (Seedling × Peace.) Height to 60 cm (2 ft). Well scented.

LAGERFELD, STARLIGHT A violet-grey Hybrid Tea. Raised by Christensen in USA, launched 1976. Height to 75 cm (2½ ft). Some scent.

SILVER STAR A grey-pink Hybrid Tea. Raised by Kordes in Germany, launched 1966. Repeat flowering. Height to 75 cm (2½ ft). Some scent.

The garden of Kim Rupert just outside Los Angeles. Kim has an extraordinary collection of grey, brown, violet and striped roses; many of the photographs on these two pages were taken in his garden.

AMBER LIGHT A strong-growing, golden-brown Floribunda. Raised by LeGrice in Britain, launched 1962. ((Seedling × Lavender Pinocchio) × Marcel Bourgouin.) Flowers continuously. Height to 75 cm (2½ ft). Good scent.

BROWNIE A Floribunda. Raised by Boerner and launched by Jackson & Perkins in USA 1959. Height to 75 cm (2½ ft). Some scent. Photograph by Kim Rupert.

VESPER An orange-brown Floribunda. Raised by LeGrice in Britain, launched 1966. Repeat flowering. Height to 75 cm (2½ ft). Some scent.

GREY DAWN A sturdy Floribunda with warm greyish coloured flowers. Raised by LeGrice in Britain, launched 1975. Height to 60 cm (2 ft). Some scent.

CAFÉ A Floribunda. Raised by Kordes in Germany, launched 1956. Height to 60 cm (2 ft). Some scent. Photograph by Kim Rupert.

The House of Archer in Kent. The nursery grounds are now, alas, a wheat field. Archer was an imaginative breeder with a passion for simple single roses.

ELLEN WILLMOTT A delicate, single Hybrid Tea which makes a good bushy plant. Raised by Archer in Britain, launched 1936. (Dainty Bess × Lady Hillingdon.) Flowers continuously. Height to 60 cm (2 ft). Some scent.

LAGOON A delicate, pale lilac Floribunda. Raised by Harkness in Britain, launched 1973. (Lilac Charm × Sterling Silver.) Free-flowering over a long period. Height to 60 cm (2 ft). Fragrant.

IMPORTANT ROSE BREEDERS (XXVI)

William Edward Basil Archer was a furniture designer from Yorkshire, who started breeding roses as a hobby. With his wife, two sisters and daughter he moved to Monk's Horton near Sellindge, Kent, in the early 1920s. The Archer family's most famous rose, Dainty Bess, named after his late wife and launched in 1926, is still available, as is a climbing sport of it. In 1929 they won a gold cup offered by the *Daily Mail* for the best scented rose. Alas, The Daily Mail Scented Rose has disappeared. Its flowers were dark, velvety red and very well scented but it was a poor grower. Ellen Willmott, named after the great gardener and author of *The Genus Rosa*, was launched in 1936. Miss Willmott is said to have ordered 400! Dainty Bess and Ellen Willmott appear to be the only two Archer roses still extant although they raised several others including several hybrid Polyanthas. Another single Hybrid Tea, Bonny Jean, raised in 1933, was described as carmine-cerise fading to white at the base; it would be worth re-finding. William's daughter, Muriel, died in about 1950 and he sold the business to Aloric Allen, a radar engineer. After one disastrous season when Allen planted the wrong stocks against local advice and could not fulfil his orders, the business closed in 1952.

IRISH ELEGANCE A delicate, subtly coloured Hybrid Tea. Raised by Dickson in Northern Ireland, launched 1905. Repeat flowering. Height to 75 cm (2½ ft). Fragrant.

FESTIVAL PINK A delicate-flowered sport of Festival Fanfare, which is itself a sport of Fred Loads. Raised by Rupert in USA, launched 1991. Repeat flowering. Height to 90 cm (3 ft). Little scent.

WHITE WINGS A delicate, single Hybrid Tea. Raised by Krebs in USA, launched 1947. (Dainty Bess × seedling.) Flowers continuously. Height to 110 cm (3½ ft). Scented. Photographed at Hidcote Manor, Gloucestershire.

FRANCES ASHTON A richly coloured, single Hybrid Tea. A charming rose that is very difficult to buy. Raised by De Puy, launched 1937. Height to 75 cm (2½ ft). Good scent.

NEARLY WILD A free-flowering, delicate, single Floribunda. Raised by Brownell in USA, launched 1941. (Dr W Van Fleet × Leuchtstern.) Height to 75 cm (2½ ft). Good scent.

ISOBEL A long-budded Hybrid Tea. Raised by McGredy in Northern Ireland, launched 1916. Height to 75 cm (2½ ft). Some scent.

KIRSTEN POULSEN A richly coloured single with a white eye, originally classed as a Poulsen Rose, but later classified as one of the first Floribundas. Raised by Poulsen in Denmark, launched 1924. Height to 60 cm (2 ft). Little scent.

ORIENTAL CHARM An almost single, tall-budded Hybrid Tea. Raised by Duehrsen, launched 1961. Height to 75 cm (2½ ft). Some scent.

CHAPTER ELEVEN

Standards

In France, especially in the Bagatelle Rose Garden, Paris, excellent use is made of very lovely standards. Weeping standards follow.

Rows of standard roses line the canal in the Generalife Gardens, Granada, Spain.

BONICA Modern Shrub. In going from garden to garden to do this book we found this rose to be a terrific flowerer and repeat flowerer everywhere. Makes an excellent standard. Raised by Meilland in France, launched 1982. *Rosa sempervirens* is one parent. Some scent. Also illustrated in Ground Cover Roses (page 222).

JOSEPH'S COAT A Floribunda normally grown as a shrub or low climber. Makes a striking standard. Raised by Armstrong & Swim in USA, launched 1964. (Buccaneer × Circus.) Flowers continuously. Little scent. Also illustrated in Climbers (page 137).

GOLD BUNNY, GOLD BADGE, RIMOSA 79 A very free-flowering Floribunda. Raised by Paolino in France, launched 1978. (Poppy Flash × (Charleston × Allgold).) Flowers continuously. Susceptible to blackspot. Some scent.

AMBER QUEEN A free-flowering, healthy Floribunda. Makes a super standard. Raised by Harkness in Britain, launched 1984. (Southampton × Typhoon.) Flowers continuously. Good scent. Photographed in the Bagatelle Rose Garden, Paris.

COCKTAIL A low Climber or Shrub Rose, which makes a superb standard. Raised by Meilland in France, launched 1959. ((Independence × Orange Triumph) × Phyllis Bide.) Flowers continuously. As a Shrub it will grow to 150 cm (5 ft). Not very hardy. Scented.

Standards burst through pot-grown roses in a mad scramble at Sharon Van Enoo's garden, Los Angeles.

RUSTICA A lovely, creamy Floribunda. Here grown and shown off to its best as a standard. Raised by Meilland in France, launched 1981. Repeat flowering. Some scent. Photographed in the Bagatelle Rose Garden, Paris.

RED CASCADE A free-flowering, climbing Miniature Rose. Raised by Moore in USA, launched 1976. Repeat flowering. Here illustrated as an incredible standard.

PAUL NOËL A low Climber. Raised by Tanne in France, launched 1913. A Wichuraiana hybrid that makes the most superb weeping standard. Some scent. I would love to grow this as a climber or a weeping standard.

RED MEIDILAND A Ground Cover Rose. Raised by Meilland in France, launched 1989. Flowers continuously. To 60 cm (2 ft) high × 150 cm (5 ft) wide.

ALBERTINE A large-flowered Rambler. Makes an ideal weeping standard. Raised by Barbier in France, launched 1921. (*Rosa wichuraiana* × Mrs A.R. Waddell.) Summer flowering. Very well scented. Also illustrated in Climbers (page 120).

AVIATEUR BLÉRIOT A Rambler. Raised by Fauque in France, launched 1910. This standard plant is about 40 years old. Summer flowering. Scented.

AUGUSTE GERVAIS A large-flowered Rambler. Raised by Barbier in France, launched 1918. (*Rosa wichuraiana* × Le Progrès.) Summer flowering. Well scented. Also illustrated in Climbers (page 120).

Rosary, Roserie A Multiflora hybrid Rambler. Another wonderful rose that has disappeared from commerce except in France. Raised by Witterstaetter, launched 1917. Summer flowering. Photographed in the Roseraie de l'Haÿ, Paris.

City of York, Direktor Benschop A Modern Climber. Makes a fine standard. Raised by Tantau in Germany, launched 1960. (Prof. Grau × Dorothy Perkins.) Summer flowering. Scented.

Pearl Meidiland A large, Ground Cover or Landscaping Rose that forms a mound. Raised by Meilland in France, launched 1989. Repeat flowering. To 60 cm (2 ft) high × 180 cm (6 ft) wide. Grown here in the Meilland rose fields as a weeping standard.

Nozomi A rampant spreading Miniature Rose that can be grown as a ground cover or a low climber or, as here so successfully, a weeping standard. Raised by Onodera in Japan, launched 1968. Summer flowering. Photographed at the Vintage Gardens Nursery, California.

Sissinghurst Castle, Kent. Vita Sackville-West adored white shrub roses.

SALLY HOLMES A modern Hybrid Musk. Raised by Holmes in Britain, launched 1976. (Ivory Fashion × Ballerina.) Repeat flowering. Good disease resistance. To 200 cm (7 ft) high × 150 cm (5 ft) wide.

MME D'ARBLAY A rambling climber or shrub of trailing growth, sometimes classed as a Hybrid Musk. Raised by Wells in Britain, launched 1835. (*Rosa multiflora × Rosa moschata*.) Summer flowering. To 180 × 180 cm (6 × 6 ft). Well scented.

CHAPTER TWELVE

Shrub Roses

Roses from the Hybrid Musk and other diverse groups that are normally grown as shrubs, ranging from small plants to really rampant giants that could be classed as climbers. They are arranged by colour: white, pink, red and yellow.

PAX A large Hybrid Musk. Flowers are often better in autumn. Raised by Pemberton in Britain, launched 1918. (Trier × Sunburst.) Flowers continuously. To 180 cm (6 ft) high × 150 cm (5 ft) wide. Well scented.

Dawn in the garden at Rose Acres, California. The white rose is SALLY HOLMES.

JACQUELINE DU PRÉ A large, free-flowering Modern Shrub. Raised by Harkness in Britain, launched 1989. (Radox Bouquet × Maigold.) Flowers continuously. To 180 cm (6 ft) high × 150 cm (5 ft) wide. Good scent.

PLEINE DE GRÂCE An outstanding, enormous, very free-flowering Modern Shrub or climber. Raised by Lens in Belgium, introduced by Austin in Britain 1983. Summer flowering. To 200 cm (7 ft) high × 400 cm (13 ft) wide. Well scented.

BALLERINA An excellent, small Hybrid Musk. Probably raised by Pemberton, launched by Bentall in Britain 1937. A *Rosa multiflora* seedling. Flowers continually right through to winter. To 120 cm (4 ft) high × 75 cm (2½ ft) wide. Some scent. Photographed in the garden at Rose Acres, California.

NEVADA A large bush in Eccleston Square, London.

HAWKEYE BELLE A full-flowered Modern Shrub. Obtainable from specialist nurseries in USA. Raised by Buck in USA, launched 1975. Height to 150 cm (5 ft). Scented.

SUSAN LOUISE A delicate, large-flowered shrub. Rare but worth searching out. Raised by Adams, launched 1929. Summer flowering. To 150 × 150 cm (5 × 5 ft). Some scent.

IMPORTANT ROSE BREEDERS XXVII

Pedro Dot (1885–1976) is the most famous of Spanish rose breeders. His father was a nurseryman on the Mediterranean coast of Spain, and Pedro was apprenticed to a firm of rose growers. Later he worked at the Bagatelle Gardens in Paris, before returning to his father's nursery where he started to breed roses in 1915. His early introductions were mainly Hybrid Teas, but in 1925 he began using the pollen of wild roses. The famous shrub rose Nevada is from this group of crosses. It is said to come from *Rosa moyesii* but is more like a Spinosissima hybrid in appearance. Dot's other early crosses include the lovely, large-flowered Climber Mme Grégoire Staechelin and, from 1935, a group of Miniatures of which Baby Gold Star was the first. Pedro Dot died in 1976 aged 91, and his son and grandsons continue to grow and breed roses.

CORNELIA A vigorous Hybrid Musk. In summer the flowers (as in our picture) are often fairly pale, in autumn the colour will be a stronger pink. Raised by Pemberton in Britain, launched 1925. Good disease resistance. To 150 × 150 cm (5 × 5 ft). A sweetly musky scent. Photographed in the Brompton Cemetery, London.

A mixed group of shrub roses including GREAT MAIDEN'S BLUSH, BUFF BEAUTY, FRITZ NOBIS and CONSTANCE SPRY.

BUFF BEAUTY An excellent, very floriferous Hybrid Musk. Raised by Bentall in Britain, launched 1939. (Unknown × William Allen Richardson.) Flowers continuously. Good disease resistance. To 150 × 150 cm (5 × 5 ft). Deliciously scented.

NEVADA

MARGUERITE HILLING

FRANCESCA A graceful Hybrid Musk. The flowers are more yellow in autumn. Raised by Pemberton in Britain, launched 1928. (Danaë × Sunburst.) To 180 × 180 cm (6 × 6 ft). Richly scented.

NEVADA An extremely free-flowering shrub. The late flowers often show pink tinges. Raised by Dot in Spain, launched 1927. Probably a hybrid of *Rosa moyesii*, but Jack Harkness thinks it is a *Rosa pimpinellifolia* hybrid × La Giralda. Main burst of flowers in spring and intermittent flowers later. Good disease resistance. 240 × 240 cm (8 × 8 ft). Light scent.

MARGUERITE HILLING A superb pink Modern Shrub. A sport of Nevada found in three different locations. Discovered by Graham Thomas, launched by Hilling in Britain 1959. Main bursts of flowers in spring and intermittent flowers later. To 210 × 210 cm (7 × 7 ft). Light scent.

DAYBREAK A delicate yellow Hybrid Musk. Raised by Pemberton in Britain, launched 1918. (Trier × Liberty.) Flowers through to autumn. To 120 cm (4 ft) high × 90 cm (3 ft) wide. Strong musky scent.

DENTELLE DE MALINES A lovely Modern Shrub. Raised by Lens in Belgium, introduced by Austin in Britain 1983. Once flowering. To 120 × 120 cm (4 × 4 ft). Some scent.

PROSPERITY A free-flowering Hybrid Musk with tall arching stems. Raised by Pemberton in Britain, launched 1919. (Marie-Jeanne × Perle des Jardins.) Flowers continuously. To 200 cm (7 ft) high × 150 cm (5 ft) wide. Good scent.

IMPORTANT ROSE BREEDERS XXVIII

Joseph Pemberton lived at Havering-atte-Bower in Essex. His early interest, encouraged by his sister, was in growing and showing roses, especially the then popular Hybrid Perpetuals, and he was one of the early members of the National Rose Society. Joseph was ordained in 1887, but continued showing roses while a curate in Romford, where he later had charge of the parish of the Church of the Ascension. He was not only interested in new roses, but actively encouraged the growing of early nineteenth-century ones, which were already considered old-fashioned by the end of the century. He started breeding roses after his retirement, using Trier, a Polyantha-Noisette hybrid raised by Lambert in Germany in 1904. By crossing Trier with Hybrid Teas, Pemberton raised Danaë and Moonlight, the first of what later came to be called Hybrid Musks, though the musk rose formed only a small part of their ancestry. Both were introduced in 1913. Pemberton died in 1926 and his sister introduced Robin Hood, the seed parent of Iceberg, in 1927 and Felicia in 1928. The Pembertons' gardener, J.H. Bentall, started his own nursery and raised, among others, Ballerina (1937).

MANY HAPPY RETURNS A delicate, free-flowering Modern Shrub. Raised by Harkness in Britain, launched 1988. Flowers continuously through summer. A good show of hips. Height to 75 cm (2½ ft). Good scent.

KATHLEEN A free-flowering Hybrid Musk. Raised by Pemberton in Britain, launched 1922. (Daphne × Perle des Jardins.) To 240 cm (8 ft) high × 120 cm (4 ft) wide. Fragrant.

PENELOPE Hybrid Musk with frilly-edged, creamy-pink flowers and pinky-orange buds. Raised by Pemberton in Britain, launched 1924. (Ophelia × Trier.) Flowers continuously. Some mildew. To 180 cm (6 ft) high × 150 cm (5 ft) wide. Slight scent.

FELICIA One of the best Hybrid Musks. Raised by Pemberton in Britain, launched 1928. (Trier × Ophelia.) Repeat flowers well. To 150 cm (5 ft) high × 270 cm (9 ft) wide. Sweetly scented. Photographed in the garden of Kiftsgate Court, Gloucestershire.

PEARL DRIFT A low, compact Modern Shrub that can be used as a ground cover. Raised by LeGrice in Britain, launched 1980. (Mermaid × New Dawn.) Continuous flowering through summer. To 90 cm (3 ft) high × 120 cm (4 ft) wide. Good scent.

SPARRIESHOOP A very free-flowering, vigorous Modern Shrub, that can be used as a climber. Remarkable for the enormous heads of flowers. Raised by Kordes in Germany, launched 1971. ((Baby Château × Else Poulsen) × Magnifica.) Repeat flowering. Height to 300 cm (10 ft). Scented.

PINK POLYANNA An elegant Modern Shrub. Raised by Warriner in USA, launched 1984. Height to 150 cm (5 ft). Well scented. Photographed in the garden of Dr Ernest Scholtz, California.

THE SECKFORD ROSE An upright-growing Modern Shrub. Raised by Kordes in Germany, launched 1987. A pink form of Kordes' Robusta. Height to 180 cm (6 ft). Good scent.

FRANCIS E. LESTER A rambling Hybrid Musk that can be grown as a gigantic shrub or trained as a rambler. Raised at Lester Rose Gardens in USA, launched 1946. A seedling of Kathleen. Summer flowering. To 300 × 300 cm (10 × 10 ft). Strongly scented.

FRITZ NOBIS A rampant Modern Shrub that can be trained as a climber. The Old-Rose style, quartered flowers tend to hang down and are therefore better trained to flower above eye-level. Raised by Kordes in Germany, launched 1940. (Joanna Hill × Magnifica.) Summer flowering. To 180 cm (6 ft) high × 120 cm (4 ft) wide. Well scented.

SURF RIDER A rambling Modern Shrub; seems to be unobtainable only in the country of its origin. Raised by Holmes in Britain, launched 1976. Summer flowering. To 150 cm (5 ft). Some scent.

LAVENDER LASSIE A Hybrid Musk. The flowers are lavender-pink; getting the colour to show up on film seems to be impossible. Raised by Kordes in Germany, launched 1959. (Hamburg × Mme Norbert Levavasseur.) Flowers continuously. To 150 cm (5 ft) high × 120 cm (4 ft) wide. Good scent. Photographed at Kiftsgate Court, Gloucestershire.

HANSEAT A large-flowered, single Modern Shrub. Difficult to obtain but worth it. Raised by Tantau in Germany, launched 1961. Height to 150 cm (5 ft). Scented.

ÉTOILE DE PORTUGAL An old Shrub Rose grown in our picture as a climber. Raised by Cayeux in Portugal, launched 1898. A *Rosa gigantea* hybrid. Summer flowering. Height to 300 cm (10 ft), nearly as wide. Well scented. Photographed in the Huntington Rose Garden, Los Angeles.

Miriam Wilkins, founder of the American Rose Group, in her garden near San Francisco, California.

AMERLOCK A Modern Shrub or low climber with pendulous flowers. Raised by Warriner and launched by Jackson & Perkins in USA 1970. Height to 180 cm (6 ft). Scented.

YESTERDAY, TAPIS D'ORIENT A low, very free-flowering Modern Shrub sometimes called a Polyantha or a Floribunda. Raised by Harkness in Britain, launched 1974. Ballerina is one of its parents. Flowers continuously. To 100 × 100 cm (3 × 3 ft).

ROMANCE, ROMANZE A large-flowered Modern Shrub. Raised by Tantau in Germany, launched 1985. Height to 120 cm (4 ft). Scented.

ST NICHOLAS A Damask Shrub put in this chapter as it is such a comparatively modern rose. A chance seedling found by Robert James, St Nicholas, Yorkshire in 1950. Possibly a cross between a Damask and a Gallica. Repeat flowering. Height to 180 cm (6 ft). Richly scented.

ANGELA A free-flowering Modern Shrub with a delicate loose habit of growth. Raised by Lens in Belgium, launched 1983. To 150 cm (5 ft) high × 180 cm (6 ft) wide.

ANGELINA A very free-flowering, low, Modern Shrub. Raised by Cocker in Scotland, launched 1976. Flowers continuously. Height to 75 cm (2½ ft). Scented.

VANITY A Hybrid Musk with rather sparse foliage. Raised by Pemberton in Britain, launched 1920. (Château de Clos Vougeot × seedling.) Flowers continuously. To 120 × 120 cm (4 × 4 ft). Fragrant.

Hybrid Musks in the rose border at Knightshayes Court, Devon.

Rush A delicate, single shrub. Raised by Lens in Belgium, launched 1985. Photographed in the Bagatelle Rose Garden, Paris.

WEIHENSTEPHAN A low-growing Modern Shrub, rare and difficult to obtain. Raised by Kordes in Germany, launched 1964. Flowers continuously. Height to 90 cm (3 ft). Scented.

WILHELM, SKYROCKET A Hybrid Musk. Raised by Kordes in Germany, launched 1934. (Robin Hood × J.C. Thornton.) Flowers well in summer but even better in autumn. Height to 180 cm (6 ft). Slightly scented.

ALL THAT JAZZ A low, almost single-flowered Modern Shrub. Raised by Twomey in USA, launched 1991. Repeat flowering. Height to 90 cm (3 ft). Some scent.

CARDINAL HUME An interesting, rich purple Modern Shrub. Raised by Harkness in Britain, launched 1984. Repeat flowering. Height to 90 cm (3 ft). Good scent.

ROCKY A Modern Shrub that can also be trained as a low climber. Raised by McGredy in New Zealand, launched 1979. Repeat flowering. Height to 150 cm (5 ft). Some scent.

DORNRÖSCHEN A large-flowered Modern Shrub. Raised by Kordes in Germany, launched 1960. Height to 120 cm (4 ft). Scented.

Décor Arlequin, Meilland Décor Arlequin A strong-growing, orange-flowered Modern Shrub. Raised by Meilland in France, launched 1986. Repeat flowering. Height to 180 cm (6 ft). Some scent.

Will Scarlet A Hybrid Musk, a sport of Wilhelm but with bright red flowers. Launched by Hilling in Britain, 1947. Flowers continuously. Height to 180 cm (6 ft). Slightly scented.

MARJORIE FAIR, RED BALLERINA, RED YESTERDAY A good, small Modern Shrub. Raised by Harkness in Britain, launched 1978. (Ballerina × Baby Faurax.) Repeat flowering. Height to 120 cm (4 ft).

CASTELLA A Modern Shrub. Raised by Tantau in Germany, launched 1985. Continues to flower throughout summer. Height to 150 cm (5 ft). Some scent.

BERLIN A Modern Shrub. Raised by Kordes in Germany, launched 1949. (Èva × Peace.) Flowers over a long period. Height to 150 cm (5 ft). Light scent.

TANGO A Floribunda or low Modern Shrub. Raised by McGredy in New Zealand, launched 1989. A seedling of Sexy Rexy. Keeps on and on flowering. Height to 60 cm (2 ft). Scented.

FRÜHLINGSZAUBER The smallest of Kordes' *Rosa pimpinellifolia* hybrids. Launched in Germany 1942. Spring flowering. To 150 cm (5 ft). Fragrant.

STADT KIEL A Modern Shrub. Raised by Kordes in Germany, launched 1962. Flowers over a long period. Height to 120 cm (4 ft). Some scent.

CERISE BOUQUET A massive shrub, well worth a place in any large garden. Raised by Tantau in Germany in 1937, launched by Kordes 1958. (*Rosa multibracteata* × Crimson Glory.) Summer flowering. To 270 cm (9 ft) high × 180 cm (6 ft) wide. Sweetly scented. Photographed at Kiftsgate Court, Gloucestershire.

CERISE BOUQUET A detail to show the flowers.

LAVENDER DREAM A low, very free-flowering Modern Shrub. Available all over the world except Britain. Raised by Interplant in France, launched 1984. Repeat flowering. Height to 60 cm (2 ft). Some scent.

LUCIA A little-known but interesting Hybrid Musk. Raised by Kordes in Germany, launched 1966. Repeat flowering. Height to 150 cm (5 ft). Scented.

DANAË A Hybrid Musk; changes to buffy-cream with age. Raised by Pemberton in Britain, launched 1913. (Trier × Gloire de Chédane-Guinoisseau.) Flowers continuously. To 150 cm (5 ft) high × 120 cm (4 ft) wide. Scented.

FRÜHLINGSMORGEN Shown in the morning light.

FRÜHLINGSSCHNEE Shrubby creamy-yellow buds that open to nearly pure white flowers. Raised by Kordes in Germany, launched 1954. (Golden Glow × Rosa pimpinellifolia altaica.) Spring flowering. To 180 cm (6 ft) high × 120 cm (4 ft) wide. Well scented.

ZITRONENFALTER A large-flowered Modern Shrub. Raised by Tantau in Germany, launched 1956. Height to 150 cm (5 ft). Scented.

GOLDEN WINGS

FRÜHLINGSGOLD

FRÜHLINGSMORGEN

GOLDEN WINGS A tall shrub. The yellow flowers have red stamens. Raised by Shepherd in USA, launched 1956. (Soeur Thérèse × (*Rosa pimpinellifolia* Grandiflora × Ormiston Roy).) Flowers through to autumn. Height to 180 cm (6 ft). Scented.

FRÜHLINGSGOLD A tall shrub with open yellow flowers that fade to white. Stamens are yellow. Raised by Kordes in Germany, launched 1937. (Joanna Hill × *Rosa pimpinellifolia* Hispida.) Spring flowering. To 200 cm (7 ft) high × 150 cm (5 ft) wide. Scented.

FRÜHLINGSMORGEN A tall shrub. Raised by Kordes in Germany, launched 1942. ((E.G. Hill × Catherine Kordes) × *Rosa pimpinellifolia altaica*.) One of the first roses to come into flower every year. Height to 180 cm (6 ft). Scented.

A view of the Landscape Rose trial grounds at Meilland Roses in southern France.

Jacques Mouchotte is the man responsible for many of the new roses at Meilland, especially the Meidiland Landscape Roses.

CHAPTER THIRTEEN

Ground Cover Roses

Landscape Roses are followed by the smaller Ground Cover Roses.

The first part of this chapter deals with the innovative large rose bushes, often known as Landscape Roses, which grow into huge shrubs that spread out to obliterate everything in their path. Look at the shed disappearing under them in the picture below! Meilland in France have made a speciality of breeding these roses, which they call their Meidiland range. In the area near Meilland's demonstration garden at Domaine-de-St-André, where the photographs on these two pages were taken, the local authority has planted Landscape Roses on the roadsides and roundabouts to great effect.

MAGIC MEIDILAND A new Ground Cover or Landscape Rose. Raised by Meilland in France, launched 1992. Flowers throughout summer. Very disease resistant. To 90 × 90 cm (3 × 3 ft). Light scent.

ALBA MEIDILAND A dense-growing Ground Cover or Landscape Rose. Raised by Meilland in France, launched 1987. Clusters of small flowers throughout summer. Good disease resistance. To 90 cm (3 ft) high × 120 cm (4 ft) wide. Some scent.

SWANY A dense Ground Cover or Landscape Rose. Raised by Meilland in France, launched 1978. (*Rosa sempervirens* × Mlle Marthe Carron.) Flowers throughout summer. To 75 cm (2½ ft) high × 180 cm (6 ft) wide. Light scent.

FERDY A dense Ground Cover or Landscape Rose. Raised by Suzuki in Japan, launched 1984. (Climbing seedling × Petite Folie.) Flowers throughout summer. Good disease resistance. To 120 cm (4 ft) high × 90 cm (3 ft) wide. Slight scent. Photographed covering the tool shed at Meilland Roses in southern France.

FIONA A rather large-flowered Ground Cover Rose. Raised by Meilland in France, launched 1982. (Sea Foam × Picasso.) Flowers throughout summer. Good disease resistance. To 90 cm (3 ft) high × 150 cm (5 ft) wide. Scented.

LA SEVILLANA A Floribunda with dark green foliage and a bushy habit that can be used as a Ground Cover or Landscape Rose. Raised by Meilland in France, launched 1982. Repeat flowers well. To 120 cm (4 ft) high × 150 cm (5 ft) wide. Little scent.

ROTE WOGE MEINIRLO A strong-growing, free-flowering Ground Cover or Landscape Rose. Flowers are large for this type of rose. Raised by Meilland in France, launched 1993. Flowers continuously. To 90 cm (3 ft) high × 120 cm (4 ft) wide. Perfume slight.

BONICA The most free-flowering, best repeating rose we have seen on our travels. It can be grown as a shrub, Patio or Ground Cover Rose. Raised by Meilland in France, launched 1982. *Rosa sempervirens* is one parent. Good disease resistance. To 90 cm (3 ft) high × 150 cm (5 ft) wide. Some scent. Also illustrated in Standards (page 200).

FAIRYLAND A delicate pink Ground Cover or Patio Rose. Raised by Harkness in Britain, launched 1980. (The Fairy × Yesterday.) Flowers continuously. To 60 cm (2 ft) high × 150 cm (5 ft) wide. Some scent.

GROUSE A strong, healthy, ground-hugging shrub that spreads and spreads. The growth is rather untidy. Raised by Kordes in Germany, launched 1982. (The Fairy × *Rosa wichuraiana* seedling.) Repeat flowering. Good disease resistance. To 45 cm (1½ ft) high × 300 cm (10 ft) wide. Fragrant.

HAPPENSTANCE A dwarf sport of Mermaid that makes an interesting Ground Cover Rose. It was found in California growing from the roots of an old Mermaid plant that had been cut back right to the ground. Photographed in the Huntington Rose Garden, Los Angeles.

SMARTY A very delicate pink Ground Cover Rose. Raised by Ilsink in The Netherlands, launched 1979. (Yesterday × seedling.) Repeat flowering. To 90 cm (3 ft) high × 120 cm (4 ft) wide. Some scent.

PAULII A trailing shrub that makes a very good ground cover. Very thorny. Raised by Paul in Britain, launched before 1903. (*Rosa arvensis* × *Rosa rugosa*.) Summer flowering. To 90 cm (3 ft) high × 180 cm (6 ft) wide. Slightly scented.

SURREY

WARWICKSHIRE

AVON

KENT

SURREY, SUMMER WIND A very free-flowering Ground Cover Rose. Raised by Kordes in Germany, launched 1987. Repeat flowering. To 60 cm (2 ft) high × 120 (4 ft) wide.

WARWICKSHIRE A dense, spreading Ground Cover. Red flowers with a white eye, give it a painted rose look. Raised by Kordes in Germany, launched 1991. Flowers continuously. To 45 cm (1½ ft) high × 90 cm (3 ft) wide. Some scent.

AVON A low Ground Cover or Patio Rose with pink buds that open very pale whitish-pink. Raised by Poulsen in Denmark. Repeat flowering. To 30 cm (1 ft) high × 90 cm (3 ft) wide.

KENT, WHITE COVER A Ground Cover Rose. Raised by Poulsen in Denmark, launched 1988. Repeat flowering. To 45 cm (1½ ft) high × 90 cm (3 ft) wide.

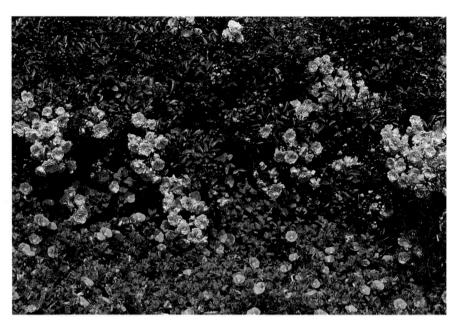

PINK BELLS A small shrub Ground Cover Rose. Raised by Poulsen in Denmark, launched 1983. (Mini-Poul × Temple Bells.) Summer flowering. Good disease resistance. To 60 cm (2 ft) high × 120 cm (4 ft) wide. (See page 235).

THE FAIRY A Polyantha, now used as ground cover. One of the first hybrids to have this trailing habit. Raised by Bentall in Britain, launched 1932. (Paul Crampel × Lady Gay.) Flowers continuously. Good disease resistance. To 60 cm (2 ft) high × 120 cm (4 ft) wide. Little scent.

FLOWER CARPET A Ground Cover Rose. Raised by Noack in Germany, launched 1990. Flowers continuously. To 45 cm (1½ ft) high × 120 cm (4 ft) wide.

ROSY CUSHION A low shrub or Ground Cover Rose with long arching stems. Raised by Ilsink in The Netherlands, launched 1979. (Yesterday × seedling.) Repeat flowering. To 75 cm (2½ ft) high × 120 cm (4 ft) wide. Some scent.

EYEOPENER, TAPIS ROUGE, ERICA A very free-flowering Ground Cover Rose. Raised by Ilsink in The Netherlands, launched 1987. Flowers throughout summer. To 45 cm (1½ ft) high × 120 cm (4 ft) wide.

MAGIC CARPET A free-flowering Ground Cover Rose. Introduced by Jackson & Perkins in USA 1993. Repeat flowering. To 60 cm (2 ft) high × 120 cm (4 ft) wide.

CHILTERNS

PHEASANT

SUFFOLK

CHILTERNS A vigorous Ground Cover or Patio Rose. Raised by Kordes in Germany, launched 1992. Repeat flowering. To 45 cm (1½ ft) high × 150 cm (5 ft) wide. Some scent.

PHEASANT, HEIDEKÖNIGIN A Patio Rose that makes a wide-spreading ground cover. Raised by Kordes in Germany, launched 1986. (Zwergkönig 78 × *Rosa wichuraiana* seedling.) Repeat flowering. To 60 cm (2 ft) high × 300 cm (10 ft) wide.

SUFFOLK, BASSINO A Patio or Ground Cover Rose with scarlet flowers and prominent golden stamens. Raised by Kordes in Germany, launched 1988. Repeat flowering. To 45 cm (1½ ft) high × 90 cm (3 ft) wide.

A new red Ground Cover Rose being tested in the rose field at Jackson & Perkins, California.

STAR DELIGHT A Miniature with delicate pointed petals. Raised by Moore in USA, launched 1990. A Rugosa Hybrid. Repeat flowering. Height to 45 cm ($1\frac{1}{2}$ ft). Scented.

MR BLUEBIRD A little China Patio Rose or Miniature. Raised by Moore in USA, launched 1960. (Old Blush × Old Blush.) Flowers throughout summer. Height to 30 cm (1 ft). Some scent.

SWEET CHARIOT A Miniature that can be used as ground cover or grown in a hanging basket. Raised by Moore in USA, launched 1984. Repeat flowering. Height to 45 cm ($1\frac{1}{2}$ ft). Scented.

CHAPTER FOURTEEN

Miniatures and Patios

This chapter starts with Miniature and Patio Roses raised by Ralph Moore in the USA and goes on to show work by other breeders.

GREEN ICE A free-flowering Miniature, good in hanging baskets. Raised by Moore in USA, launched 1971. ((*Rosa wichuraiana* × Floradora) × Jet Trail.) Height to 45 cm ($1\frac{1}{2}$ ft). Some scent.

RISE 'N' SHINE, GOLDEN SUNBLAZE A very free-flowering Patio Rose or Miniature. Raised by Moore in USA, launched 1978. (Little Darling × Yellow Magic.) Flowers continuously. Very healthy. Height to 45 cm ($1\frac{1}{2}$ ft).

IMPORTANT ROSE BREEDERS XXIX

Ralph S. Moore of Visalia, California, has been in the forefront of the development and popularization of Miniature Roses since 1937. A robust eighty-six-year-old with short, cropped, dazzling white hair, he started growing rose seedlings while still at high school in the 1920s. In 1927 he sowed seeds from a huge plant of Climbing Cécile Brünner in the garden next door. One of the seedlings had tiny white flowers on a bush about 90 cm (3 ft) tall, but there was little interest in Miniatures at this time and that plant was lost.

A few Miniatures have been around since before the nineteenth century. Centifolia Parvifolia or Pompom de Bourgogne, a dwarf Centifolia, has been grown since 1664. Pompom de Paris was a popular pot-plant in the Paris flower markets in the mid-1800s but is now usually grown in its climbing form. A single miniature China had been introduced from Canton in around 1800 but was believed to be lost. However, in 1917, it or its descendant was rediscovered growing in pots on a window-sill in Switzerland, and named Rouletti after its finder. Soon it was being used for hybridizing by one or two breeders, notably Pedro Dot in Spain. Baby Gold Star was one of his early crosses. Ralph Moore first saw *Rosa rouletti* in 1935. Soon after, he bought plants of Tom Thumb, raised by de Vink in the Netherlands, and Oakington Ruby, raised by Bloom, and his enthusiasm for Miniatures was rekindled. From these roses, Ralph began the breeding programme that is still going strong today. One of his important parent seedlings, code-named Zee, was raised from the Miniature Tom Thumb and Carolyn Dean, an early Moore Climber with perfectly shaped, single, coppery-pink flowers. Zee was the pollen parent of such important Miniature Climbers as Yellow Doll and Pink Cameo. Since those early days the colour range of his Miniatures has been

PLAYGIRL A little Floribunda (patio-size plant) with almost single flowers. Raised by Moore in USA, launched 1986. Repeat flowering. Height to 45 cm ($1\frac{1}{2}$ ft). Scented. Photographed at Ralph Moore's nursery.

Ralph Moore, a tower of strength, at work in his greenhouse.

POMPOM DE PARIS A China that is now classed as a Miniature. There is also a climbing form. Used by Ralph Moore as one of his first breeding stocks. Flowers continuously. Height to 60 cm (2 ft). Some scent.

MILLIE WALTERS A sprawling, free-flowering Patio or low ground cover rose. Raised by Moore in USA, launched 1983. Repeat flowering. Height to 30 cm (1 ft).

CHAPEAU DE NAPOLÉON, CRESTED MOSS, *ROSA CENTIFOLIA* CRISTATA This very early Moss Rose is not a Miniature but is in the Ralph Moore chapter because he used it to develop his Miniatures. Raised by Vibert in France, launched 1827. Summer flowering. To 150 cm (5 ft). Fragrant.

CRESTED JEWEL A low-climbing Moss that proved very valuable in raising further crested Mosses. Raised by Moore in USA, launched 1971. (Little Darling × Chapeau de Napoléon.) Summer flowering. Height to 150 cm (5 ft). Scented.

CRESTED SWEETHEART An Old Rose flower that makes a low Climber with superb cresting on the buds. Raised by Moore in USA, launched 1988. Height to 120 cm (4 ft). Fragrant.

extended to include bicolours such as Magic Carousel (1972), greens like Green Ice (1971) and mauves like Lavender Lace (1968).

Ralph himself describes his rose breeding as a joyful journey and adventure, and a visit to his nursery and seedling houses is an exciting experience. He is always looking for some new character or combination of characters thrown up by his widely based breeding programme. When we visited him we saw roses with petals like oak leaves, with red eyes, picotee edges and stripes; and flowers with curved, fluted petals like *Clematis texensis* hybrids. Ralph is prepared to keep all these and, if possible, develop them into something new. He has also introduced other species into his programme to get roses that look really different. *Rosa bracteata, Rosa rugosa* and the old Hybrid Perpetual Paul Neyron have all produced exciting seedlings. Crosses with very different roses seem to take well on Miniatures. One other speciality of Ralph's must be mentioned: the breeding of modern Moss and Crested Roses. Since 1948, by patience and careful selection, he has introduced Miniature Roses that have the added attraction of mossy, scented buds. Some of them have crested sepals derived from Chapeau de Napoléon. One of the early parents in this programme was Golden Moss, a Pedro Dot seedling of Floribunda type. In turn, this led to the first yellow-flowered modern Moss, Goldmoss, introduced by Moore in 1972. William Lobb was also used as a parent, and the two lines came together to produce Dresden Doll, a lovely pink Miniature with glandular, mossy buds. New roses with crested buds are being bred using a Climber, Crested Jewel, raised from Chapeau de Napoléon and Little Darling.

Although he has been raising roses for over sixty-five years, Ralph Moore's energy and enthusiasm are unabated. He works long hours in the seedling houses at temperatures of over 38°C (100°F), unflagging while younger men, including us, wilt. Ralph has more new roses planned than ever before – enough ideas to keep him going until he is 100!

A superb new CRESTED MOSS with deep red-purple striping, another development to look forward to from Ralph Moore.

A striped MOSS seedling in Ralph Moore's greenhouse. It is very free flowering, like a Floribunda.

STRAWBERRY SWIRL Another new break, a striped Mini Moss or Patio Rose. Raised by Moore in USA, launched 1978. Repeat flowering. Height to 45 cm ($1\frac{1}{2}$ ft). Some scent.

RED MOSS RAMBLER A miniature mossy Rambler. Raised by Moore in USA, launched 1990. Height to 30 cm (1 ft) spreading to cover up to 120 cm (4ft). Some scent.

SCARLET MOSS A strong red Miniature Moss or Patio Rose. Raised by Moore in USA, launched 1988. Height to 45 cm ($1\frac{1}{2}$ ft). Scented.

TOPAZ JEWEL, YELLOW FRU DAGMAR HARTOPP, GELBE DAGMAR HASTRUP, RUSTICA A fine yellow Rugosa hybrid. Raised by Moore in USA, launched 1987. Repeat flowering. Height to 150 cm (5 ft). Scented.

GOLDEN MOSS The only yellow Moss. Ralph Moore has used it extensively in his Mini Moss breeding. Raised by Dot in Spain, launched 1932. Summer flowering. Height to 150 cm (5 ft). Scented.

Our visit to the greenhouses of Ralph Moore in Visalia, California, showed how the creative breeder's imagination can call forth the most exquisite combinations. On these two pages are some of Ralph's newer roses, plus seedlings that he is working on right now. Some will be launched in the near future but many will be only a step in his breeding programme.

RALPH'S CREEPER A shrub or small Ground Cover Rose. Our picture shows Ralph trying it out as a weeping standard. Raised by Moore in USA, launched 1988. Height to 30 cm (1 ft). Some scent.

SEQUOIA JEWEL A Patio Rose or Miniature. Raised by Moore in USA, launched 1989. (Sheri Anne × Paul Neyron.) Height to 60 cm (2 ft). Scented.

CHERRY MAGIC A Miniature. Its distinctive feature is the way the petals recurve, giving it a soft cushiony appearance. Raised by Moore in USA, launched 1988. Height to 60 cm (2 ft).

LAVENDER MINI A Miniature Climber. Its cup-shaped flowers have delicately pointed petals like a waterlily. Repeat flowers well. A new seedling in Ralph Moore's greenhouse.

PEACH HALO × RED EYE A red-eyed seedling with a delicately double display of petals. In Ralph Moore's greenhouse.

One of Ralph Moore's latest developments: seedlings with oak-leaf petals.

Just a few of the striped seedlings that Ralph Moore is developing in his greenhouses.

A delicately striped seedling that is starting to show the dividing of the petals, as does the oak-leafed petalled seedling.

HULA HOOP A small Floribunda with picotee-flowers well marked with cerise-pink. Raised by Moore in USA, launched 1990. Height to 75 cm ($2\frac{1}{2}$ ft).

HALO A most interesting, red-eyed seedling in Ralph Moore's greenhouse.

A view of a seedling bed in one of Ralph Moore's greenhouses, showing some of the crosses made with Angel Face, New Penny and Anytime.

An Angel Face cross with delicate colour changes and ruffled petals. In Ralph Moore's greenhouse.

WANAKA, LONGLEAT, YOUNG CALE
A free-flowering Miniature that makes an excellent low ground cover. Raised by McGredy in New Zealand, launched 1978. (Anytime × Trumpeter.) Height to 45 cm (1½ ft).

ANGELA RIPPON A Patio or Miniature. Raised by de Ruiter in The Netherlands, launched 1978. (Rosy Jewel × Zorina.) Flowers continuously. Height to 30 cm (1 ft). Good scent.

PURPLE BUTTONS A very free-flowering Miniature. Raised by Rupert and launched by Moore in USA 1993. A seedling of the Shrub Rose, Cardinal Hume. Height to 45 cm (1½ ft). Very good scent.

MANDARIN A large-flowered, very free-flowering Miniature or Patio Rose. Raised by Kordes in Germany, launched 1987. Height to 30 cm (1 ft).

MARY GAMMON A large-flowered Miniature. Raised by Fryer in Britain. Height to 30 cm (1 ft).

ESTHER'S BABY A bushy Miniature or Patio Rose. Raised by Harkness in Britain, launched 1979. Repeat flowering. Height to 45 cm (1½ ft).

NEW FASHION A Patio Rose. Roses in pots are very useful as they can be moved at will. Repeat flowering. Height to 45 cm (1½ ft).

COLIBRI A Miniature. Raised by Meilland in France, launched 1958. (Goldilocks × Perla de Montserrat.) Flowers continuously. Susceptible to blackspot. To 30 cm (1 ft).

SWEET DREAM A delicate, cup-shaped Floribunda or Patio Rose. Raised by Fryer in Britain, launched 1987. Flowers continuously. Height to 45 cm (1½ ft). Slight scent.

BABY MASQUERADE, BABY CARNIVAL A very free-flowering Miniature. Raised by Tantau in Germany, launched 1956. (Peon × Masquerade.) Flowers continuously. Height to 45 cm (1½ ft). Some scent.

STARGAZER A Floribunda or Patio Rose. Raised by Harkness in Britain, launched 1976. (Marlena × Kim.) Flowers continuously. To 45 cm (1½ ft). Scented.

MINIJET A delicate Miniature. Raised by Meilland in France, launched 1977. (Seventeen × (Mon Petit × Perla de Montserrat).) Height to 30 cm (1 ft).

PANDEMONIUM, CLAIRE RAYNER A free-flowering small Floribunda or Patio Rose. Raised by McGredy in New Zealand, launched 1988. Repeat flowering. Height to 45 cm (1½ ft).

HOLY TOLEDO A Miniature or Patio Rose. Rather tender. Raised by Christensen in USA, launched 1978. (Gingersnap × Magic Carrousel.) Height to 45 cm (1½ ft).

TIP TOP A Miniature or small Floribunda. Our illustration shows the climbing sport. Raised by Tantau in Germany, launched 1963. Flowers continuously. Height of Miniature to 45 cm (1½ ft), climber to 120 cm (4 ft). Some scent.

DOROLA, BENSON & HEDGES SPECIAL A bushy, healthy Miniature or Patio Rose. Raised by McGredy in New Zealand, launched 1982. (Minnuetto × Mabella.) Flowers continuously. Height to 30 cm (1 ft). Some scent.

PINK PETTICOAT A free-flowering Miniature. Raised by Strawn, launched 1979. Height to 45 cm (1½ ft). Some scent.

LITTLE ARTIST, TOP GEAR A delicate Miniature. Raised by McGredy in New Zealand, launched 1982. (Eyepaint × Ko's Yellow.) Flowers continuously. Height to 30 cm (1 ft).

GOLD SYMPHONIE A large-flowered Miniature with strong unfading yellow flowers. Raised by Meilland in France, to be launched by Selection Meilland in 1994. Repeat flowering. Height to 45 cm (1½ ft). Light scent.

CINDERELLA (CLIMBING) A Miniature in climbing form. The climbing sport was launched by Sequoia in USA 1975. (Cécile Brünner × Peon.) Flowers continuously. To 100 cm (3½ ft). Scented.

TOP MARKS A healthy, free-flowering Miniature. Raised by Fryer in Britain, launched 1992. Repeat flowering. Height to nearly 60 cm (2 ft). Some scent.

BABY BIO A low Floribunda or Patio Rose. Raised by Smith in Britain, launched 1977. (Golden Treasure × seedling.) Flowers continuously. Height to 45 cm (1½ ft). Some scent.

GENTLE TOUCH A free-flowering Miniature or Patio Rose. Raised by Dickson in Northern Ireland, launched 1986. Flowers continuously. Height to 30 cm (1 ft). Some scent. Photographed in the patio at Eccleston Square, London.

PEEK-A-BOO, BRASS RING A spreading Miniature with flowers that fade to pink with age. Raised by Dickson in Northern Ireland, launched 1981. ((Bangor × Anabell) × Nozomi.) Flowers continuously. Height to 45 cm (1½ ft).

HAKUUN Patio Rose or small Floribunda with dense clumps of flowers. Raised by Poulsen in Denmark, launched 1962. (Seedling × (Pinocchio × Pinocchio).) Height to 45 cm (1½ ft).

PINK BELLS A Miniature perhaps better classed as a ground cover. A twin of White Bells. Raised by Poulsen in Denmark, launched 1983. (Mini-Poul × Temple Bells.) Summer flowering. To 60 cm(2 ft) high × 120 cm (4 ft) wide. Some scent.

WHITE BELLS A Miniature often used as ground cover. A twin of Pink Bells. Raised by Poulsen in Denmark, launched 1983. (Mini-Poul × Temple Bells.) Summer flowering. To 60 cm (2 ft) high × 120 cm (4 ft) wide. Some scent.

235

CHAPTER FIFTEEN

English Roses

David Austin's breeding plants are followed by his roses arranged by colour: white, pink, red and yellow.

David Austin in the rose fields at his nursery in Albrighton, Shropshire.

DAINTY MAID A lovely, almost single, Floribunda that Austin has used in his breeding. Raised by LeGrice in Britain, launched 1940. (D.T. Poulsen × unknown.) Continues to flower through summer. Height to 80 cm (2½ ft). Scented.

Mother plants in David Austin's greenhouse show tapes that key back to the date of the cross and the male parent used to fertilize the seed.

David Austin has the rare distinction of creating a completely new class of rose, which he has called English Roses. As a young man farming in the early 1950s, he was struck by the beauty of Old Roses, especially the Gallicas, Centifolias and Damasks raised in nineteenth-century France and then being collected by his friend Graham Thomas at Hillings Nurseries.

From the time he started crossing roses David Austin has aimed to combine the grace, scent, shape and muted colours of Old Roses with the perpetual flowering habit and health of Modern Roses. He has paid particular attention to the shape of the open flower which had been rather ignored in Hybrid Teas, bred for perfection in the unfolding bud.

The first cross which produced seedlings of note was between the Floribunda Dainty Maid and Belle Isis, a Gallica or Gallica-Centifolia hybrid. This resulted in the sumptuous, large-flowered, tall shrub or climber named Constance Spry after the great English flower-arranger.

David now crossed Constance Spry with recurrent-flowering roses such as the Floribunda Ma Perkins, the Hybrid Tea Monique, and the old Hybrid Tea Mme Caroline Testout (page 87). This group of crosses produced a pink-flowered strain which has continued until the present. One of the seedlings from this group was Wife of Bath (1969). In the next generation, stronger growing, repeat-flowering roses appeared, notably Heritage (1984) and Perdita in 1983 (page 247). Newer roses in this group include Bibi Maizoon (page 242), with very cupped flowers, and Charles Rennie MacKintosh (page 243) which has huge flowers with a hint of lilac pink.

CHAUCER One of the earliest of the English Roses. For the first ten years many of Austin's roses had names from Chaucer. Launched in Britain 1970. (Duchesse de Montebello × Constance Spry.) Repeat flowering. Height to 90 cm (3 ft). Good myrrh scent. Photographed in the garden of Sharon Van Enoo, Los Angeles.

GRAHAM THOMAS A tall English Rose, named after Graham Thomas, the leading Old Rose enthusiast. Launched in Britain 1973. (Charles Austin × Iceberg seedling.) Repeats quite well. Height to 175 cm (6 ft). Good scent.

MRS DOREEN PIKE A new pink, double Rugosa hybrid. David Austin, like many other breeders, is doing a lot with *Rosa rugosa*. Launched in Britain 1993. Repeats. To 90 cm (3 ft). Strong Old Rose scent.

CONSTANCE SPRY David Austin's first English Rose. A large shrub or climber. Launched in Britain 1961. (Belle Isis × Dainty Maid.) David Austin admits he made a lucky start by getting a rose that combined Modern Rose health and vigour with Old Rose shape and scent. Only once flowering, in summer, but worth a place in every garden. Good disease resistance. Height to 400 cm (13 ft) but to 200 × 200 cm (7 × 7 ft) if left as a shrub. Well scented; Graham Thomas has compared the scent to myrrh.

CONRAD FERDINAND MEYER A Rugosa hybrid. Used by Austin in his breeding programme. (Gloire de Dijon × (Duc de Rohan × *Rosa rugosa*).) Repeat flowers well. Height to 300 cm (10 ft). Very fragrant.

BELLE ISIS An unusually delicate pink Gallica, included here as it was a parent of Constance Spry, Austin's first rose. Raised by Parmentier in Belgium, launched 1845. Summer flowering. Height to 120 cm (4 ft). Good scent of myrrh.

COMTE DE CHAMBORD A Portland Rose. Another rose that Austin has used in breeding English Roses. Raised by Moreau-Robert in France, launched 1863. (Baronne Prévost × Portland Rose.) Repeat flowers well. Height to 120 cm (4 ft). Good Damask scent.

FRANCINE AUSTIN Medium-sized Noisette-like shrub that can be used as a ground cover. Raised by Austin in Britain, launched 1988. (Alister Stella Gray × Ballerina.) Continues to flower over a long period. To 120 × 120 cm (4 × 4 ft). Little scent.

SHROPSHIRE LASS A large, summer-flowering English Rose that can also be grown as a climber. Raised by Austin in Britain, launched 1968. (Mme Butterfly × Mme Legras de St Germain.) Height to 250 cm (8 ft) or twice that on a wall. Well scented.

WINCHESTER CATHEDRAL A shrub, a sport of Mary Rose. Raised by Austin in Britain, launched 1988. Flowers continuously. To 120 cm (4 ft). Scented.

A view of David Austin's rose garden at Albrighton, Shropshire. The pale pink rose on the right is SCINTILLATION. The pink Rambler is MAY QUEEN.

SCINTILLATION A low shrub or ground cover. Raised by Austin in Britain, launched 1968. (Rosa macrantha × Vanity.) Flowers over a long period in summer. Height to 100 cm (3½ ft), spreading to cover 120 cm (4 ft). Well scented.

GLAMIS CASTLE Austin's favourite white English Rose to date. The flowers are the shape of Graham Thomas with a delicate, white-tinged buff colour. Raised by Austin in Britain, launched 1992. (Graham Thomas × Mary Rose.) Flowers continuously. Height to 90 cm (3 ft). Myrrh scent.

PEACH BLOSSOM A semi-double English Rose. Raised by Austin in Britain, launched 1990. (The Prioress × Mary Rose.) Continues to flower through summer. Height to 120 cm (4 ft). Slight scent.

EMILY A small English Rose. The outer petals flatten out leaving the inner petals in a cup formation. Raised by Austin in Britain, launched 1992. Repeat flowering. Height to 70 cm (2½ ft). Strong scent.

To get a red strain, David Austin crossed Dusky Maiden (page 169), a deep red single, with Tuscany (page 22), a deep purplish-red Gallica. This early cross produced The Knight and Chianti. Later, Château de Clos Vougeot, an early hybrid Tea, was introduced into the strain; it produces good red flowers but rather weak shrubs. This meant the plants in the red 'family' have tended to be small so David Austin is now concentrating on breeding much stronger-growing reds.

Yellow has proved to be the most unpredictable of all the colours to raise. Graham Thomas, probably David Austin's most famous yellow, was raised from Charles Austin (page 247) and an Iceberg seedling in 1973. Some other yellows were raised using the pink Conrad Ferdinand Meyer which has Gloire de Dijon (page 142) in its ancestry. The yellow colour has appeared again in Tamora, a pale apricot, and been reinforced in Jayne Austin, a hybrid of Tamora and Graham Thomas. Jayne Austin has the character of some of the old Noisette Roses and even has the controversial Tea Rose fragrance.

DOVE A low-spreading English Rose. Raised by Austin in Britain, launched 1984. (Wife of Bath × Iceberg seedling.) Flowers especially well in dry autumns. Height to 75 cm (2½ ft). Some scent.

One criticism of English Roses is that they are reproductions of Old Roses and, by analogy with paintings, therefore inferior, or at least not genuine, compared with the antique Gallicas, Albas and Centifolias. David Austin has always been aware of this and, as he says in *Old Roses and English Roses*, has not attempted to breed new Gallicas or Albas, although this would be perfectly possible: 'and worthwhile if done with care and good taste.' His intention has always been to breed new groups for beauty first and health and toughness second. This is quite contrary to the practice of other breeders who are almost obsessive about disease and reject otherwise lovely roses if they show the slightest sign of infection.

And what of the future? David Austin has more seedlings coming on than ever before and is introducing new types of roses into his breeding programme. Unlike very large breeders, he is his own master and can introduce and sell anything he considers beautiful. He does not have to get his roses past a committee which considers only those that they think will sell by the hundred thousand. He does not have to aim for one flower shape or rose type and, like Ralph Moore in the USA, is always ready to find a new break among his seedlings and introduce it or give it a trial in the garden.

FAIR BIANCA An upright English Rose. Raised by Austin in Britain, launched 1983. Parentage includes Belle Isis. Repeat flowers well. Height to 90 cm (3 ft). Good scent.

LEANDER A tall, very healthy, summer-flowering English Rose that can also be grown as a climber. Raised by Austin in Britain, launched 1982. A Charles Austin seedling. Summer flowering. Height to 200 cm (7 ft), double that as a climber. Good fruity scent.

ELLEN A vigorous, free-flowering English Rose. Raised by Austin in Britain, launched 1984. Flowers continuously. Height to 130 cm (4 ft). Strongly scented.

LUCETTA A semi-double English Rose. Makes a large shrub or climber. Raised by Austin in Britain, launched 1983. Repeat flowers well. Height to 140 cm (5 ft), more as a climber. Good scent.

SWEET JULIET A free-flowering English Rose. Raised by Austin in Britain, launched 1989. (Graham Thomas × Admired Miranda.) Flowers continuously. May get some mildew. Height to 110 cm ($3\frac{1}{2}$ ft). Well scented.

REDOUTÉ An English Rose. A free-flowering sport of Mary Rose. David Austin compares the colour to the delicate pink shades of the Alba Roses. Raised by Austin in Britain, launched 1992. Height to 120 cm (4 ft). Light scent.

SAINT CECILIA A low-growing English Rose. Raised by Austin in Britain, launched 1986. A Wife of Bath seedling. Continues to flower into autumn. May get a little mildew but this will not really affect the superb flowering. Height to 90 cm (3 ft). Good myrrh fragrance.

KATHRYN MORLEY A low-growing, bushy English Rose. Raised by Austin in Britain, launched 1990. (Mary Rose × Chaucer.) Repeat flowers very well. Height to 70 cm (2½ ft). Good scent.

SHARIFA ASMA One of the most delicate of the English Roses. Raised by Austin in Britain, launched 1989. (Mary Rose × Admired Miranda.) Repeat flowers well. Height to 90 cm (3 ft). Strong scent.

COUNTRY LIVING An English Rose with well-quartered flowers. Raised by Austin in Britain, launched 1991. (Wife of Bath × Graham Thomas.) Flowers continuously. Height to 120 cm (4 ft). Fragrant.

ST SWITHUNS A delicate pink English Rose. Raised by Austin in Britain, launched 1993. Repeat flowers well. Good disease resistance. Height to 90 cm (3 ft). Strong myrrh scent.

ABRAHAM DARBY A large English Rose with enormous flowers that often hang down, thus best trained as a low climber or left to grow into a tall shrub. Raised by Austin in Britain, launched 1985. (Aloha × Yellow Cushion.) Repeat flowers well. Height to 150 cm (5 ft), taller as a climber. Strong fruity scent. Photographed in David Austin's rose garden at Albrighton, Shropshire.

WARWICK CASTLE A small English Rose shrub. Raised by Austin in Britain, launched 1986. (Lilian Austin × The Reeve.) Repeat flowers until autumn. Height to 75 cm (2½ ft). Wonderful scent.

DAPPLE DAWN A Modern Shrub with delicate single flowers. Raised by Austin in Britain, launched 1983. A sport of Redcoat. Repeat flowers well. Height to 150 cm (5 ft). Lightly scented. Photographed in the Huntington Rose Garden, Los Angeles.

PRETTY JESSICA A low, bushy English Rose. Raised by Austin in Britain, launched 1983. A Wife of Bath seedling. Flowers continuously. Height to 75 cm (2½ ft). Good scent.

THE REEVE A wide, sprawling English Rose with very prickly stems. Raised by Austin in Britain, launched 1969. (Lilian Austin × Chaucer.) Repeat flowering. Height to 90 cm (3 ft). Good scent.

BIBI MAIZOON A perfect pink English Rose, unfortunately not a very free flowerer. Raised by Austin in Britain, launched 1989. (The Reeve × Chaucer.) Repeat flowering. Height to 90 cm (3 ft). Well scented.

A general view of the rose garden at David Austin's nursery in Albrighton, Shropshire. A lovely mixture of Old Roses and English Roses, the garden is well worth a visit.

THE COUNTRYMAN English Rose with rather loose peony-form flowers. Raised by Austin in Britain, launched 1987. (Lilian Austin × Comte de Chambord.) If pruned it will repeat flower in autumn. Height to 90 cm (3 ft). Excellent scent.

WIFE OF BATH A low, bushy English Rose. Raised by Austin in Britain, launched 1969. (Mme Caroline Testout × (Ma Perkins × Constance Spry).) Flowers continuously. Height to 90 cm (3 ft). Strong myrrh scent

MARY ROSE A bushy English Rose that can be left to grow large or pruned hard. Raised by Austin in Britain, launched 1983. (Wife of Bath × The Miller.) Good repeat flowering. Height to 120 cm (4 ft). Fragrant.

CHARLES RENNIE MACKINTOSH A strong, bushy English Rose. Raised by Austin in Britain, launched 1988. (Chaucer × Conrad Ferdinand Meyer.) Flowers throughout summer. Height to 110 cms (3½ ft). Strongly scented.

GERTRUDE JEKYLL A vigorous, free-flowering English Rose. Raised by Austin in Britain, launched 1986. (Wife of Bath × Comte de Chambord.) Flowers over a long period. Disease resistant. Height to 150 cm (5 ft). Strong Damask scent – so good that experiments have been made with growing this rose commercially to produce perfume. Photographed in David Austin's rose garden at his nursery in Albrighton, Shropshire.

CHARMIAN A large English Rose shrub that can be trained as a low climber. Raised by Austin in Britain, launched 1982. (Lilian Austin × seedling.) Flowers continuously. Height to 120 cm (4 ft), more if trained. Strong scent.

SIR EDWARD ELGAR A medium-sized English Rose. Raised by Austin in Britain, launched 1992. (Mary Rose × The Squire.) Repeat flowering. Height to 90 cm (3 ft). Light scent.

HILDA MURRELL A large-flowering English Rose. Raised by Austin in Britain, launched 1984. (Seedling × (Parade × Chaucer).) Repeat flowering. Height to 125 cm (4 ft). Strong Old Rose scent.

PROSPERO A lovely, small English Rose. To prosper it seems to need very good soil. Raised by Austin in Britain, launched 1983. (The Knight × Château de Clos Vougeot.) Flowers continuously. Height to 75 cm (2½ ft). Strong scent. Photographed in the garden of Sharon Van Enoo, Los Angeles.

LILIAN AUSTIN An excellent Modern Shrub. Raised by Austin in Britain, launched 1973. (Aloha × The Yeoman.) Flowers continuously up to winter. Good disease resistance. Height to 100 cm (3½ ft). Good scent.

WILLIAM SHAKESPEARE A strong-growing English Rose. Raised by Austin in Britain, launched 1987. (The Squire × Mary Rose.) Repeat flowers well. Some blackspot. Height to 120 cm (4 ft). Good Old Rose scent.

THE SQUIRE A really good deep red
English Rose. Raised by Austin in Britain,
launched 1977. (The Knight × Château de
Clos Vougeot.) Repeat flowering. Rather
subject to disease. Height to 90 cm (3 ft).
Very fragrant.

THE DARK LADY A medium-sized
English Rose with big, peony-like flowers.
Raised by Austin in Britain, launched
1991. Repeat flowering. Height to
110 cm (3½ ft). Strong Old Rose scent.

TRADESCANT

FISHERMAN'S FRIEND

FISHERMAN'S FRIEND A tough,
exceptionally hardy English Rose that is
really good in cold climates. Raised by
Austin in Britain, launched 1987. (Lilian
Austin × The Squire.) Height to 110 cm
(3½ ft). Strong scent.

TRADESCANT An exceptionally rich dark
red English Rose. Raised by Austin in
Britain, launched 1993. Good repeat
flowering. Height to 70 cm (2½ ft). Good
Old Rose scent.

OTHELLO A large, upright-growing
English Rose with very large blooms that
darken to purple with age. Raised by
Austin in Britain, launched 1986. (Lilian
Austin × The Squire.) Repeat flowers well.
Slight tendency to mildew. Height to
120 cm (4 ft). Strong scent.

REDCOAT A Modern Shrub. Raised by Austin in Britain, launched 1973. (Parade ×
an English Rose.) Flowers profusely throughout summer. Height to 120 cm (4 ft) when
pruned as a shrub or 180 cm (6 ft) if left to grow freely. Little scent.

GOLDEN CELEBRATION A strong, healthy English Rose. Raised by Austin in Britain, launched 1992. (Charles Austin × Abraham Darby.) Repeat flowering. Height to 120 cm (4 ft). Strong scent.

JAYNE AUSTIN An English Rose with an upright growth habit. Raised by Austin in Britain, launched 1990. (Graham Thomas × Tamora.) Good repeat flowering. Height to 120 cm (4 ft). Very fragrant.

YELLOW BUTTON A low-growing English Rose. Raised by Austin in Britain, launched 1975. (Wife of Bath × Chinatown.) Flowers continuously. Height to 90 cm (3 ft). Good scent.

SYMPHONY A reliable English Rose. Raised by Austin in Britain, launched 1986. (The Knight × Yellow Cushion.) Flowers continuously. Very disease resistant. To 100 cm ($3\frac{1}{2}$ ft). Scented.

ENGLISH GARDEN A free-flowering English Rose with real Old Rose flowers. Raised by Austin in Britain, launched 1986. Parentage includes Lilian Austin, Iceberg and Wife of Bath. Height to 120 cm (4 ft). Good scent.

BREDON A very free-flowering, small, upright English Rose. Raised by Austin in Britain, launched 1984. (Wife of Bath × Lilian Austin.) Flowers continuously. Height to 90 cm (3 ft). Good scent.

CHARLOTTE Light yellow, deeply cupped flowers, similar to Graham Thomas from which it was bred. Raised by Austin in Britain, launched 1993. Height to 90 cm (3 ft). Strong Tea Rose scent.

HAPPY CHILD A deep rich yellow English Rose with dark green, glossy foliage. Raised by Austin in Britain, launched 1993. Height to 100 cm ($3\frac{1}{2}$ ft). Tea Rose fragrance.

PERDITA A free-flowering English Rose. The colour tends more towards yellow in the first flowering and more towards pink in later flowers. Raised by Austin in Britain, launched 1983. (The Friar × (seedling × Iceberg).) Flowers continuously. Excellent disease resistance. Height to 90 cm (3 ft). Very good scent.

CHARLES AUSTIN

YELLOW CHARLES AUSTIN

THE PILGRIM Extremely strong, healthy English Rose. Very free flowering. Raised by Austin in Britain, launched 1991. (Graham Thomas × Yellow Button.) Flowers continuously. Height to 110 cm (3½ ft). Some scent.

CHARLES AUSTIN A tall-growing English Rose. Raised by Austin in Britain, launched 1973. (Chaucer × Aloha.) Needs strong pruning to encourage repeat flowering. Height to 150 cm (5 ft). Strong fruity scent.

YELLOW CHARLES AUSTIN An English Rose. A yellow sport of Charles Austin. Raised by Austin in Britain, launched 1981. Repeat flowers well if firmly pruned. Height to 150 cm (5 ft). Well scented.

TAMORA A small English Rose. Sharon Van Enoo recommends it for California. Raised by Austin in Britain, launched 1983. (Chaucer × Conrad Ferdinand Meyer.) Repeat flowers profusely. Height to 90 cm (3 ft). Rich myrrh scent.

CLAIRE ROSE A vigorous, upright English Rose. The petals open pink and fade to white. Raised by Austin in Britain, launched 1986. (Charles Austin × (seedling × Iceberg).) Repeat flowering. Height to 130 cm (4 ft). Good scent.

CHAPTER SIXTEEN

Roses for the Future

This chapter describes some current developments and future possibilities in rose breeding.

Keith Zary with some of the new seedlings being developed at Jackson & Perkins in Somis, California.

The Jackson & Perkins greenhouses with a new cut rose that is being tested. Green buds give way to a well-formed white rose flushed a delicate pink. The scent is excellent.

Crystalline A pure white Hybrid Tea. Raised by Christensen-Carruth 1987. Makes a fine cut rose. Here being checked out in the greenhouse at Jackson & Perkins.

At Somis in southern California, Jackson & Perkins have an intensive programme for the development of new cut roses under their director of research, Keith Zary. Worldwide the trade in these greenhouse roses for flower shops is enormous: about half the total trade in roses. Most major breeders devote a great deal of time to developing longer lasting, longer stemmed, better scented roses with thorn-free stems for this trade.

A pale yellow rose with distinct red markings on the petals, being developed for the cut-flower trade at Jackson & Perkins.

Blue is Beautiful

Some companies believe a blue rose would be beautiful and a very great deal of money and time has gone into research to develop one that is a true blue. The problem is that there is no rose with a pure blue gene in its make-up, so no natural blue rose can ever be developed. Scientists are therefore now attempting to take a gene from another group of plants and implant it into roses. Delphiniums have strong, dominant blue genes (no pun intended), and it is this gene that is currently being used in experiments with roses. However, not only will it have to become established in the breeding lines of roses, it will also have to prove itself dominant enough to throw up pure blue flowers. At the moment this scientific work is still in the experimental stage. Personally, I hope it remains there for a few hundred years yet.

Smooth Perfume A thornless Hybrid Tea developed by Harvey Davidson in California. Davidson is one of a number of smaller breeders attempting to raise thornless roses. Photographed by Harvey Davidson.

SMOOTH PRINCE A thornless Hybrid Tea bred by Davidson in California. Apart from breeding thornless roses he is attempting to grow ones with shiny, deep green foliage. Photographed by Harvey Davidson.

A thornless Landscape Rose, not yet ready to be launched, under development at Meilland in the south of France. This rose is well scented and a good repeater. Let's hope they release it or its progeny soon.

BLUE MOVIES These roses are not yet for sale and I hope they never will be. If there is a need for Blue Roses, is there also a need for pigs with eight legs to get more meat? No, no, no. Roses have the most wonderful range of subtle colours, so do delphiniums and forget-me-nots. Let's keep blue for Blue Jeans and not use Blue Genes to confuse plants one with another. Our photograph is a fake.

Recommended Roses

A short list of roses that are readily available, easy to grow and healthy.

MODERN ROSES

Alexander (page 158)
Anisley Dickson (page 158)
Chicago Peace (page 182)
Double Delight (page 191)
English Miss (page 153)
Ernest H. Morse (page 169)
Eyepaint (page 192)
Freedom (page 188)
Grandpa Dickson (page 184)
The Lady (page 182)
Mountbatten (page 188)
Olympiad (page 170)
Peace (page 187)
Pink Favourite (page 164)
Polar Star (page 149)
Princess Michael of Kent (page 188)
Queen Elizabeth (page 157)
Red Devil (page 172)
Savoy Hotel (page 157)
Sexy Rexy (page 156)
Silver Jubilee (page 178)
Southampton (page 177)
The Times Rose (page 168)
Tynwald (page 150)

CLIMBERS

Albertine (page 120)
Alchemist (page 140)
Aloha (page 129)
Compassion (page 122)
Constance Spry (page 237)
Eden Rose 88 (page 128)
Gloire de Dijon (page 142)
Golden Showers (page 138)
Maigold (page 138)
Mermaid (page 140)
New Dawn (page 130)
Rosa filipes Kiftsgate (page 78)

OLD ROSES

Blush Noisette (page 84)
Celestial (page 19)
Charles de Mills (page 30)
Comte de Chambord (page 82)
Felicité Hardy (page 15)
Hermosa (page 105)
Mme Grégoire Staechelin (page 87)
Great Maiden's Blush (page 19)
Mutabilis (page 102)

SHRUB ROSES

Buff Beauty (page 207)
Canary Bird (page 65)
Cerise Bouquet (page 217)
Complicata (page 35)
Cornelia (page 206)
Graham Thomas (page 237)
Lilian Austin (page 244)
Nevada (page 206)
Penelope (page 208)
Rosa rugosa (page 68)
Roseraie de l'Haÿ (page 68)
Sally Holmes (page 204)
Stanwell Perpetual (page 63)

GROUND COVER ROSES

Alba Meidiland (page 220)
Bonica (page 222)
Ferdy (page 221)
Fiona (page 221)
Grouse (page 222)
Magic Meidiland (page 220)
Pink Bells (page 235)
The Fairy (page 224)

Further Reading

FOR THE NAMES OF THE ROSES WE HAVE FOLLOWED:
Dobson, Beverly R & Schneider, Peter, *Combined Rose List 1992,* available from Peter Schneider, PO Box 16035, Rocky River, OH 44116 USA.

Main works on roses consulted:
Austin, David, *Old Roses and English Roses,* Antique Collectors' Club, Suffolk, 1992.
Beales, Peter, *Roses,* Harvill, London, 1992.
Bean, W.J., *Trees & Shrubs Hardy in the British Isles,* eighth edition.
Dickerson, Brent C. *The Old Rose Advisor,* Rimer Press, Oregon, 1992.
Fearnley-Whittingstall, Jane, *Rose Gardens,* Chatto & Windus, London, 1989.
Griffiths, Trevor, *My World of Roses Vols 1 & 2,* Whitcoulls, New Zealand, 1986.
Harkness, Jack, *Roses,* Dent, London, 1978.
Harkness, Jack, *The Makers of Heavenly Roses,* Souvenir Press, London, 1985.
Krüssmann, Gerd, *Roses,* Batsford, London, 1982.
Phillips, Roger & Rix, Martyn, *Roses,* Pan Books, 1988.
Thomas, Graham Stuart, *The Old Shrub Roses* and *Climbing Roses Old and New,* Dent, London, 1983.

Historical Works:
D'Arneville, Marie-Blanche, *Parcs et Jardins sous le Premier Empire,* Tallandier, 1981.
Bennett, Emmett L Jr., *The Olive Oil Tablets of Pylos,* 1958.
Bretschneider, E, *History of European Botanical Discoveries,* two vols, Leipzig, 1962.
Thompson, R Campbell, *Dictionary of Assyrian Botany,* London, 1941.
Drower, Margaret Flinders Petrie, *A Life in Archaeology,* Gollancz, 1985.
Keimer, Ludvig, *La Rose Egyptienne* in *Études d'Egyptologie IV,* Cairo, 1943.

Knapton, Ernest John, *Empress Josephine,* Harvard University Press, 1964.
Needham, J, *Science and Civilization in China Vol VI,* Cambridge University Press, 1954.
Oppenheim, A Leo, *Ancient Mesopotamia,* University of Chicago Press, 1977.
Rix, Martyn & Alison, *The Redouté Album,* Studio Editions, 1990.
Rix, Martyn, *The Art of the Botanist,* Lutterworth Press, 1981.
Rose, Graham, King, Peter & Squire, David, *The Love of Roses,* Quiller Press, London, 1990.
Shirazi, J K M, *Life of Omar al-Khayyámi,* 1905.
Tourtier-Bonazzi, Chantal & Tulard, Jean, *Napoléon, Lettres d'Amour à Joséphine,* Fayard, 1981.
Unschuld, Paul U, *Medicine in China,* University of California Press, 1986.
Warner, Ralph, *Dutch and Flemish Flower and Fruit Painters of the XVII and XVIII Centuries,* Mills and Boon, 1928.
Woolley, Sir Edward, *Ur of the Chaldees,* revised and updated by P R S Moorey, The Herbert Press, 1982.

Rose Nurseries

AUSTRALIA
Langton Roses, Lot 2, Rocky Waterhole Road, PO Box 19, Mudgee 2850, NSW
Ross Roses, St Andrews Tce, PO Box 23, Willunga, Australia 5172
Roy H. Rumsey Pty Ltd, Box 1, Dural 2158, NSW
Swane Bros Pty Ltd, 490 Galston Road, PO Box 29, Dural, NSW 2158
The Rose Garden Pty Ltd, PO Box 18, Watervale, South Australia 5452
Treloar Roses Pty, Keillers Road, Portland, Victoria 3304, Australia

Index

In this index, the common names of the roses are in Roman type; scientific names are in *italics*. Breeders, gardens and other significant entries are in **bold** type.

INDEX

The Rose Family

A very much simplified family tree of the main groups and some of the forms behind Modern Roses. Many more forms and a great many unnamed seedlings are involved and also many of the details of parentage are unknown. However this family tree will give some idea of the parentage of the roses of today.

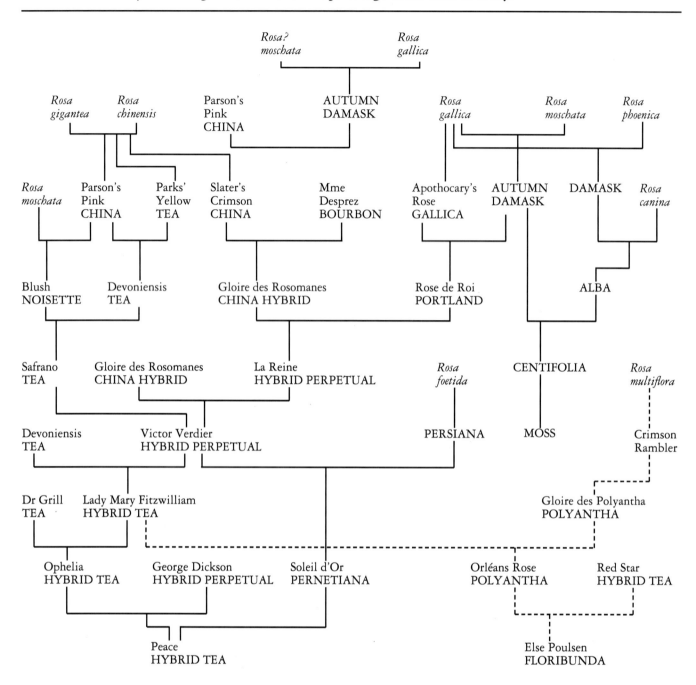